D0772629

A GUIDE TO
GREEK TRADITIONS AND
CUSTOMS IN AMERICA

A *Guide To* Greek Traditions And Customs In America

Marilyn Rouvelas

Rev. Dr. George Papaioannou
Religious Editor

Illustrations by Olga Angelo Deoudes

Nea Attiki Press
Bethesda, Maryland

A Guide to Greek Traditions and Customs in America.
Copyright © 1993 by Marilyn Rouvelas. All Rights Reserved.

Published by Attica Press, Bethesda, Maryland
    First printing, November 1993
    Second printing, March 1994
    Third printing, July 1994
Published by Nea Attiki Press (Reg. U.S. Pat. Off.)
P.O. Box 34008, Bethesda, Maryland 20827
    Fourth printing, December 1994
    Fifth printing, November 1995
    Sixth printing, October 1996
    Seventh printing, March 1998
    Eighth printing, October 1999

Cover and book design:
    Alicia A. Angelides, Design Power Inc., Herndon, Virginia

Rouvelas, Marilyn.
    A guide to Greek traditions and customs in America / Marilyn Rouvelas ;
George Papaioannou, religious editor ; illustrations by Olga Angelo Deoudes. —
Bethesda, Md. : Attica Press, c1993.
    xiv, 320 p. ; ill. ; 27 cm.
    Includes bibliographical references (p. 301-306) and index.
    ISBN 0-9638051-0-X : $25.00

    1. Greek Americans—Social life and customs. I. Papaioannou, George,
1933–   II. Title.

E184.G7R65 1993   973'.0489—dc20   93-72728
                                                   AACR 2 MARC

Printed in the United States of America by
    Automated Graphic Systems, White Plains, Maryland

To my koumbára, *Pitsa Papadakes, whose loving example showed me the joy of Greek traditions and customs.*

To my husband, Emanuel — my true love since that first glass of retsína.

MAY THEIR MEMORY BE ETERNAL:

Mary Rouvelas (1921-1992)
Elias (Louie) Spyridis (1946-1993)

Presvytera Maria Papaioannou (1932-1993)

CONTENTS

PREFACE

ACKNOWLEDGEMENTS

INTRODUCTION: GREEK AMERICANS PAST AND PRESENT

 PART ONE

THE ENDURING TRADITIONS OF ORTHODOXY

The Church 9
The Seven Sacraments 31
    Baptism and Chrismation 33
    Marriage 45
    Confession 63
    Communion 67
    Holy Unction 71
    Holy Orders 75
Saints 81
Name Days 96
Icons 103
The Church of the Home 113
Special Blessings, Prayers, and Appeals 118
Religious Breads 123
Fasting 128
Death and Mourning 133

PART TWO

CUSTOMS OF EVERYDAY LIFE

Greek-American Values 154
Birth of Children 163
Selecting a Name 169
Greek School 173
As the Greeks Say 177
Food and Drink 183
Popular Music 189
Folk Dancing 194
Proverbs and Sayings 199
Superstitions 201
Community Life 208
Visiting Greece 219

PART THREE

FEAST DAYS, FASTS, AND HOLIDAYS

Annual Calendar 231

AUTUMN 232

*The Nativity of the Mother God • The Exaltation of
the Holy Cross • Oxi Day • Christmas Lent •
The Presentation of the Mother of God in the Temple*

WINTER 237

*Christmas, New Year, and Epiphany • Feast Day of
the Three Hierarchs • The Presentation of Jesus
Christ in the Temple*

SPRING 257

*The Easter Season: Pre-Lent • Great Lent •
The Annunciation of the Mother of God and Greek
Independence Day • Holy Week • Holy Pascha
(Easter) • The Ascension of Jesus Christ •
Pentecost*

SUMMER 294

*Holy Apostles Lent • Feast Day of Saints Peter and
Paul • Feast Day of the Holy Apostles • Dormition
of the Mother of God Lent • The Transfiguration of
Jesus Christ • The Dormition of the Mother of God*

BIBLIOGRAPHY

INDEX

NOTES

PREFACE

When I met my Greek-American husband in 1965, everything from the food to the church services was literally foreign. One of our first dates was at a small Greek nightclub in Seattle, pulsing with the exotic sound of *bouzoúki* music. We nibbled on unidentifiable tidbits and drank a strange wine called *retsína* (the only time it tasted good to me!). I was gradually introduced to his family, at first as his sister's friend so as not to alarm the grandmother who expected her grandson to marry someone Greek. Raised a Lutheran, my early years of marriage required considerable adjustment. Over time, however, I converted to Orthodoxy and began to love the many wonderful qualities of Greek-American life: the meaning of a special love called agape, the symbolism in Orthodoxy, the closeness of the family, Greece's legacy to our own democracy, to say nothing of the indescribable desserts like *galaktoboúriko*. These special gifts have inalterably changed my life and the lives of our two children, who love their Greek heritage.

My hope is that this book will explain the meaning and beauty of Greek customs and foster the appreciation they deserve. As a practical guide it will provide useful information on those traditions and customs as practiced in America.

The book is written for both Greeks and non-Greeks. Many Greek Americans are gradually dropping the customs of their forbearers. Their parents lament the loss, but do not know what to do. Some found that strict adherence to old-country traditions made their children, eager to assimilate, spurn their heritage completely. The children in turn may feel guilty about turning their backs on their heritage. For those Greek Americans, this book may spark new enthusiasm and understanding.

I hope this book will be helpful to non-Greeks who, like me, have converted to Greek Orthodoxy and/or married into the faith. This latter group is on the rise. Non-Greeks often feel excluded and perplexed because they do not understand the language or the traditions. Although not born Greek, they will see that they can share the Orthodox faith and recognize it as a powerful bond that transcends geography and ancestry.

The Orthodox faith and the church are central to this book. Most of the Greek customs described here have a religious basis. This is because the church is significantly involved in so many events of life: birth, baptism, marriage, death. Church holidays are occasions of great celebration and family gatherings. And here in the United States, the church is the primary social and cultural center for most Greek Americans.

The combination of religious and ethnic customs within the Greek Orthodox church in America is a controversial and emotional issue. There are those who firmly believe that the church should retain the Greek language and influence. Others argue that the Orthodox church has survived because it has adapted to the language and culture of the country in which it is located. In my opinion, the United States offers a unique setting for Greek Orthodoxy because Americans are not homogeneous. The country gains from its diversity. But special Greek qualities that can enhance Orthodoxy will do so only if they are understood. And if this means compromising on the issue of language by accepting both Greek and English usage in the church, then let us do so.

The idea for this book came to me during my engagement in 1966. I needed a single reference to grasp quickly the basics of Greek-American living. Such a book did not exist, and the reason is apparent to me now. With the exception of some of the church traditions, few customs are consistently practiced by everyone in Greece. There are great differences among the geographic areas: each island and each region has its own subculture. There are differences too, between the villages and the cities. Many village customs, for example, are left behind when a villager moves to town. Sometimes the villager feels "backward" practicing those customs in a cosmopolitan city. This diversity of social behavior was a challenge to me.

Yet I was determined to find some method of capturing the essence of the practices. The first hurdle was to accept the reality that this would *not* be a complete and comprehensive history of all Greek customs and traditions. It is a snapshot of how customs and traditions are practiced in America in the late twentieth century. A comparison with how things are done in Greece and a history of the practice are included when they enhance the subject.

When it came to church traditions, however, the task was easier. Most church tradition is clearly defined despite changes through the centuries. Where a tradition is controversial, the varying positions are usually presented. I hope that the use of this book will give you a clearer direction on how and why things are done a certain way.

Few Greek Americans practice every custom and tradition. (It is impossible even to know them all!) And there is a large difference between significant traditions and the lesser ones. For example, you cannot be in good standing with the church (and participate in the sacraments) if your marriage was not performed in the Orthodox church. Your good standing, however, will not be jeopardized if you do not burn the disposable items from special church services (the palm cross, *epitáphios* flowers, etc.) on Holy Thursday as prescribed in the chapter *The Church of the Home*. Most people do what they can according to their own conviction and time. And since I was unable to include every tradition, you may want to add other traditions that are important to your family and acquaintances. Write them down at the end of the book in the blank section, *Notes*.

I hope you will find joy and new meaning in the wonderful Hellenic and Orthodox heritage as you use this reference book. May you and your family share these traditions with love.

ACKNOWLEDGEMENTS

Centuries of concern by thousands of individuals have preserved Greek traditions and customs to the present day. We are fortunate in America to have vigilant custodians who have given generously of their knowledge and time to make this book possible. Without their cooperation, the book could not have been written. The support, knowledge, and wisdom of my parish priest, Rev. Dr. George Papaioannou of the Greek Orthodox Church of Saint George, Bethesda, Maryland, were invaluable. How fortunate I was to have him — the noted author of several books and the "Tell Me Father" column in the *Orthodox Observer* — as religious editor. The liveliest source was a group of women from St. George who spent countless evenings with me and my tape recorder, fondly recalling customs and traditions from various regions of Greece. My deepest thanks to our Presvytera Maria Papaioannou (Mitilini), Presvytera Moscha Despotides (Sifnos), Rea Assimakopoulos (Constantinople), Sylvia Basdekas (Thessaloniki), Martha Gourdouros (Peloponnesus), Roula Hunter (Athens), Julia Inglesis (Constantinople), Maria Koutrouvelis (Peloponnesus), Mary Merrill (Peloponnesus), Helen Hadgis Pappas (Asia Minor/Sea of Marmara region), Mary Tsangaris (Dodecanese Islands), and Georgia Volakis (Simi/Dodecanese Islands).

The project was blessed with a very talented book production team: Olga A. Deoudes (illustrator), Alicia A. Angelides (book designer), Jeanne Moody (editor and indexer), Helen Petropoulos (Greek editor), and Alice Padwe, Helen Panarites and George Anthan (editors). For review of specific subjects, I relied on Evelyn Bilirakis, Tom Brady, Jennifer Calomiris, Trianthe Dakolias, Lambros Hatzilambrou, Mary Ann Jobe, Maria Kouroupas, Elaine Lailas, Kally Lulias, Julie Markee, John Markos, Lily Menou, Nitsa Morekas, Aphrodite Pallas, Rena and Harilaos Papapostolou, Janet Peachey, Jude Schmidt, Pauline Spyridis, Gina Stevens, Presvytera Sophronia Tomaras, Kathy Tompros, Eva Catafygiotu Topping, Peggy Tramountanas, Irene Vagelos, and Eva Vatakis. The staff of the Theodore J. George Library of Annunciation Cathedral in Baltimore, Maryland, graciously shared its valuable resources.

My husband, Emanuel, helped any time day or night and was a remarkable resource and booster. I thank God for him, my son, Eleftherios, and my daughter, Mary, all of whom gave constant encouragement and suggestions. My sincere gratitude to the Larry Rouvelas and Elias Spyridis families in Seattle and the Harry Papadakes family in Norristown, Pennsylvania, who embraced me from the beginning. With love I also thank my mother, Mary Edmunds, for the gift of religious faith.

Special Acknowledgement

All book-sale profits will be donated to the Greek Orthodox Cultural Center at St. George in Bethesda, Maryland. With gratitude, the church acknowledges the generous support of Rev. Nicholas and Presvytera Moscha Despotides, the Falls Run Family Foundation, and the Ladies Philoptochos Society of St. George, Bethesda, Maryland, for making the production of *A Guide to Greek Traditions and Customs in America* possible.

PRONUNCIATION GUIDE

The Greek words in this book have been transliterated to render pronunciation in standard modern Greek. In some cases, however, a word may be shown with the popular English spelling. These exceptions are included when the word is widely used and accepted such as "*Oxi.*" In such cases the correct pronunciation will be shown in parentheses: *Óxi* (pron. *óchi*).

Greek Capital Letter		Transliteration	Pronounced as
A	*Álpha*	*a*	a in father
B	*Víta*	*v*	v in vase
Γ	*Gámma*	*g* or *y*	g in got or y in yes
Δ	*Thélta*	*th*	th in the
E	*Épsilon*	*e*	e in ten
Z	*Zíta*	*z*	z in zip
H	*Íta*	*i*	i in police
Θ	*Thíta*	TH	th in thin
I	*Ióta*	i	i in police
K	*Káppa*	*k*	k in bike
Λ	*Lámvtha*	*l*	l in laugh
M	*Mi*	*m*	m in me
N	*Ni*	*n*	n in no
Ξ	*Ksi*	*ks* or *x*	ks in rocks or x in ax
O	*Ómikron*	*o*	o in row
Π	*Pi*	*p*	p in piece
P	*Ro*	*r*	r in roll
Σ	*Sígma*	*s*	s in same
T	*Taf*	*t*	t in talk*
Y	*Ípsilon*	*i* or *y*	i in police
Φ	*Fi*	*f* or *ph*	f in farm or ph in photo
X	*Hi*	*h* or *ch*	h in hit or German "ch"
Ψ	*Psi*	*ps*	ps in caps*
Ω	*Oméga*	*o*	o in row
Dipthong:			
OY	*Ómikron ípsilon*	*ou*	ou in coup

*When "t" or "p" are combined with "s" at the beginning of a Greek word, the "t" or "p" is pronounced, *not* left silent as in the English pronunciation of "psychology."

INTRODUCTION:
GREEK AMERICANS
PAST AND PRESENT

When a young Greek-American boy in grade school told one of his classmates that his background was Greek, the classmate responded, "Oh, do you believe in Zeus?" For many the perception of Greek Americans stops with classical Greece — ancient gods, the birthplace of democracy, the Parthenon, and famous philosophers such as Plato and Socrates.

What non-Greeks may not be aware of is the heritage that shaped the Greek Americans after the classical period: the Orthodox faith, four-hundred years of Turkish occupation, numerous wars in the twentieth century, the struggles of immigration to America, and the triumph of developing a Greek-American way of life. Greek Americans come from a rich past. But who are they today?

Are there distinguishing attitudes, habits, and beliefs? Is it ethnicity, history, language, religion, food, music, and dancing? The answer may be found partly by looking back to the first Greek Americans, the early immigrants and their dreams, difficulties, values, and successes.

Early Greek Immigrants

GREEK IMMIGRANTS

Although individuals and small groups came earlier, a Scotsman recruited the first large number of Greeks from Mani in southern Greece as indentured laborers with the promise of land. Approximately 400 to 500 immigrants arrived in 1768 and settled south of St. Augustine, Florida, in a community named New Smyrna. These immigrants endured great hardships and many died. Eventually they left the area, were formally granted freedom in 1777, and moved to St. Augustine. The St. Photios National Shrine in St. Augustine now commemorates the house where they worshiped and serves as a monument to those first immigrants, the equivalent of a Greek-American Plymouth Rock. During the next 100 years, individuals and other small groups arrived, but the first church with a priest, Holy Trinity, was not established until 1864 in New Orleans, Louisiana.

According to a leading Greek-American sociologist, Charles Moskos, at the end of the nineteenth century around 15,000 Greeks had immigrated to the United States. Between 1890-1917, the largest wave of Greek immigrants, 450,000, arrived in America.[1] They came primarily for economic reasons, initially settling mainly in large cities. Eventually, though, Greeks could be found in most cities and in every state. In the big cities they held jobs in factories, restaurants, shoeshine parlors, candy shops, and produce stands. In New England they were blue-collar workers at textile and shoe factories; and in the Midwest and West, many worked in mines and helped build railroads.[2] Smaller groups went South also, to Alabama, North Carolina, Georgia and Florida.[3] The tremendous flow slowed in 1924 when national quotas were set by the American government. The Immigration Act of 1965 ended ethnic quotas, however, and the second largest wave of Greek immigrants (160,000) arrived between 1966 and 1979. All together, 810,000 Greek immigrants came to America between 1873 and 1989.[4]

TRANSPLANTING THE GREEK ETHOS

While many immigrants originally intended to return to Greece, a substantial number stayed and began to recreate the society they had left. A Greek ethos was transplanted to America, a way of life built on the family, church, and ethnic heritage. Early immigrants fiercely tried to perpetuate these values. A close family was the primary base. Parents sacrificed for their children, and children were expected to defer to their elders. Greek Orthodox churches were established to perpetuate the faith and provide a center for cultural and social needs. In addition many immigrants strove to preserve their Greek heritage: the language, history, food, dancing, music, and cultural achievements.

The early immigrants faced enormous challenges. American society discriminated against foreigners, treating them as second-class citizens, contemptuous of their language and life style. The inability to speak English was a substantial barrier to acceptance. Riches flowing in the American streets could be garnered only through hard work, long hours, poor working conditions, and sacrifice. The immigrants, however, believed in the promise of America and the ability of the individual and his family to succeed. Through education, hard work, and the opportunity of an open society, Greeks became highly successful in the United States. They managed to develop a Greek-American way of life rooted in Orthodoxy, Hellenism (Greek secular culture), and American society. Life style and values reflected both Greek and American ways: family, religion, ethnic pride, education, personal honor, and the work ethic. (See *Greek-American Values*)

GENERATIONAL DIFFERENCES

While there are broad values held in common by Greek Americans, the practice of these values, traditions, and customs differs enormously. "Greekness" varies with individual and family circumstances. In general, however, as sociologist Alice Scourby notes in her book *The Greek Americans*, there are significant differences among generations. For example, the first generation of Greek Americans — those born in Greece — vigorously tried to preserve values from the motherland. The second generation — those born in America but having at least one parent born in Greece — was more assimilated but often felt ambivalent about being Greek American. Some rejected the Greek aspects and others overcompensated. The third generation — both parents born in America — usually felt comfortable as Americans with their Greek heritage.[5]

DEFINING ANCESTRY

The issue of ancestry poses a thorny problem. How far removed can one's Greek ancestors be for one to still be Greek — fifth generation, tenth? The United States Bureau of the Census adopted the policy of letting people define themselves. It asked each American to indicate his or her ancestry. In 1990, just over one million claimed to have Greek ancestors.[6] But what of the future? A new infusion of Greek immigrants is unlikely. Marriages between Greek Orthodox and non-Greek Orthodox are on the rise: thirty percent in the 1960s, and sixty percent in the 1980s.[7]

Without learned culture and heritage, does a person with Greek ancestors remain Greek? What parts of the heritage — the religion, food, dancing, music, history, language, values — are essential to maintaining the identity? These are questions facing Greek Americans today. Should the Greek-American way continue to evolve and change as it has since those early immigrants? Does change mean its demise or can it be a positive transformation? Is preservation desirable and possible? These questions are being addressed by the church, the community, and the individual. I believe that the heritage can and should be preserved.

PRESERVING ORTHODOXY AND HELLENISM

Many Greek Americans are preserving their identity and culture through numerous organizations. The church has been in the forefront of the movement to preserve Hellenism. Until 1948 it actively advised against marriage between Greeks and non-Greeks. Use of the English language in services was officially discouraged until 1970. The church has sponsored Greek language classes for generations and continues to express its concern. A two-year study published in 1991 by the Archdiocese concludes that the best structure for maintaining Greek identity is on a strong spiritual base fostered in active church life.[8]

Greek-American community organizations also play a substantial role in preserving the Hellenic heritage. Regional societies attract members who are from the same parts of Greece, such as Thessaly, Athens, Crete. Many community organizations sponsor Hellenic cultural affairs. Greek professionals may come together for mutual benefit, bonding because of their ethnic background. The Greek-American media (print, radio, and television) keep Hellenism and

Orthodoxy visible. "Greek Towns" in some large cities perpetuate a Greek life style. To a large extent, however, defining who is Greek American comes down to the individual. Each person must evaluate the merits, attractiveness, and reasons for the traditions and customs.

This book describes the Greek traditions and customs in use today in America. It explains contemporary Greek-American values and how they developed. It provides useful and meaningful information on the many religious practices of Orthodoxy: the seven sacraments, the beliefs, fasting, icons, death and mourning, saints, name days, the home *ikonostási,* and the highlights of major holidays, including Greek Independence Day. The dynamism of Greek-American secular life is covered in chapters on food, music, dancing, superstitions, proverbs, vacationing in Greece, and participating in the community.

I hope this book will provide you with the insight, appreciation, and information to follow in the footsteps of the earlier generations who kept the Greek spirit alive.

---

1. Charles C. Moskos, *Greek Americans: Struggle and Success,* 2d. ed. (New Brunswick, N.J.: Transaction Publishers, 1989), 156.

2. Ibid. 13.

3. Ibid. 25.

4. Ibid. 156.

5. Alice Scourby, *The Greek Americans* (Boston: Twayne Publishers, 1984), 73-74.

6. U.S. Bureau of the Census, *1990 Detailed Ancestry Groups for States,* CPH-L-97, 1.

7. "Future Theological Agenda of the Archdiocese — Conclusion," *Orthodox Observer,* March, 1991.

8. Ibid.

PART ONE

The Enduring Traditions of Orthodoxy

Holy Cross Chapel
Brookline, Massachusetts

✤ *The Church*

The Greek Orthodox church plays a major role in Greek-American life. Many traditions and customs have a religious basis, and most churches offer a broad range of secular activities such as dances, festivals, and cultural events. At the church's core remains a treasury of tradition: beliefs, history, art, architecture, language, music, and services. That tradition satisfies the deep religious needs of Orthodox believers. Others may find the church some-what intimidating and inaccessible. Through understanding, how-ever, a new appreciation and faith may develop.

ORTHODOX BELIEFS

ORIGIN

Orthodoxy remains virtually unchanged since its beginnings al-most two thousand years ago. The church began with the descent of the Holy Spirit to Christ's twelve apostles fifty days after his Resurrection, filling them with the grace, will, and ability to carry on his message. Through the Holy Spirit, God's will continues to be revealed and interpreted for the church on earth. This continu-ity and stable tradition are essential characteristics of Orthodoxy, giving it an "air of antiquity [and] changelessness" as described by Timothy Ware in his classic work on the church, *The Orthodox Church*.[1]

Over time a vast "Holy Tradition" developed. Ware explains that Tradition "means the books of the Bible; it means the Creed; it means the decrees of the Ecumenical Councils and the writings of the Fathers; it means the Canons, the Service Books, the Holy Icons — in fact, the whole system of doctrine, Church govern-ment, worship, and art which Orthodoxy has articulated over the ages."[2] The literal interpretation of the word "Orthodoxy" reflects this long Tradition: *orthós* (correct) and *dóxa* (belief).

DOCTRINE (DOGMA)

Doctrine (dogma) is a belief revealed by God as contained in the Bible or formulated by the church. The faithful accept it as a final and unchangeable truth. These doctrines are strictly connected with the basic beliefs of the faith and as such cannot be altered or replaced by other teachings. For example, the belief that Jesus Christ is the incarnate Son of God was revealed by God to man at Christ's baptism. This is a doctrine. Changing this belief is to change basically the Christian religion. For a comprehensive explanation of Orthodox theology read *The Orthodox Way* by Kallistos Ware.[3]

The most important statement of the faith is the Nicene Creed, recited by the parishioners during each Divine Liturgy.

The Nicene Creed

I believe in one God, the Father, the almighty, creator of heaven and earth, and of all things visible and invisible.

And in one Lord, Jesus Christ, the only begotten Son of God, begotten of the Father before all ages. Light of light, true God of true God, begotten, not created, of one essence with the Father, through whom all things were made.

For us and for our salvation, he came down from heaven and was incarnate by the Holy Spirit and the Virgin Mary and became man. He was crucified for us under Pontius Pilate, and he suffered and was buried. On the third day he rose according to the scriptures. He ascended into heaven and is seated at the right hand of the Father. He will come again in glory to judge the living and the dead. His kingdom will have no end.

And in the Holy Spirit, the Lord, the giver of life, who proceeds from the Father, who together with the Father and the Son is worshiped and glorified, who spoke through the prophets.

In one, holy, catholic, and apostolic church.
I acknowledge one baptism for the forgiveness of sins.
I expect the resurrection of the dead.
And the life of the age to come. Amen.

To Sýmvolon tis Písteos (To Pistévo)

Pistévo is éna THeón, Patéra, Pantokrátora, Piitín
ouranoú ke yis, oratón te pánton ke aoráton.
Ke is éna Kírion Iisoún Christón ton Ión tou THeoú,
ton monoyení, ton ek tou Patrós yenniTHénta pró pánton
ton eónon. Fós ek fotós, THeón aliTHinón, ek THeoú
aliTHinoú yenniTHénta, ou piiTHénta, omooúsion to
Patrí, thi ou ta pánta eyéneto.

Ton thi imás tous anTHrópous ke thiá tin imetéran
sotirían katelTHónta ek ton ouranón, ke sarkoTHénta,
ek Pnévmatos Ayíou ke Marías tis ParTHénou ke
enanTHropísanta. StavroTHénta te ipér imón epí Pontíou
Pilátou ke paTHónta ke tafénta. Ke anastánta ti tríti
iméra katá tas grafás. Ke anelTHónta is tous ouranoús
ke kaTHezómenon ek thexión tou Patrós. Ke pálin
erhómenon metá thóxis kríne zóntas ke nekroús, ou tis
vasilías ouk éste télos.

Ke is to Pnévma to Áyion, to Kírion, to zoopión, to ek
tou Patrós ekporevómenon, to sin Patrí ke Ió simpros-
kinoúmenon ke sinthoxazómenon to lalísan thiá ton
profitón.

Is mían, ayían, kaTHolikín ke apostolikín ekklisían.
Omologó en váptisma is áfesin amartión.
Prosthokó anástasin nekrón.
Ke zoín tou méllontos eónos. Amín.

CANON LAW

Canons are the rules concerning church sacramental, disciplinary, and administrative practices developed over the centuries by council decrees and individual church fathers. These rules deal with the earthly life of the church: fasting, marriage of priests, political administration, etc., and serve to discipline both the clergy and the people. The most widely used English translation containing approximately 1,000 canon laws is *The Rudder* by D. Cummings.[4]

The Church

Changing Canon Law

Unlike immutable dogma, canons can be changed by church councils, regional synods, and individual church fathers. Many of the existing canons are not applicable to contemporary situations and thus have become obsolete. The church realizes this, and for many years a pan-Orthodox group, representing different churches of Orthodoxy throughout the world under the leadership of the Ecumenical Patriarchate of Constantinople, has been working diligently to prepare a list of canons to change, add, and omit at a future meeting. Since the Orthodox church has not been administratively unified for centuries, the last council of the entire church administration was the Seventh Ecumenical Council convened in 783.

Oikonomía

Oikonomía (pron. *ikonomía*) means the act of mercy concerning the canons in extraordinary cases. For example, a canon states that a man and woman who have the same godparent cannot marry because they are considered brother and sister spiritually. The church may use *oikonomía* as an act of mercy to allow the marriage. Only a bishop and a higher church authority may make such decisions.

THE ORTHODOX CONCEPT OF *THÉOSIS*

The purpose of Orthodoxy is to help and guide the individual to reach safely the destination of *théosis* (pron. *THéosis*), a complete identification with God. *Théosis* is derived from the basic teaching of the Bible as stated in Gen. 1:26: "Let us make man in our image, after our likeness..." Your personal challenge, therefore, throughout your life is to find and reveal the godlike image within you.

Achieving *Théosis*

The task, though difficult, is not impossible. Sin gets in the way, blurring God's perfect image. God, however, did not abandon man to struggle alone and combat sin, but sent his son, Jesus Christ, to serve as a model and lead one to that destination. God became man so that man could become God, as stated by St.

Athanasios in the fourth century. By emulating Christ's life, you can become like Christ and therefore like God. This is a difficult task and requires the grace of the Holy Spirit. It is within the established services of the church and in your relationship with others that *théosis* can be approached.

Théosis through Participation in the Sacramental Life of the Church

You should attend church regularly, participate in the sacraments, pray to God, and read the Bible. In the Divine Liturgy you can identify with your fellow Christians and participate in Holy Communion, sharing the Body and the Blood of Christ. Through the Divine Liturgy and other services, you are helped to live a life worthy of this high calling, your own *théosis.* Private prayer, reading the scriptures, the practice of giving to charity, the use of the sacrament of confession, and the guidance of a spiritual father help you reach your goal.

In addition, the church provides many opportunities to emulate Christ through services that reenact the major events in his life: the forty-day blessing, baptism, fasting, burial, the achievement of eternal life. Just as Christ was brought to church after forty days by his mother, so are you. As Christ received the Holy Spirit at his baptism, so do you. Even the Divine Liturgy is a symbolic reenactment of Christ's life every time it is offered.

Théosis through Relations with Others

In addition to regular participation in the church, you should act towards others as Christ did: kind, tolerant, helpful, forgiving, and loving. Christ's love of humanity is one of his greatest qualities, and he is referred to in the Divine Liturgy as *philánthropos*, (lover of man). His example of Christian charity and love is a model for daily living.

ARCHITECTURE AND ART

Orthodox churches are noted for the beauty and elegance of their Byzantine architecture. The grandest prototype is the cathedral of St. Sophia erected in Constantinople in the sixth century. Here can be seen the classic Byzantine style dominated by two elements, the dome and the church proper shaped like a cross. This form influences the design of most Orthodox churches though each has its own distinct style ranging from the modern Church of the Annunciation designed by Frank Lloyd Wright in Milwaukee, Wisconsin, to the classic St. Sophia Cathedral in Washington, D.C., to a modest hut with a thatched roof in Kenya.

CLASSIC BYZANTINE ARCHITECTURE

The main features of classic Byzantine architecture on the outside include a square on ground level, a cross on the second, and a dome on the third.

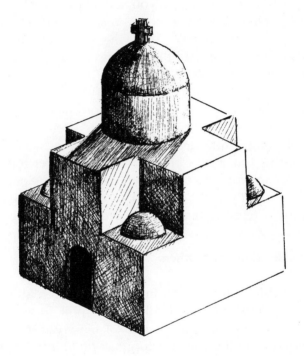

Classic Byzantine Architecture

On the inside the basic features are an entry section called the narthex for the purpose of assembly, lighting candles, and revering icons; a nave where parishioners worship; and the sanctuary with the altar for clergy and assistants.

NARTHEX

The entry point of the church, the narthex, provides an area of preparation for worship with its candlestand and icons. After making a donation, each visitor lights a candle in honor of Christ and for individuals to be remembered. Icons of the Virgin Mary holding Christ and the saint or event for which the church was named are prominently displayed. The visitor makes the sign of the cross and kisses one or more icons before proceeding into the nave.

During the first centuries of Christianity the purpose of the narthex was to accommodate the catechumens, those who were not already baptized. When the second part of the liturgy was to begin, the catechumens were ordered by the deacon to leave the nave and go to the narthex. Today this practice is still followed in a service called the Liturgy of the Presanctified Gifts. In addition, the first part of the sacrament of baptism takes place in the narthex.

NAVE

The beautiful, often elaborate, Byzantine interior transports the worshiper to a level of spiritual exaltation. It strives to create heaven on earth so the faithful may worship together with God and the saints. The floor symbolizes earth and the dome symbolizes heaven where the worshipers are reminded that although they reside on earth, their final and certain destination is heaven.

Large full-length icons of Christ, Mary, and other saints immediately engage those entering the nave. The saints serve as examples to the ordinary faithful that they too can attain the destiny of heaven if they live according to the teachings of the church. Just as these saints have achieved *théosis*, so can the parishioner. Other icons may depict important events in the life of Christ.

The church icons are arranged in a standard pattern. The dome displays the icon of Christ as the Pantokrator (omnipotent God), holding the Gospel and blessing the congregation with his raised hand. Additional icons can be found in different parts of the church but most notably on a large screen called the *ikonostásion* (icon stand) that separates the nave from the altar area. The icons are arranged in prescribed tiers. All churches have a bottom tier that includes (as viewed from left to right): the Archangel Michael, the saint or event for which the church was named, the Virgin Mary, the Royal Gates with the four evangelists, Jesus Christ, St. John the Baptist, and the Archangel Gabriel. Icons relating to the twelve great feast days of Orthodoxy, the disciples, and the Virgin Mary may be included in additional tiers.

Church Interior

Icons of other saints and significant Biblical events may be added to the walls of the church in frescoes, mosaics, and moveable boards. They, too, contribute to the extended family of saints that worship with the congregation.

Two other prominent features of the nave are the pulpit and the bishop's chair. From the pulpit the primary teachings of the day are delivered to the parishioners through the reading of the Gospel and the delivery of the sermon. The elaborate bishop's chair is reserved for a visiting bishop or archbishop.

SANCTUARY

The sanctuary, separated from the nave by the *ikonostásion*, is always located on the east side of the church because Christ, the light of the world, will arise again in the east. The sanctuary has four main features: the altar, the table of oblation, the Platytera, and the crucifix.

It is here that the greatest mystery of the church — the changing of the bread and wine into the Body and Blood of Jesus Christ — takes place. The central element is the altar which represents his tomb. The other elements are complementary to the altar, such as the table of oblation placed to the left of the altar. The table normally stands in a concave area that represents Christ's manger. The icon is that of the Nativity. The oblation table is where the priest conducts the *proskomithí* during the *órthros* service, in which he prepares the bread and the wine to be used for Holy Communion (Eucharist).

Most of the Divine Liturgy is conducted around the altar, usually made of stone or marble in keeping with the practice of the early Christians who used the tombs of their deceased brethren for tables to perform the Eucharist. Relics of saints are even placed in each altar to replicate those early tables. One or more columns support the altar. The one column signifies the foundation of the world, Jesus Christ. Four columns signify the four evangelists: Matthew, Mark, Luke, and John. On the altar the changing of the bread and wine takes place, the church's most important mystery. On the top of the altar lie the Gospel book and the *artophórion*, a large four-sided box made of precious metal with a cross on top that contains the consecrated bread immersed in the Blood of Jesus. This is reserved for emergencies and for the offering following the sacrament of baptism. Behind the altar stands a large crucifix on which the body of Christ hangs, a reminder of his sacrifice for mankind.

The ceiling above the altar shows the Platytera ton Ouranon (wider than heaven), depicting the Virgin Mary with open arms and with the Christ Child on her lap. She is called Platytera because in her womb she held the omnipotent God. Her outstretched arms welcome and encompass the worshiper.

As a usual practice, only clergy and male laymen go beyond the *ikonostásion* and into the altar area. More recently the individual parish priest may make allowances, for instance when a female baby is brought for the forty-day blessing. (See *Birth of Children*)

*Byzantine
Cross*

*Greek
Cross*

CROSSES

The primary symbol of Christianity, the cross, appears throughout the church. Many styles are used, including crosses with equal sides, T shapes, and decorative variations. None is more Byzantine or Orthodox than the other, but art historians have applied the term "Greek" to the cross with equal sides and "Byzantine" to the one with a longer vertical.

The cross holds a special place in the life of the church and each individual Christian. Orthodox Christians have crosses in their homes and wear them around their necks, not as ornaments but as a symbols of protection and constant reminders of their identification with the sacrifice of the Lord.

BYZANTINE MUSIC

CHARACTERISTICS

Mystical, non-Western music distinguishes the Greek Orthodox church service. It wafts and echoes through the church expressing the soul's longing to communicate with God and the saints. Deceptively simple, it integrates theology, text, and music to express the purpose of the church service and transport the listener into another realm. Classic Byzantine music has a single-line melody with a parallel background tone. It is based on an eight-mode system with non-Western rhythm and notation. The single-line melody (plain chant) represents a direct prayer to God from the heart, through the mouth. Traditionalists maintain that only the human voice can adequately express the feelings to be communicated. The chanter (*psáltis*) interprets text, turning it into worship. Even individuals singing in groups should use one voice like the angelic choirs in heaven.

The eight modes are varying scales, expressing different moods. Unlike the West where an entire song is composed in one time (such as 4/4), Byzantine music is tonic, i.e., it follows the syllables and accents of prose text and thus has no consistent rhythm. The musical notation bears no resemblance to that of the West either. In the nineteenth century, reformers made substantial revisions, resulting in the neo-Byzantine music system in use today.

VARIATIONS

In the United States, radical changes were made in Byzantine music during the twentieth century with the blessing of the church hierarchy. Today a typical Divine Liturgy features three types of Byzantine-based music: single-melody chants by one *psáltis*, chants in free harmony by several *psáltes*, and full harmony works sung to organ accompaniment by a choir with men and (unlike Greece) women. The choral works may combine Western music style and the Byzantine chant. One of the most popular choral liturgies today was written in 1951 by Greek-American Frank Desby. Other Greek-American composers have also written liturgies, most of them more Westernized than Desby's. Close to the Byzantine tradition is the music of Anna Gallos. Even more Byzantine is the music of Harilaos Papapostolou, choir director of St. Sophia Cathedral in Washington, D.C. In most parishes, the priest, *psáltes*, and choir perform the music in the Orthodox service. The congregation rarely sings, except for those parishioners familiar enough with the liturgy to "sub-sing" in low voices to themselves.

Use of the organ in America is a radical departure from Byzantine tradition. Many early parishes acquired existing non-Orthodox churches with organs and began using them. Archbishop of North and South America Athenagoras (1931-1948) believed that a similar instrument had been used at St. Sophia Cathedral in Constantinople and approved its use.

HYMNS

A wealth of hymns contributes to the treasury of Orthodox tradition and elevates worshipers with their elegant poetic style. The *psáltes* and choir sing most hymns, but many may be followed in the four primary hymn books: *The Lenten Triodion, The Festal Menaion*, the *Pentecostarion,* and the *Parakletike*. All may be purchased for personal use, and the first three have been translated into English.[5]

LANGUAGE

Today the majority of Greek Orthodox churches in the United States conduct services in Greek and English, alternating the two languages as the service progresses. Certain portions of the service such as the Gospel, Epistle, Nicene Creed, and Lord's Prayer may be repeated in both languages. This accommodation is relatively recent, coming into widespread practice during the 1960s.

The introduction of English into the Greek Orthodox services has been a divisive and difficult problem. Factions adamant about preserving the Greek language dominated for three-quarters of the twentieth century. They feared the loss of Greek identity and important religious traditions. During his tenure as Archbishop of North and South America, the Ecumenical Patriarch Athenagoras insisted that Greek always be used in the church services and the sermons.

A large wave of new immigrants to the United States after World War II increased the number of Greek-speaking church members, reinforcing the anti-English sentiment. In 1950 English was allowed in the Sunday schools, but official English usage stopped there. Meanwhile parishes themselves began introducing English into the services, and the practice became sufficiently widespread that in 1970 a new Archbishop, Iakovos, proposed the use of English where needed in the service and sermons. It was resisted by many groups and disapproved by the highest church authority, the Ecumenical Patriarch Athenagoras. After the furor subsided, however, the clergy did what best suited their individual parishes, resulting in the combination today of both English and Greek. Various English translations of the liturgy have been in use for years, but the prevailing English version is the liturgy prepared by the members of the faculty of Hellenic College/Holy Cross Greek Orthodox School of Theology.[6]

Byzantine Greek comprises most of the liturgy, except for koine (common — pron. *kiní*) used in the Gospels. Koine — the Greek language of the Hellenistic and Roman periods — was used to write the New Testament.

SERVICES

The Orthodox church holds many services, ranging from the daily morning matins (*órthros*) and evening vespers to the glorious Easter service at midnight. But the most important and most frequently attended service is the Divine Liturgy held throughout the world every Sunday and on special feast days. The same service conducted centuries ago at the center of Orthodoxy in Constantinople is conducted the same way today. Generation after generation appreciates and loves its beauty and consistency.

There are four liturgies in the Greek Orthodox church:
St. John Chrysostom (most frequently used)
St. Basil (ten times a year)
St. James (on October 23)
Liturgy of the Presanctified Gifts (Wednesday and Fridays of Lent and the first three days of Easter Holy Week)

PURPOSE OF THE DIVINE LITURGY

The primary purpose of the Divine Liturgy is the offering of the Eucharist in which bread and wine are transformed into the Body and Blood of Christ (the holy Gifts). The faithful unite with Christ and one another during the service. Christ instituted this tradition at the Last Supper to establish an ongoing communion between himself and his followers. It provides a way for them to constantly receive renewal and grace. The entire liturgy leads to that moment when the parishioners come to the front of the church to take the sacrament (see *Communion*).

ROLE OF THE PRIEST

Between the congregation and God stands the priest. He is human, one of the congregants, but vested with the authority to offer the sacrament. In this capacity the priest offers the liturgy and acts in the place of Christ who is the real celebrant of the Eucharist.

AN INTELLECTUAL AND EMOTIONAL EXPERIENCE

Intellectually, the service enables one to communicate with God: offering praise, asking mercy, and learning lessons of life conduct. Emotionally, the prayers of the service penetrate deeply into the soul of the worshiper, stimulating the fervent desire to elevate oneself to a higher level of existence, the unreachable, the sublime. The senses are stimulated by many elements. The beauty of the icons, vestments, and architecture have visual appeal. The incense, symbolically lifting prayers to God, stimulates the sense of smell. The bells on the censer and the hymns please the ear.

The taste of the holy Gifts satisfies the palate. These sensual experiences transport the worshiper to the spiritual world and are part of the Orthodox way of teaching God's message and bringing the faithful into union with him.

INVOLVEMENT IN THE DIVINE LITURGY

Some parishioners complain about their passive role in the liturgy. The priest, chanter, and choir appear to do everything. Work and concentration are required on your part to make the service meaningful.

- Follow the text in the service book. The priest's petitions and prayers are also yours.
- Learn from the Gospel and the Epistle.
- Recite the Creed and the Lord's Prayer.
- Understand the symbolism in the service.
- Make the sign of the cross and kneel where appropriate (see "Church Etiquette" below).
- Take communion as often as possible.

DIVINE LITURGY OF ST. JOHN CHRYSOSTOM

The following guide summarizes the most frequently attended service, the Divine Liturgy of St. John Chrysostom.

In the first part, the "Liturgy of the Word," the priest guides the people in their prayers and supplications to God for a peaceful Christian life. They ask for mercy for the saints, civil and religious leaders, for good harvests, and help for those who suffer. People are asked to commit themselves to God and to be saved through the intercessions of the Virgin Mary. Then the Gospel bound in a large gold book is brought in during the Small Entrance, symbolizing Christ's coming to earth as a teacher. A reading from the Epistles of St. Paul or the Acts of the Apostles gives worshipers advice on how to conduct their lives according to Christ's life. The Gospel reading then relates a specific teaching from Christ's life. This may be followed by the sermon, ending the teachings for the day. For practical reasons, because not all of the worshipers are in church at this time, it has become customary in America for the sermons to be given at the conclusion of the entire liturgy.

The second part, the "Liturgy of the Faithful," prepares worshipers to receive communion. It is known as the Liturgy of the Faithful because it was intended for those who have been baptized. In an earlier time, the unbaptized were ordered to depart from the nave after the first part of the service. Today the faithful are implored to put away worldly cares, and God is asked to cleanse them, making them worthy to receive the holy Gifts. The Great Entrance then begins with the priest, preceded by altar boys, bringing the holy chalice with the wine and water and the holy paten holding the bread, into the nave of the church. The priest represents Christ carrying his cross on the way to Golgotha. He returns to the altar with the holy Gifts and begins a set of petitions that culminate with the recitation of the Creed, the twelve basic articles of the Christian faith. A singing dialogue begins among the priest and the people, represented by the choir and/or chanter, as they prepare for the consecration of the holy Gifts. The eucharistic prayer gives thanks for the gifts and offers them to God. The climax of the liturgy occurs when the bread and wine are consecrated. With the priest and congregation kneeling, the Holy Spirit transforms the elements into the Body and Blood of Christ. After the recitation of the Lord's Prayer (Pater Imon), comes the communion prayer asking for purification and forgiveness. The priest takes communion and then offers it to those who have prepared themselves by repenting and fasting. Closing prayers follow, and a piece of bread is distributed to everyone in the church as a blessing and an expression of love and fellowship.

THE LORD'S PRAYER

Our Father, who art in heaven, hallowed be thy name. Thy kingdom come. Thy will be done, on earth as it is in heaven. Give us this day our daily bread; and forgive us our trespasses, as we forgive those who trespass against us; and lead us not into temptation, but deliver us from evil.

Priest only: For thine is the kingdom and the power and the glory of the Father, and the Son, and the Holy Spirit, now and forever and to the ages of ages. Amen.

Páter Imón

Páter imón, o en tís ouranís, ayiasTHíto to ónomá sou,
ElTHéto i vasilía sou. YeniTHíto to THélimá sou, os en
ouranó ke épi tis yís. Ton árton imón ton epioúsion,
thós imin símeron. Ke áfes imín ta ofilímata imón, ós
ke imís afíemen tís ofilétes imón. Ke mí isenégis imás ís
pirasmón, alla ríse imás apo tou piroroú.

Priest only: *Óti soú estín, i vasilía ke i thínamis ke i*
thóxa tou Patrós ke tou Ioú ke tou Ayíou Pnévmatos,
nín ke aí ke is tous eónas ton eónon. Amín.

CHURCH ETIQUETTE

PURPOSE

If you were not raised in the Orthodox church, you may vividly
recall your first service. There was a bewildering number of "do's"
and "don'ts": Enter only at certain times; stand and sit sporadi-
cally; parishioners making the sign of the cross; English and Greek
interwoven. What is the logic of it all? The rules of conduct in
the church are external gestures that help you express and foster
your faith. Their repeated habit can provide a sense of stability.
The following suggestions will help you understand and master
church etiquette.

ATTIRE

Since you are meeting God at church, it is respectful to present
yourself in a clean and neat manner. For church services, dresses
and skirts are preferred for women and jackets for men. In American Greek Orthodox churches, head and shoulder coverings for
women are no longer required, but modesty is strongly recommended. If you plan to take communion, do not wear lipstick.

ARRIVAL TIME

Orthodox church services begin on time, but few parishioners are
ever there! Parishioners arrive throughout the service. This is a
matter of individual choice, of course, but late church arrival is a

bad habit — bad for you and for your fellow parishioners who are interrupted. The Divine Liturgy usually lasts about an hour and a half. Do your best to arrive within the first half hour to hear the Epistle and Gospel.

ENTERING THE NARTHEX

When you enter the narthex, stop all talking. This is a time to prepare for worship. Bow your head, make the sign of the cross, and make an offering for a candle. Light the candle from another one at the candle stand. Venerate the icons by making the sign of the cross before kissing them. If there are two major figures in the same icon, such as the Virgin Mary holding Christ, kiss them both if you wish. Many parishioners say short prayers during these preparations.

CANDLES

The lighted candle is a constant symbol in the Orthodox church. It represents the light of Christ according to Jesus' own words, "I am the light of the world; he who follows me will not walk in darkness, but will have the light of life." John 8:12.

When you light a candle, say a brief prayer that your life will shine as Christ commanded in Matt. 5:16: "Let your light so shine before men, that they may see your good works and give glory to your Father who is in heaven." Light a candle to honor him and reaffirm that you are a follower in the faith. It is also common to light one for someone in need, to honor a saint, or to commemorate a deceased loved one.

SIGNING THE CROSS

Meaning

The cross is the most powerful symbol in Christianity for it was on the cross that Christ died. In a sign of mutual recognition, an early Christian could quickly make the sign of the cross for identification. Today it is used in a variety of situations: to show the believer's faith, to invoke God's presence, to begin and end a prayer, to protect against evil and to show thanksgiving. The cross can be made with a spoken or silent prayer.

How to Make the Sign

The proper Orthodox cross is made by holding the thumb and first two fingers of the right hand together and resting the remaining two fingers on the palm.

The three fingers together represent the Father, Son, and Holy Spirit, and the remaining two fingers the dual nature of Christ as God and man. The fingers and thumb are placed first on the forehead, then the center of the chest, the right shoulder, then the left shoulder. (The right shoulder is touched first because Christ sits at the right hand of God.) The motion should be continuous and distinct, done either once or three times consecutively. At the end the hand is then opened and placed on the center of the chest. Always make your cross distinctly and with conviction. A poorly executed cross is disrespectful. Sometimes a parishioner will bow, make a cross and then touch the floor (repeating the sequence three times). This is known as a *metánia*. On occasion a devout parishioner may kneel, make a cross, and kiss the ground numerous times.

Hand position for signing the cross

Young children are first taught to make their cross while saying and singing the "Ayios O Theos" (pron. *THeós* — Holy God).[7]

When to Make the Sign of the Cross

1. Whenever you feel the need
2. Before and after any prayers
3. When you enter and leave the narthex and nave
4. Before you kiss an icon, cross, or the Gospel book
5. When you pass the altar
6. When you hear any of the following phrases:
   - "The Father, and the Son, and the Holy Spirit"
   - *"Áyios O Theós, Áyios Ischirós, Áyios ATHánatos, eléison imas."* (Holy God, Holy Mighty, Holy Immortal, have mercy on us.)
   - "Theotokos," "Panayia," or "Virgin Mary"
   - The name of a saint
7. When the censer is moved in your direction
8. After the reading of the Epistle and the Gospel
9. Near the end of the Nicene Creed at the phrase "In one, holy catholic, and apostolic church"
10. After kneeling for the consecration during the Divine Liturgy

11. At the end of the Lord's Prayer while the priest says, "For Thine is the kingdom and the power and the glory forever. Amen."
12. Whenever the priest makes the sign of the cross
13. Immediately before and after receiving communion
14. Before receiving *antídoron* (see below)

Ayios o Theos

A - yi - os o The - ós, A - yi - os I - schi - rós,

A - yi - os A - THá - na - tos, e - lé - i - son i - más.

Thóxa Patrí ke ió ke Ayío Pnév - ma - ti

ke nin ke aí ke is tous eónas ton e - ó - non. A - min.

A - yi os A - THá - na - tos, e - lé - i - son i - más. Thí - na - mis.

Holy God, Holy Mighty, Holy Immortal, have mercy on us. Glory to the Father, and the Son and the Holy Spirit, now and forever and to the ages of ages. Amen. Holy Immortal, have mercy on us. [Give us] strength.

ENTERING THE NAVE

Make the sign of the cross when entering the main part of the church, the nave. If a service is not in progress, you should go to the front, make the sign of the cross and kiss the icon of Christ and then Mary in the *ikonostásion* and any other icons you wish. If a service is in progress, especially the Divine Liturgy, enter at the proper time (see "Etiquette for the Divine Liturgy"). If you are unsure, ask an usher if you may proceed. You may sit anywhere you wish, unless seats are reserved or a memorial service is scheduled. Normally the first several rows on the right-hand side of the church in front of the icon of Christ are reserved for the family and friends of a deceased person.

GENERAL DECORUM

General church decorum has changed through the years. The earliest churches in the United States were similar to those in Greece. There were no pews, and people were constantly moving around, in and out, frequently bowing and touching the floor while making their crosses. Except for the separation of men to the right side of the church and women to the left, there was an uninhibited quality to Orthodox worship. Occasionally this former style of worship is still seen in some American churches. For example, you may see a parishioner standing through most of the service with his or her body bent forward in a reverent bow, making the cross frequently, touching the ground, and singing the liturgy in a low voice. Today's American congregation, in contrast, is more reserved, perhaps because of the addition of pews.

ETIQUETTE FOR THE DIVINE LITURGY

1. Arrive in time to hear the Epistle and the Holy Gospel.
2. Enter the narthex as described above, make your cross, light a candle, and kiss the icons.
3. Enter the nave any time except during the following:
    *   Beginning of the service when the priest says: "Blessed is the Kingdom of the Father, Son, and Holy Spirit."
    *   During the Small Entrance with the Gospel
    *   During the reading of the Epistle and the Gospel
    *   During the Great Entrance with the chalice

- During the recitation of the Nicene Creed
- During the transformation of the bread and wine when parishioners are kneeling
- During the recitation of the Lord's Prayer

4. Make the sign of the cross at the appropriate places.

5. Stand during the Small Entrance, the reading of the Gospel, the Great Entrance, Nicene Creed, and the Lord's Prayer. For additional times follow the service book and watch for the priest's signal (a bell, light, or hand sign).

6. Kneel during the consecration of the Gifts (when the bread and the wine are being changed into the Body and Blood of Christ — except during the first forty days after Easter).

7. If you are taking communion, be prepared by fasting and confessing privately or by sacrament. Women should not wear lipstick. Go to the front of the church when the priest says, "With fear of God, faith and love, draw near." When you reach the priest, make the sign of the cross, tell him your baptismal name, hold the red cloth under your chin, and he will put a spoon containing the Gifts in your mouth. Hold the cloth for the next person. Make the sign of the cross again and take the bread offered by the altar boy.

8. At the end of the service, take the *antídoron*, a small piece of bread. Everyone, Orthodox and non-Orthodox, receives it as an expression of love and Christian fellowship. *Antídoron* (pron. *andíthoron*) is a compound word meaning "Instead of the gift." It is not consecrated but blessed at the altar. Go to the front of the church where the priest hands out the small pieces of bread. Make the sign of the cross while approaching the priest and kiss his hand as he gives it to you. Walk down the center aisle and as you leave the nave, turn and bow toward the altar, make the sign of the cross, and exit.

1. Timothy Ware, *The Orthodox Church* (1963; reprint, London: Penguin Books, 1987), 203. The book covers the political history of the Orthodox church and explains its beliefs and traditions.

2. Ibid. 204.

3. Kallistos [Timothy] Ware, *The Orthodox Way* (1979; reprint, Crestwood, N.Y.: St. Vladimir's Seminary Press, 1986).

4. D. Cummings, *The Rudder* (Chicago: The Orthodox Christian Educational Society, 1957).

5. Hymns for nine great feast days have been translated in *The Festal Menaion,* trans. Mother Mary and Kallistos Ware (1969; South Cannan, Pa.: St. Tikhon's Seminary Press, 1990). Hymns for Lent through Holy Week may be found in *The Lenten Triodion,* trans. Mother Mary and Kallistos Ware (1978; reprint, London: Faber and Faber, 1984). Hymns for Easter through the Sunday of All Saints are contained in the *Pentecostarion,* trans. Holy Transfiguration Monastery (Brookline, Mass.: Holy Transfiguration Monastery, 1990). The *Parakletike,* trans. Holy Transfiguration Monastery (Brookline, Mass.: Holy Transfiguration Monastery, 1990) contains hymns for each day of the year in Greek.

6. Members of the Faculty of Hellenic College/Holy Cross Greek Orthodox School of Theology, trans. *The Divine Liturgy of Saint John Chrysostom* (Brookline, Mass.: Holy Cross Orthodox Press, 1985).

7. "Ayios o Theos" adapted from Nick and Connie Maragos, eds. *Sharing in Song: A Songbook for Greek Orthodox Gatherings* (Sherman Oakes, Calif.: The National Forum of Greek Orthodox Church Musicians, 1988), 3.

❧ *The Seven Sacraments*

The Orthodox believe that God should be present in all facets of life. Life is a continuous striving for perfection and sanctification. To help individuals reach that perfection, the church provides its members the sacraments *(mystírion)*, seven of its most important services. These seven sacraments are the jewels of Orthodox spirituality:

- Baptism
- Chrismation
- Confession
- Communion
- Marriage
- Holy Unction
- Holy Orders

The term "mystery" describes the miraculous way that the grace of God and the Holy Spirit come to worshipers through the sacraments, enabling them to perfect themselves in God's image *(théosis)*. In confession and communion, for example, God's healing forgiveness cleanses the individual of sins, and the Body and Blood of Christ replenish the sacred self. In marriage the grace of God's love nurtures the sacred union of husband and wife.

The sacraments are administered only by priests to the Orthodox who have been baptized in the church and who remain in good standing. Egregious violation of church policy, such as marrying outside the church, affects standing, and sacraments cannot be administered. To experience Greek Orthodox life fully, be an active participant in its sacramental offerings. Baptism, chrismation, confession, and communion are considered essential.

Infant Baptism

BAPTISM AND CHRISMATION

Baptisms bring great happiness to the Greek family. The special church service with the naked infant immersed in the baptismal font and anointed with holy oil is often followed by a joyful celebration of feasting and dancing. Family and friends celebrate the "rebirth" of the young child and the birth of the new relationship with the godparent.

The Sacrament of Baptism

The sacraments of baptism and chrismation were instituted by Christ himself when he commanded his apostles, "Go therefore and make disciples of all nations, baptizing them in the name of the Father and of the Son and of the Holy Spirit." (Matt. 28:19) For centuries these sacraments have initiated the individual into the Greek Orthodox church. Baptism cleanses the soul of the original sin transmitted to the human race by Adam and Eve when they disobeyed God. Chrismation transmits the gifts of the Holy Spirit. Through these two sacraments, the individual takes the first steps toward *théosis* (becoming like God). Symbolically, Christ's baptism, death, and Resurrection, plus the gift of the Holy Spirit to the apostles at Pentecost, are reenacted.

Baptism begins in the church narthex where the unbaptized originally congregated. The godparent speaks on behalf of the child and forcefully rejects Satan, including blowing three times in the air and symbolically spitting three times on the floor.

Turning toward the altar, the godparent professes a belief in Christ and recites the Nicene Creed, a summary of the basic beliefs of the Greek Orthodox Christian. Then using the child's baptismal name for the first time, the priest asks God to make the candidate worthy of baptism by cleansing away old sins and filling the child with the Holy Spirit.

The priest, child, and godparent proceed to the front of the church to the large baptismal font that represents the divine womb in which the child receives a second birth as a child of God. The godparent promises to raise the child as a good Christian.

The priest blesses the water in the baptismal font, adding a small amount of olive oil that the godparent has brought to the church. The fruit of the olive tree has been a symbol of peace and reconciliation between God and humans since a dove brought an olive branch to Noah at the end of the great flood described in the Old Testament.

The child is undressed, symbolizing the removal of old sin. The priest makes the sign of the cross with oil on various parts of the infant, and the godparent rubs oil over the child's body. The oil serves as a silent prayer to God: "O, God, let there be peace always between this child and you." The priest immerses the child three times into the font, symbolizing the three days Christ spent in the tomb. He declares, "The servant of God [name] is baptized in the name of the Father, and of the Son, and of the Holy Spirit. Amen." This dramatic event is a reenactment of Christ's baptism, death, and Resurrection. Like Christ, the child is resurrected and reborn. The priest places the child in the open arms of the godparent, who holds a new white sheet as a symbol of the soul's purity.

THE SACRAMENT OF CHRISMATION

Immediately following the baptism, the priest administers a second sacrament, chrismation. Like the early apostles, the child receives the gift of the Holy Spirit during chrismation, a gift of grace from God to help the child lead a Christian life. The priest anoints the child with *miron*, a special oil blessed by the Ecumenical Patriarch, and says, "The seal of the gift of the Holy Spirit. Amen." Three locks are tonsured from the child's hair in the form of a cross. This gift to God shows gratitude and obedience.

Oil of Chrismation and Scissors for Tonsuring

The priest blesses a piece of the child's new clothing, then puts it on the child with these words, "The servant of God [name] is clothed with the garment of incorruptibility." Relatives or friends then dress the child, and the priest puts a necklace with a cross on the child's neck, saying, "If any man would come after me, let him deny himself and take up his cross and follow me." Mark 8:34

After lighting the decorated baptismal candle, the priest, the godparent holding the infant, and a few selected children walk around the font symbolizing a dance of joy for the new Christian who has been added to the church.

Following the dance and a reading of scriptures, the priest administers a third sacrament, communion, to the child. The child's parents approach the front of the church where the godparent hands the infant to them with these traditional words, "I present to you your son/daughter baptized and confirmed, dedicated to God." The parents kiss the hand of the godparent and receive their child.

PREPARING FOR THE CEREMONY

WHEN TO BAPTIZE

Baptize your baby as soon as possible after the forty-day blessing. (See *Birth of Children*) Baptism is essential for entering heaven and participating in other church sacraments. Since the fate of an unbaptized individual is unknown, parents who neglect to have their child baptized bear a heavy responsibility.

Baptisms are not permitted on the following holidays:

> December 25 through January 6, and Easter Holy Week (dates vary). Other dates, such as major feast days, may be inconvenient or inappropriate. Exceptions must be approved by the diocesan bishop.

CHOOSING THE GODPARENT

Significance

Give substantial time and thought to selecting the godparent. The godparent is responsible for the spiritual upbringing of your child and becomes a "member of the family." A lifelong relationship of love and friendship should develop between your two families. The relationship, sanctioned by God, is very special, and being a godparent is as close as one can come to being a family member. Many times parents select other family members as godparents.

Qualifications

The church requires that all godparents be baptized Orthodox Christians who are in good standing with their parish and in full sacramental communion. They should be exemplary Christians. Although officially there is only one godparent, many priests allow a second person to assist. A godparent should set a good religious example and take an interest in the religious upbringing of the godchild.

Godparent of Firstborn Child

Traditionally, the *koumbáros* (male) and/or *koumbára* (female), the Orthodox witness(es) at the parents' wedding, will baptize the couple's first child. (See *Marriage*) Sometimes the *koumbáros* is much older than the parents, and it is in the child's best interest to have a younger godparent who will be available throughout the child's life. In such a situation, do not ignore the tradition, but be courteous and discuss the matter with the *koumbáros*.

Godparent for Additional Children

If the *koumbáros* is not going to baptize your baby or if this is your second child, it is customary to wait for someone to offer. Since being a godparent entails religious, emotional, and financial commitments, it is both a favor and a great honor. If you are concerned that no one will offer to be the godparent, subtle hinting may be necessary. In America's mobile society, however, parents may need to ask someone outright or consult their parish priest for suggestions.

If you receive more than one offer to baptize your child, select the most suitable person or use the method in the next paragraph.

Random Selection of Godparent

In rare instances a child's godparent is determined in the nave of the church. It may be impossible for the parents to choose among various offers of baptism. Or sometimes a child has been born after a *táma* to a saint. (See *Special Blessings, Prayers, and Appeals*) In those instances, the baby is placed on the church floor under the icon of Christ or the Virgin Mary during a Divine Liturgy, and the first person to pick up the child becomes the godparent. In Tinos, Greece, at the Church of the Evangelistria which is dedicated to the Virgin Mary, tourists who are not Christian Orthodox are warned not to lift any babies from the floor since non-Orthodox are not permitted to baptize.

Baptism of Male and Female Children

In Greece, godparents baptize only children of the same sex, because adults with the same godparents are not allowed to marry. In the eyes of the church, they are related. This rule, however, has been relaxed in the United States, and godparents can baptize both male and female children.

What to Call Each Other

Godparents and parents address each other as *"koumbáre"* (male), *"koumbára"* (female), or *"koumbári"* (plural). A godchild addresses a godfather as *"nouné"* and a godmother as *"nouná."* In America the masculine terms *"koumbáro"* and *"nounó"* are popularly used, but this is gramatically incorrect.

PREPARATIONS BY THE PARENTS

Celebration

The parents are responsible for the celebration after the baptismal ceremony. When composing the baptismal invitation, do not use the child's name because it is not given until the sacrament is performed. The correct wording would be that the parents are inviting guests to the baptism of their daughter or son. Celebrations for baptisms vary from small receptions of coffee and sweets to luncheons or dinners with dancing; budget and circumstances should prevail.

Selection of Assistants

Select two people to undress and dress the baby at the ceremony. It is customary to ask the baby's grandmothers to share this honor. If they are not available, ask other family members or close friends to assist. Also choose two or more children to walk with candles around the font at the prescribed time during the ceremony.

Bonboniéres

In some cases, furnish candy favors (see *"Bonboniéres"* below). Discuss this matter with the godparent.

Gift

Give the godparent a present to show your appreciation.

Optional Explanation

Provide guests with an explanation of the service. You may either reprint the explanation above or ask your priest for text.

PREPARATIONS BY THE GODPARENT

Name Selection

Select a name for your godchild that is acceptable to the church and the parents. Generally, names must be both Christian and Greek, and the child is named during the baptismal ceremony. (See *Selecting a Name*)

The following custom in many villages and towns in Greece exemplifies the naming prerogative of the godparent. As the ceremony begins, all the village children huddle in the narthex, listening for the godparent to say the child's name after recitation of the Nicene Creed. After hearing the name, the children run as fast as they can to the parents' home where the mother waits to learn her baby's name. The mother gives the child who delivers the news a reward of money and/or food. The parents then go to the church to receive the newly baptized child from the godparent. A variation of this custom is still practiced in some American churches. The father or mother waits outside the church proper and hands a coin to the first child to announce the baby's name, or the godparent gives a silver coin to the first person who calls the baby by name.

Items Needed for the Baptism

Proof of Good Standing

Provide proof of your current good standing and membership in a Greek Orthodox church to the priest baptizing the baby. If married, provide proof of your marriage in the Orthodox church.

Items for the Priest

Bring the following to the priest in advance on the day of the ceremony:

  2 white hand towels
  1 white bath towel
  1 white sheet
  1 small bottle of olive oil
  1 small bar of soap
  3 or more white candles described below
  1 set of new white clothing described below
  1 gold cross and chain
  (*Optional:* Inscribe cross with child's initials)

Baptismal Candle

Baptismal Candles. The godparent provides one large decorated candle for the ceremony, which the godchild keeps. The other smaller white candles, decorated or undecorated, are carried by the children who circle the font during the ceremony.

The traditional decoration for the godchild's candle is made by securing a large bow of ribbon or tulle with streamers on a large white candle and placing an artificial decoration such as a flower at the center of the bow (see *illustration*). The color blue remains popular for boys, and pink for girls. More elaborate decorations have evolved over the years and may be made at home or purchased at a Greek specialty store.

New White Clothing. The child is dressed in new white clothing during the ceremony to signify purification and new life from the rebirth of baptism. The outfit includes diaper, underwear, dress or suit, socks, shoes, two hats (one should be an absorbent liner) and possibly a coat, depending on the season. The clothing should cover the child as much as possible to absorb the holy oil from the ceremony. The godparent must carefully rub oil all over the baby's body during the ceremony. Some believe the superstition that any unoiled part will smell for the rest of the child's life!

Martirikấ

Martirikấ are the small lapel crosses distributed at the end of the baptismal ceremony and worn by the guests as proof of witnessing the baptism (see *illustration*). The traditional *martirikó* (singular) features a simple cross with a pin on the back and plain ribbon tied on the front. Over a period of time, more elaborate pins have become popular. The ribbon, traditionally blue or pink, surrounding a tiny cross, little metal icon, etc., is printed with the child's name, birth, and baptismal dates on one side, and the godparent's name on the other. These are commercially prepared and can be ordered through Greek specialty stores. The godparent or designated people distribute the *martirikấ* at the front of the church, in the narthex, or at the reception.

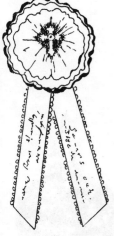

Martirikấ

Bonboniéres

Bonboniéres are the almond-candy favors given to each guest after the baptism. Since custom varies as to whether the parents or godparent should provide them, discuss this when making plans. Styles range from simple puffs of tulle tied with ribbon to elaborate containers to hold the candies. The most traditional are understated and easy to make. Place an odd number, usually five or seven, of candy-coated almonds (*kouféta*) in three layers of fine tulle cut in circles at least eleven inches in diameter. The edges can be scalloped for a softer look. Customarily white *kouféta* are used, but colored candies have become popular. Tie with a blue or pink ribbon and insert a small decorative item, such as an artificial flower at the bow (see *illustration*). Ready-made *bonboniéres* can also be purchased from a Greek specialty store.

The favors can be handed out by selected assistants in the narthex as guests leave the church or distributed at the reception personally by whoever provides them. They may also be placed at the tables where the guests will be sitting. Use your imagination!

Some say *koufêta* are given in the hope that a sweet future awaits the child and the guests. Many people also believe that using an odd number is good luck and that seven *koufêta* represent the seven sacraments.

Gratuities

Thank the priest, chanter, and sexton for their assistance by giving them either money or a present after the ceremony. Check with other parishioners for specific recommendations. Such compensation is not a church regulation, but is an accepted gesture of thanks for services rendered.

Optional. Give a silver coin to the first person who says the godchild's name to you.

COMMON EXPRESSIONS

Common expressions for congratulating the family may be found in *As the Greeks Say.* If the baby cries during the ceremony, guests say, *"O thêmonas fêvgi"* ("The devil is fleeing").

ONGOING RESPONSIBILITIES OF THE GODPARENT

The godparent's primary responsibility is to keep the godchild within the guidelines of the church and encourage him or her to live in the Orthodox way. Godparents must set a good example for it is said that children take on many of the characteristics of the people who anointed them with oil. It is common to remark that a godchild is like his or her godparent: *"Émiase tou nounú/tis nounás"* ("Took after his/her godfather/godmother").

IMMEDIATE RESPONSIBILITIES

- If convenient, give the baby the first bath after the baptism and wash the baptismal sheet, towel, and clothes. Because the wash water will contain holy oil, it should be poured some place outside where it will not be stepped on, such as the foot of a tree or a corner of the house. In the village of Sifnos, Greece, baptismal items are always washed in the sea. In Constantinople, the godparent puts a gold coin or jewelry in the baby's bathtub.

- Place all the baptismal articles in a box and give them to the godchild's family for safekeeping. Centuries ago the baptismal candle was brought to church for special occasions in the child's life such as his or her name day, wedding, and funeral. It was a reminder that the light of Christ was always in the person's life. An old custom on Mitilini was to save the baptismal sheet and use it as a shroud for burial.

- Take the child to church for communion after the baptism. The child should receive communion three times. However, if communion was given at the baptism, take the child only twice. Be sure to bring the baptismal candle, lighting it just before communion and carrying it and the child to the front for the sacrament.

LATER RESPONSIBILITIES

- Remember the child's name day, birthday, and special occasions such as Easter and Christmas.

- Provide information to the godchild about the patron saint for whom he or she was named. Give the child an icon of the saint and encourage emulation as a role model.

- Attend church together if possible, especially on godparents' Sunday (variable date).

- Become the *koumbáros/a* at the godchild's wedding, circumstances permitting. (See *Marriage*)

SPECIAL SITUATIONS

ADULT BAPTISM AND CHRISMATION

Adults can be baptized in the Orthodox church after study and discussion guided by a priest. The priest approves baptism when he believes that true understanding has been reached by the individual. For those who have been baptized in another Christian faith such as a Roman Catholic or a Trinitarian Protestant denomination, only the chrismation service need be performed along with a shorter study and discussion session.

Women candidates should wear all white at the ceremony and men should wear a white shirt. Holy water will be either sprinkled or poured over the candidate's head, depending on the priest's preference. The godparent for the adult provides a cross and a candle.

EMERGENCY BAPTISM

In an emergency, such as severe illness or an accident, an infant can be baptized by any Orthodox person in several ways.

By Air

Lift the child into the air, making the sign of the cross with the child's body, saying, "The servant of God [name] is baptized in the name of the Father (lift straight up), and the Son, (lift to the right), and the Holy Spirit (lift to the left)."

By Water

Pour or sprinkle water on the individual while making the sign of the cross and saying, "The servant of God [name] is baptized in the name of the Father, and the Son, and the Holy Spirit."

Dance of Isaiah
Marriage Ceremony

MARRIAGE

Greek weddings sparkle. There is joy, laughter, loud *bouzoûki* music, mountains of food, and coiling lines of boisterous dancers. In the United States, most of the social customs surrounding the wedding festivities are American, with a few Greek customs here and there. However, the wedding ceremony itself remains pristinely Greek Orthodox, unchanged for centuries. It incorporates human joy with the joy of heaven when two people are united in holy matrimony.

THE SACRAMENT OF MARRIAGE

Through the sacrament of marriage the Orthodox church joins a man and a woman in the sacred union of husband and wife. During the ceremony they commit themselves to one another and to raising a Christian family in a Christian home. God, in turn, bestows his love (agape) on them that they may live in harmony and peace for life. The service consists of beautiful hymns and prayers extolling marriage and emphasizing its responsibilities.

The service is conducted around a small table on which wedding crowns, the book of Gospels, two wedding rings, a cup of wine, and two white candles have been placed. These objects are used symbolically throughout the service.

THE BETROTHAL — BLESSING OF THE RINGS

In the first part of the service, the couple becomes betrothed by the church. The priest blesses the rings and touches the foreheads of the bride and groom with them. Making the sign of the cross above their heads with the rings, he proclaims to each of them, "The servant of God [name] is betrothed to the servant of God [name] in the name of the Father, and the Son, and the Holy Spirit." The rings are put on the right hands, and the official sponsor — *koumbáros* (male) or *koumbára* (female) — exchanges the rings three times, symbolizing the complimentary role of husband and wife.

THE WEDDING

The wedding proper then takes place, highlighted by the following:

The Candles

The bride and groom each hold a lighted candle during the service, similar to a parable in the Bible where five wise maidens prepare to receive Christ the Bridegroom by lighting their lamps with oil. The candles remind the couple of the light of Christ who is with them throughout the sacrament and their coming life together.

The Joining of Hands

The couple joins right hands as the priest appeals to God to make them one in spirit and flesh and grant them the joy of children.

The Crowning

Crowns (*stéphana*) joined with a ribbon are worn by the bride and groom who are to be respected as king and queen in their home and family. As this crowning takes place, the blessing of God is invoked upon the couple. "O, Lord our God, crown them with honor and glory." As these words are sung, the *koumbáros/a* exchanges the crowns three times.

The Readings

There are two designated readings from the scriptures. In the Epistle of St. Paul to the Ephesians, Paul talks of love and respect. The husband should love his wife and be prepared to give his life to protect her as Christ gave his life out of love for the church. The wife should respect her husband as the church honors and respects Christ and should submit herself to him. The second reading from the Gospel of St. John relates the story of Christ at the wedding in Cana of Galilee and his miracle of changing water into wine.

The Common Cup

Just as wine was drunk at the wedding in Cana, the bride and groom share a common cup of unconsecrated wine, symbolizing the sharing of all that life will bring — the joys, sorrows, love, and pain.

The Dance of Isaiah

Led by the priest, the couple circles the small table while wearing their crowns and holding hands. The *kourbáros(a)* follows them, holding the ribbon that joins the crowns. The dance proclaims the church's joy at the new union, similar to the joy of Isaiah the prophet who saw the Messiah in a vision nine hundred years before Christ's birth. In Greece, guests shower the couple with rose petals and rice during the dance.

Near the end of the ceremony the priest removes the crowns, charging the newlyweds: "Be magnified, O bridegroom, as Abraham, and blessed as Isaac, and increased as was Jacob. Go your way in peace, performing in righteousness the commandments of God. And you, O bride, be magnified as was Sarah, and rejoiced as was Rebecca, and increased as Rachel, being glad in your husband, keeping the paths of the law, for so God is well pleased."

The bride and the groom are proclaimed as husband and wife, at the conclusion of the service. Just before the crowns are removed from their heads, the priest invokes God's blessings once more. "O Lord, bless these your servants who, by your providence, are now joined in the communion of marriage."

[End of ceremony]

THE ENGAGEMENT PERIOD

The wedding ceremony is the culmination of an intense time of anticipation and planning before the marriage. The engagement period and the process of organizing the wedding test the bond, commitment, and values of the future husband and wife. During this time they work with their families and church, preparing for their life together.

PARENTAL PERMISSION

Unlike Greek couples generations ago, whose marriages were arranged by their parents, women and men today meet, fall in love, and choose each other. Although parents play a lesser role now, it is respectful to seek the parents' permission to marry. The prospective groom should discuss his plans with the prospective bride's parents. This is also an American tradition and begins the formal relationship on a positive note.

Many years ago Greek parents prearranged their children's marriages. Marriage was a practical business based on the background of the families, calculated prospects for success and happiness, old promises between families, and even the amount of a dowry (*príka*). Sometimes a matchmaker (*proksenítis* [m] or *proksenítra* [f]) facilitated the prearranged marriage (*proksenió*), even negotiating terms of the agreement. In Constantinople, the matchmaker would come to make an offer wearing one slipper and one shoe!

RINGS

Traditions vary regarding the rings. In America, a man sometimes gives the woman an engagement ring with a precious stone that she wears on the third finger of her left hand. The wedding bands for the bride and groom are usually inscribed with a variety of information: initials, names, dates of either the engagement or wedding. This is a matter of personal preference. In Greece, a gold band serves as both the engagement ring and the wedding ring for the man and the woman. For the engagement, the ring is worn on the left hand, but moved to the right after the marriage. The right hand is considered stronger because in the Bible it performed miracles.

ENGAGEMENT PARTY

Like Americans, Greeks celebrate the good news with an engagement party. The focal point is the blessing of the engagement and wedding rings by the priest. Prepare for the blessing by setting a table with an icon and a silver tray layered with *kouféta* (candied almonds). Put the rings on the *kouféta* for the blessing. This blessing takes the place of the binding betrothal service which is now the first part of the marriage sacrament. *Kouféta* are placed in candy dishes for the guests or distributed as *bonboniéres* (see below). Guests generally bring gifts to the party, and well-wishers congratulate the couple with, "*Kalá stéphana*" ("Good crowning") or "*Syncharitíria*" ("Congratulations").

You may want to adopt a lively tradition from some parts of the Peloponnesus. A large sweet bread shaped like a ring and decorated with fresh flowers is baked for the engaged couple. They pull it apart, and whoever gets the larger piece will have the upper hand in the marriage!

An old superstition holds that a jealous person can cast *mayá* (a spell) on the couple and break up the engagement or keep the marriage from being consummated. If such a curse is suspected, contact a priest.

PRE-MARITAL COUNSELING

The Greek Orthodox church in the United States requires pre-marital counseling, although the extent differs from one diocese to another. It is advisable for couples who are contemplating marriage to consult their priest immediately following the engagement. In addition to providing emotional support, he can answer questions about church guidelines.

GREEK ORTHODOX CHURCH GUIDELINES

The Orthodox church promulgates strict guidelines for marriage, concerning membership standing, the *koumbáros/a*, marriage to a non-Orthodox, etc. Certain criteria must be met before the priest can perform the marriage. (See "Guidelines for Marriage in the Greek Orthodox Church" below.) Be aware that the church does not recognize marriage outside the Orthodox church. If you marry in a non-Orthodox ceremony, you excommunicate yourself and are barred from the sacraments, from becoming a sponsor at a wedding or baptism, and from receiving an Orthodox funeral.

WEDDING SHOWER

American Etiquette

At a wedding shower the bride receives gifts for her new household and/or herself, depending on the kind of shower being given. Since this is an American custom, check with a wedding book for further details concerning types and etiquette.

Greek Customs Today and Yesterday

The traditional candy for weddings, *kouféta*, may be distributed in small candy dishes or as *bonboniéries*. An appropriate Greek gift is a case (*stephanothíki*) for the marriage crowns (*stéphana*) usually given by a close relative such as the mother of the bride, an aunt, or sometimes the *koumbáros/a*. According to a folk belief, if you receive scissors or knives as a gift, you should give money (like a penny or nickel) to the person who gave you the gift to avoid a quarrel!

In most cultures, women begin collecting bedding, kitchenware, and household items before the marriage. Americans call this a "hope chest." At one time young Greek women sewed, embroidered, and crocheted linens for their *príka* (dowry) and proudly displayed their work just before the wedding.

The *príka* was the money, land, and possessions a woman's family promised to bring to the marriage. The *príkes* ranged widely in value. The Greek-American author, Harry Mark Petrakis, listed his mother's *príka* in 1908 in *Stelmark: A Family Recollection*: "2,000 gold drachmas, an orchard of 37 olive trees, free and clear of debt, some adjoining orange and peach trees, and assorted household items, bedding, spreads, pots and pans, knives and forks."[1]

A woman's marriage depended on the size of her *príka*, resulting in many cruel ramifications. The birth of a girl was bemoaned because it meant providing a *príka*. Failure to provide one resulted in a loss of honor (*philótimo*) for the entire family. Brothers were pressed to earn *príkes* for their sisters before they themselves could marry. In fact many Greek men came to America simply to earn money for such obligations. Today parents of the bride in Greece help as much as they can, but it is voluntary and not legally required.

PLANNING THE WEDDING

Most Greek Orthodox weddings in the United States combine Greek and American customs. Use an American wedding etiquette book as a basic planning guide. Such books are available for purchase or may be checked out of a local library. Add the Greek customs included here — *bonboniéres, stéphana, bouzoúki,* and *baklavá* — for a unique and joyous Greek-American wedding!

SETTING THE DATE

Marriages cannot be performed on certain church feast days and during some periods of Lent. For example, do not plan to marry during Great Lent and Holy Week. (See "Guidelines for Marriage in the Greek Orthodox Church" below)

SELECTING THE *KOUMBÁROS(A)* AND OTHER ATTENDANTS

The *koumbáros* (male) or *koumbára* (female), the official sponsor of the marriage, must be Orthodox and in good standing with the church. Generally there is only one *koumbáros(a),* but some priests permit couples (*koumbári*). (In formal Greek the word *paránymphos* is used for *koumbáros[a].*)

Traditionally the groom's godparent is asked to serve first and then the godparent of the bride. If neither of them participate, ask a close friend or family member. Remember, this is an important relationship lasting a lifetime. *Koumbári* become almost like family. Consider also the suitability of the *koumbáros(a)* as a godparent, since he or she usually baptizes the first child.

The *koumbáros(a)* can be the best man or maid of honor, but this does not have to be the case. No other attendants, except the *koumbáros(a),* are required to be Orthodox.

RESPONSIBILITIES OF THE *KOUMBÁROS(A)*

The *koumbáros(a) stephanóni* the couple. *Stephánoma* is the act of exchanging the wedding crowns three times above the heads of the bride and groom during the service.

The *koumbáros(a)* should provide the following for the marriage ceremony (see explanations below):

- Proof of good standing in an Orthodox church
  (a letter from the parish priest)
- Marriage crowns (*stéphana*)

- Wedding tray layered with *kouféta* and rice
- Two candles
- Wedding rings (purchased by the couple)
- Gratuities to the priest, chanter, and sexton
- *Optional*: Wine goblet

Marriage Crowns (*Stéphana*)

The crowning of the bride and groom during the church ceremony is a highlight of the Orthodox service.

In most instances, the *koumbáros(a)* provides the *stéphana*. Selection of the *stéphana* is a matter of personal choice. Some *koumbári* buy the crowns without consulting the bride and groom. Others may go with the bride to the specialty shop and make the selection together.

Crown styles change frequently. The church requires only that they be round and joined together by ribbon. Traditional crowns are delicate and simple, a weaving of white wax flowers with beading and white leaves, linked together with a white satin ribbon (see *illustration*). They may be purchased through a Greek specialty store, a catalog, in Greece, or from an individual who makes them. Elaborate crowns are becoming more common, featuring intricate beading or metal work with designs that match the bride's gown. These can be quite expensive, however, and are not necessary. Some couples use their parents' *stéphana*, but most have their own for permanent display at home.

Wedding Tray

Put the *stéphana* on top of a tray covered with a single layer of *kouféta* and rice. The priest places the tray on a small table at the front of the church for the ceremony. The tray, usually the wedding gift from the *koumbáros(a)* to the couple, is traditionally made of silver and may include a tea and coffee service. This is changing, however, and less formal trays such as mirrored vanity sets and serving pieces make suitable wedding presents.

Candles

Decorating the candles is optional. These may be prepared at a Greek specialty store or made by tying large bows with streamers on the candles and attaching artificial flowers to them.

Gratuities

The *koumbáros(a)* customarily thanks the priest, chanter, and sexton for their services with a gratuity. Amounts vary with each parish.

Optional: Purchase of a wine goblet to be kept by the newlyweds is not required since the church provides the chalice used during the ceremony.

WEDDING GOWN AND HEADPIECE

Select a wedding gown or dress appropriate to the time and style of the wedding. Consult an American etiquette book. But keep in mind two Greek traditions during the ceremony: The *koumbáros(a)* simultaneously switches the *stéphana* three times above the heads of the bride and groom during the ceremony. The headdress should not interfere with the exchanging. Also, you will have to go around a table three times during the ceremony and may want to avoid a large, bulky dress.

Greek Americans from Constantinople write the names of unmarried female friends of the bride on the lining of the train or back hem of the wedding dress to bring them good luck in finding a husband. The names are in back of the bride, so that the friends will follow her footsteps to the altar!

In some areas of Greece it is traditional for the groom to buy the bride's entire wedding outfit. In Athens, brides usually rent modern gowns, but in remote villages elaborate native costumes are worn.

BRIDAL BOUQUET

In Epirus the bride's bouquet includes a tiny pair of scissors to cut the power of the evil eye from envious guests!

BONBONIÉRES

Bonboniéres (favors of *kouféta*), are given to guests after the wedding. The bride's parents usually provide them, but in some regions they are the responsibility of the *koumbáros(a)*. Traditionally, the bride and her bridesmaids make them together. Like the *bonboniéres* for a baptism, they can be simple, with netting and an interesting decoration or much more elaborate (see *illustration*). The almonds are always white and uneven in number, usually five or seven. Each family decides its own style and amount to spend. Traditionally each guest receives a favor, but it has become common practice at weddings to give one to female guests only.

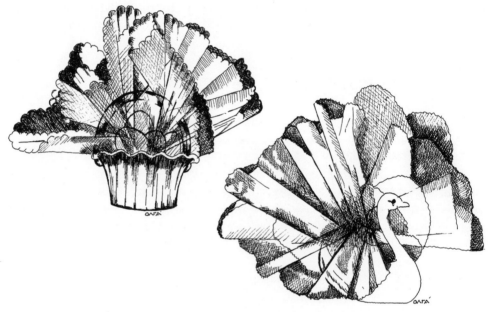

Bonboniéres

There are numerous ways of distributing the *bonboniéres*. In the United States the newlyweds sometimes hand them out at the reception, or the bridesmaids may do so. The bride and groom go from table to table with a nicely decorated basket greeting their guests and distributing *bonboniéres*. If the wedding is large and time does not permit personal distribution, the *bonboniéres* may be left at the table place settings. Sometimes each favor has a card with the guest's name and table number on it. In this case, all the favors are placed on a general table outside the hall, and guests find their table assignments by picking up their favor.

MARRIAGE SERVICE

Language

The ceremony, lasting about forty-five minutes to one hour, may be performed in both Greek and English, in whatever combination is comfortable for the couple and the priest. However, the content and wording cannot be changed in any way. Modern "I do" vows are not part of the service and cannot be added. Neither can phrases be eliminated. Couples concerned about the wording, "Wives, be subject to your husbands," should understand that this is the Orthodox approach to marriage. According to church doctrine, the husband is the head of the household, but the mother has a revered position as the cornerstone of the family and is responsible for maintaining the family unit. According to a popular folk custom, if the bride can step on the groom's foot first while this passage is being read, she will be the head of the house!

Wedding Program

A printed program that explains the Orthodox service is very helpful to your guests. You may reprint the "Sacrament of Marriage" in this chapter or ask your priest to supply text. Also include in the program the names of the bride and groom, the date, time and place, the name of the priest, names and titles of the wedding party, and special performers such as musicians.

Music

The church likes to maintain a Greek Orthodox atmosphere throughout the ceremony. It requires, for example, that only the chanter provide responses to the priest. Any singers other than the chanter and any instruments other than the organ can be used only with permission of the diocesan bishop. It has become acceptable to play appropriate, non-Orthodox music while the guests arrive, during the wedding party entrance, and as the guests leave.

Church Decorations

Consult your priest about placement of flower arrangements and other decorations. The table with the *stéphana*, arranged by the

Marriage

priest, is the focal point. You may also want to consider using a decoration common in Greece: two candles joined with fabric to symbolize the uniting of the man and the woman. Place a large candle stand with lighted candles behind and on either side of the small *stéphana* table. Connect the two candles with a large white drapery and have a young child stand by each one throughout the ceremony. The bride keeps the material and may have it made into a dress, tablecloth, or any item she chooses.

COMMUNION

It is suggested the couple take communion the Sunday before the wedding since communion is not given during the ceremony. The bride and groom drink wine from a common cup to commemorate the Biblical wedding in Cana.

WEDDING BED

If convenient, single women friends of the bride (often the bridesmaids) prepare the wedding bed. An old custom is to roll a young child on the bed and then scatter *kouféta*, rice, and money on the top for wishes of fertility and good fortune. In some small Greek villages, the marriage bed is decorated and paraded around the village before the ceremony.

WEDDING RECEPTION

Delicious food, a table laden with sweets, *bouzoúki* music, and lines of laughing dancers complete the day. Most wedding receptions are a combination of American and Greek food, music, and dancing. The music alternates between modern American songs, current Greek pop favorites, and folk music for dances like the *hasápiko* and the *kalamatianós*. Traditionally the Greek dancing begins with the bride leading a *kalamatianós* (if she wishes) with her husband next in line. Then the family members and close friends take turns "dancing the bride" by assuming the lead at the head of the line, starting with the father. The most popular wedding song is *"Oréa íne i Nýfi Mas"* ("Beautiful is our Bride"). In addition to the wedding cake, it is customary to have an assortment of Greek sweets including *baklavá* and *kourabiéthes*. Be sure to have the priest bless the food before eating. Add whatever American customs you wish — such as a receiving line, toasts by the best man and maid of honor, tossing the bride's bouquet — and enjoy!

AFTER THE WEDDING

WHAT TO SAY

See *As the Greeks Say* for typical expressions said after a wedding.

PRESERVING THE MARRIAGE CROWNS — *STEPHANOTHÍKI*

The *stéphana* are one of the most important symbols of the marriage. They remind the newlyweds that they are united in their own kingdom with the blessing of God, and they have a chance to build their own home and family together. The crowns deserve to be properly preserved. Place the crowns in the home *ikonostási* or in a special case called a *stephanothíki* (pron. *stephanoTHíki*).

The case, handmade or purchased through a Greek specialty store or catalog, may be round, rectangular, or octagonal, made of wood with a glass front (see *illustration*). Some contain an electric light and an icon of the Virgin Mary inside. Keep the *stephanothíki* by the *ikonostási* or above the marriage bed.

In some places in Greece, the crowns are brought to the church after the wedding and left on the altar for eight days for a special blessing.

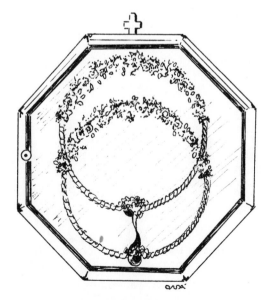

Stephanothíki

SUPERSTITIONS

Koufét́a under the Pillow

It is said that a single woman will dream of her future husband if *koufét́a* from a *bonboniéra* are put under her pillow. If *koufét́a* from the wedding tray are placed under her pillow, her chances of finding a husband greatly improve — the Greek equivalent of catching the bouquet!

Preserving the Candle Wicks

At the end of the ceremony, cut the tips off the two candles from the table with the *stéphana*. These should be saved by the bride and groom. Some say that a jealous person can take them and cast *máya* on the couple, preventing consummation of the marriage.

SPECIAL SITUATIONS

MARITAL RELATIONS

Birth Control

The church leaves the decision to use birth control up to the couple but disapproves of any device that aborts life. The church maintains that the main purpose of sexual intercourse is procreation.

Abstinence

The church recommends abstinence from sex before communion and during Holy Week.

DIVORCE

Divorce is permitted in the Orthodox church, but strongly discouraged. Every effort should be made by the couple, with the help of a priest and possibly outside counseling, to establish a harmonious relationship. If this fails, however, a civil divorce must be obtained and application made through your priest to the ecclesiastical court of your local diocese. There is no guarantee that an ecclesiastical divorce will be granted even though a civil divorce has been allowed. The only church ground for divorce is adultery, but through special mercy the church will make exceptions. An ecclesiastical divorce is essential for remarriage in the Orthodox church. Members who have not received an ecclesiastical divorce are not in good standing and cannot receive communion or be sponsors for weddings or baptisms.

SECOND AND THIRD MARRIAGES

Second or third marriages are allowed by the church, but only if both civil and ecclesiastical divorces have been granted, or if a spouse has died. A fourth is forbidden. The wedding in such circumstances is usually handled in a subdued manner with less elaborate food and clothing. Even the marriage service is different and more somber. Check with your priest and an American etiquette book for the proper approach.

GUIDELINES FOR MARRIAGE IN THE
GREEK ORTHODOX CHURCH

The following guidelines are excerpted from the Greek Orthodox Archdiocese of North and South America's *Yearbook 1999*.[2] If you have any questions, consult your priest.

> For the sacramental union of a man and a woman to be proper in the eyes of the Church, the marriage must be conducted in the Orthodox church. For such an ecclesiastical marriage to be valid, the following must be adhered to:
>
> 1. No impediment to marriage may exist.
> 2. A civil marriage license must be obtained from civil authorities.
> 3. An ecclesiastical marriage license must be obtained from the appropriate diocese.
> 4. The Sacrament of marriage must be celebrated by an Orthodox priest according to the liturgical tradition of the Orthodox Church and in a canonical Orthodox Church.

5. The priest must belong to the Greek Orthodox Archdiocese. However, marriage performed in another Orthodox jurisdiction in communion with the Greek Orthodox Archdiocese is also recognized as valid by the Greek Orthodox Archdiocese.

6. The priest must receive authorization for the marriage from his Diocesan Bishop.

7. Before requesting permission from the Bishop for the marriage the priest must verify:

    a. that the parties in question are not already married either in this country or elsewhere.

    b. that the party or parties who are members of another parish obtain a certificate of membership from the parish to which they belong.

    c. that if either or both parties are widowed, that he or she present the death certificate of the deceased spouse.

    d. that if either or both of the parties have been divorced and/or have remarried, that they present the appropriate certificates.

8. No more than a total of three marriages will be allowed by the Church, and this only by extreme mercy.

9. When one or both of the parties are divorced, they must obtain an ecclesiastical divorce as well in order to marry again in the Church.

10. In the case of an interfaith marriage, the non-Orthodox partner must have been baptized in the name of the Holy Trinity and in water. A marriage cannot take place in the Orthodox Church between an Orthodox Christian and a non-Christian.

11. In the case of interfaith marriages between an Orthodox Christian and a non-Orthodox Christian, the marriage must be celebrated by an Orthodox priest in the Orthodox Church according to the Orthodox tradition.

12. The Sponsor (koumbaros or koumbara) must be an Orthodox Christian in good standing with the Church. A person who does not belong to a parish, or who belongs to a parish which is not in communion with the Greek Orthodox Archdiocese, or who if married, is not married in the Orthodox Church cannot be a Sponsor. Non-Orthodox persons may be members of the rest of the wedding party, but may not exchange the rings or crowns.

DAYS WHEN MARRIAGE IS NOT PERMITTED

- January 5-6 (Epiphany)
- Great Lent
- Holy Week
- August 1-15 (Dormition of the Mother of God)
- August 29 (Beheading of St. John the Baptist)
- September 14 (Exaltation of the Holy Cross)
- December 13-25 (Christmas)
- The day before and on major feast days including Pentecost, Christmas, Pascha, etc.
- All Holy Days of Our Lord

A wedding may be conducted on these days only if absolutely necessary and then only by special permission of the Diocesan Bishop.

INTERFAITH MARRIAGES

It is a fact that the more things a couple holds in common, the more likely it will be that they live their married lives in peace and harmony. Shared faith and traditions spare newlyweds and their children many serious problems and strengthen the bonds between them. However, the Orthodox Church blesses interfaith marriages under the following conditions:

1. The non-Orthodox partner must be a Christian who has been baptized, in water, in the name of the Holy Trinity.
2. The couple must commit to baptize their children in the Orthodox Church and nurture them in accordance with the Orthodox faith.

The Orthodox partner should bear in mind that a married Orthodox Christian whose wedding has not been blessed by the Orthodox Church is no longer in good standing with the Church and consequently does not have the right to receive the sacraments of the Church, including Holy Communion, or to become a sponsor at an Orthodox wedding, baptism or chrismation. An Orthodox Christian who has been married outside the Church and who wishes to be reconciled to the Church, is encouraged to request from his or her local Orthodox priest that his or her marriage be blessed in the Orthodox Church.

A non-Orthodox Christian who marries an Orthodox Christian does not automatically become a member of the Church, and is therefore not permitted to receive Holy Communion or other sacraments of the Church or a Church funeral. These are privileges of the baptized or chrismated members of the Church.

PROHIBITED MARRIAGES

First Group — Parents with their own children, grandchildren or great-grandchildren, or godchildren of the same godparents.

Second Group — Brothers-in-law with sisters-in-laws.

Third Group — Uncles and aunts with nieces and nephews.

Fourth Group — First cousins with each other.

Fifth Group — Foster parents with foster children or foster children with the children of foster parents.

Sixth Group — Godparents with godchildren or godparents with the parents of godchildren.

---

1. Harry Mark Petrakis, *Stelmark: A Family Recollection* (New York: David McKay Company, 1970), 21.

2. Greek Orthodox Archdiocese of North and South America, *Yearbook 1999* (New York: Greek Orthodox Archdiocese Press, 1999), 219-20.

CONFESSION

While men and women of the Orthodox faith can express their contrition to God and beg his forgiveness at anytime or in any place, this is not always effective. Therefore loving guidance and direction may be sought in the formal sacrament of confession (*exomológisis*).

THE SACRAMENT OF CONFESSION

A person in emotional turmoil because of sins committed may need to talk to someone on a higher spiritual level with a special degree of authority who will say, "You are forgiven." Jesus knew this human weakness and established the sacrament of confession after the Resurrection:

> "Peace be with you. As the Father has sent me, even so I send you." And when he had said this, he breathed on them, and said to them, "Receive the Holy Spirit. If you forgive the sins of any, they are forgiven; if you retain the sins of any, they are retained." John 20:21-22.

During a sacramental confession, the penitent and the priest are alone in the church, usually standing side by side before the icon of Christ at the *ikonostásion* (altar screen). The priest is a witness, not a judge, and is required to keep everything in strict confidence. Three basic elements are involved: recognition of the sins, repentance, and absolution. The penitent must confess all and completely repent before forgiveness can be granted.

After confession, kneel or bow your head so that the priest may put his hand and stole on your head while repeating the prayer of absolution:

> May God Who pardoned David through Nathan the Prophet when he confessed his sins, and Peter, weeping bitterly for his denial, and the sinful woman weeping at his feet, and the publican and the prodigal son, may that same God forgive you all things, through me a sinner, both in this world and in the world to come, and set you uncondemned before His terrible Judgment Seat. Having no further care for the sins which you have confessed, depart in peace.[1]

Confession

PRELIMINARIES

WHO CAN CONFESS AND TO WHOM

Only baptized Orthodox can participate in the sacrament of confession, starting at age seven. Ideally, confess to your own priest. However, if this makes you uncomfortable, arrange to see another.

WHAT AND WHEN TO CONFESS

Grave sins such as murder, apostasy (abandoning of one's belief), adultery, and transgressions that cause extreme discord in your relationship with other people and with God should be brought before a priest immediately. Other sins can be saved until your next confession, repented in your own prayers, or confessed during the Divine Liturgy.

The frequency of sacramental confession varies greatly, and the church has no strict rule regarding this. Once a year is the minimum, but more often is recommended. Many people choose the time of Great Lent, a period of reflection and cleansing. Confession is an integral part of taking communion, and should be said, either in private or to a priest, before receiving the Gifts (see "Private Confession" below).

Although it is one of the seven sacraments of the Orthodox church, sacramental confession before a priest is not widely practiced. Even some of the most devout do not participate, despite the fact that the church considers baptism, chrismation, confession, and communion essential for complete participation in the church.

PREPARATION

An honest self-examination is essential before confession with the priest. Two Greek words associated with confession, *metánia* and *exomológisis* (pron. *eksomológisis*), describe the process of introspection. *Metánia* means a "change of mind" and therefore repentance. You acknowledge both that you are wrong and that you have had a change in your heart and mind. *Exomológisis* means "expressing it in words," i.e., an unburdening of the soul.

PENANCE AND EXCOMMUNICATION

PENANCE

Penance is not a part of the sacrament of confession, but the priest may prescribe remedies such as fasting, charitable works, restraint from communion, or additional prayers.

EXCOMMUNICATION

The harshest punishment for the Orthodox Christian is excommunication, literally the breaking of communion. Communion and all other basic aspects of religious life such as being a godparent, sponsor at a marriage, and receiving a church funeral service are denied. One breaks communion with the faith by adopting another faith, like Islam or Judaism, or marrying outside the Orthodox church. The Greek Orthodox Archdiocese of North and South America, however, considers each case separately and is very careful in imposing such a severe penalty.

Although the church appears to excommunicate, actually it is the sin of the unrepentant person that puts that person out of communion with the church. There is an ancient ritual of excommunication, but the church does not exercise that rite in modern times.

PRIVATE CONFESSION

Private confession occurs between the penitent and God, whenever you feel the need, at any time or place. This personal acknowledgement of sin is not a substitute for the sacrament of Holy Confession. However, you should always confess before taking communion. Follow carefully the Communion Prayer said during The Divine Liturgy after the priest pours water in the communion cup.

---

1. N. M. Vaporis, ed., *An Orthodox Prayer Book* (Brookline, Mass.: Holy Cross Orthodox Press, 1977), 136-137.

Receiving Communion

COMMUNION

The sacrament of communion is the most important act in the liturgical life of the church. Jesus asked his followers to remember him by participation in this dramatic ritual where the transformation of ordinary bread and wine into the actual parts of a sacred human body represents the greatest mystery of the Christian faith.

The Sacrament of Communion

Communion is given at every Divine Liturgy and at the Liturgy of Presanctified Gifts. This reenactment of Christ's Last Supper with his disciples restores spirituality and renews faith. By partaking of the Body and Blood of Christ (Eucharist or Gifts), the faithful come closer to union with God (*théosis*).

While parishioners are kneeling during the Divine Liturgy, the Holy Spirit transforms the wine and bread into the Eucharist. After the priest takes communion, he stands at the altar gate with the chalice and invites parishioners to come forward by saying: "Approach with the fear of God, faith, and love."

Participants walk slowly toward the priest. Women should remove their lipstick. When you reach the priest, make the sign of the cross, and tell him your baptismal name. Hold the red cloth of the chalice under your chin as the priest puts the spoon containing the holy Gifts in your mouth. He will say: "The servant of God [baptismal name] receives the Body and Blood of Christ for forgiveness of sins and eternal life."

Hand the chalice cloth to the person behind you and make the sign of the cross again. Take bread from the altar boy and return to your seat.

Preliminaries

ELIGIBILITY

Only baptized and chrismated Orthodox are eligible to take communion. Those who have committed extraordinary sins such as murder, adultery, and incest should consult with their priest before taking communion. Penance, including a period of abstinence from communion, may be required.

FREQUENCY

The frequency with which church members take communion has varied since the beginning of the church. For the first three hundred years every member took communion each time the Divine Liturgy was performed. However, participation declined as the worthiness of the individual was emphasized more. Later, to encourage participation, a canon was adopted in 1819 stating that the faithful should receive communion with each liturgy. Yet to this day, very few do. Why? Orthodoxy emphasizes the proper preparation of the individual to receive the holy Gifts, and strict compliance can be rigorous and inhibiting. (See "Preparation" below)

Most priests today encourage parishioners to partake more often and not feel compelled to comply with every custom of preparation such as formal confession to a priest. Thus, there has been increased participation over the widespread practice of taking communion four times a year in conjunction with the four major fasting periods in the church year: Christmas Lent, Great Lent, Holy Apostles Lent, and Dormition of the Mother of God Lent. Many parishioners take communion at a Divine Liturgy conducted during these fasting periods or on the feast day that ends the fast: the Easter Resurrection service (date varies), June 29 or 30 (Saints Peter and Paul or Holy Apostles), August 15 (The Dormition of the Mother of God), and December 25 (Christmas). In addition to these special days, parishioners should take communion as often as they wish after proper preparation.

PREPARATION

The Orthodox faith places great emphasis on the spiritual, emotional, and physical preparation to take communion. This is not a creation of the church but rather an apostolic directive, specifically passed to the church by St. Paul in his first epistle to the Corinthians.

> Whoever, therefore, eats the bread or drinks the cup of the Lord in an unworthy manner will be guilty of profaning the

Body and Blood of the Lord. Let a man examine himself,
and so let him eat of the bread, and drink of the cup. For
any one who eats and drinks without discerning the body
eats and drinks judgment upon himself. I Cor. 11:27-29

Developing this directive, Father George Mastrantonis, a Greek-
American priest, gives this advice in "Holy Communion, the Bread
of Life":

Strengthen your belief in Communion. Apply the Christian
principles of self control and sympathy for others; pray
constantly; ask the Lord to guide you; avoid temptation;
keep your stomach light, your mind sober, your flesh pure,
your relations calm — humbly in the name of the Lord.
Recognize your sins and avoid them — especially sins of
neglect. Live in prayer, almsgiving, forgiveness, and good
will.[1]

Physical preparation for communion, specifically fasting, varies
throughout the United States. All authorities agree that except in
health-threatening situations, NO FOOD OR LIQUIDS MAY BE
CONSUMED AFTER MIDNIGHT BEFORE TAKING COMMUNION,
and social activities should be moderated the prior evening. However, some communicants follow a strict fast at least three days
before receiving communion. (See *Fasting*) Others do not and
take communion frequently. Consult with your parish priest. Before an evening service, church authorities request no food or
water for six hours prior to communion. Ask forgiveness of those
with whom you are in disharmony.

A controversial canon prohibits a woman from taking communion
while she is menstruating. However, there is a movement within
the church to change such thinking on "cleanliness." Most priests
recommend that each woman decide for herself. Many women
raised with this tradition are uncomfortable taking communion
during that time, but many others are uncomfortable with the idea
that menstruation renders a woman "unclean."

At one time, all makeup was prohibited, but today only lipstick is
discouraged while taking communion. An unadorned face reflects
the clean state of the mind and body prepared for the holy Gifts.
From a practical standpoint, lipstick accumulates on the common
spoon and chalice cloth, possibly offending fellow parishioners.

COMMUNION AT NON-ORTHODOX CHURCHES

Orthodox cannot take communion at non-Orthodox churches. Major differences in the faith prevent sharing of the common cup.

CONTRIBUTING TO THE EUCHARIST

The Orthodox church invites its members to contribute the bread (*prósforo*) and wine needed for the Eucharist. You may bring these items along with a list of names of living and deceased persons you would like the priest to commemorate in the Divine Liturgy. In the closing prayer of the preparation service (*proskomidí* — pron. *proskomithí*) during the *órthros* service and during the Divine Liturgy, the priest asks God to bless those who offered the gifts and those requested to be remembered.

You may want to bake the *prósforo* yourself — a satisfying and rewarding tradition. See *Religious Breads* for the recipe and special instructions. There are no specifications regarding the wine, except that it be red; a sweet dessert wine such as mavrodaphne is customary.

Be sure to notify the priest that you would like to bring the bread. The priest will need it before the *órthros* service that precedes the Divine Liturgy.

---

1. George Mastrantonis, "Holy Communion, The Bread of Life (St. Louis, Mo.: Ologos, n.d), 10.

HOLY UNCTION

Orthodox believe in the power of God to heal both the body and the spirit. In this sacrament, the Holy Spirit is invoked to bless olive oil, an ancient Greek balm, and the ill person is anointed. Most parishioners receive the sacrament once a year on Holy Wednesday of Holy Week, but it also may be administered privately.

THE SACRAMENT OF HOLY UNCTION

The sacrament of holy unction provides both physical and mental healing with holy oil (*efchéleon*) blessed by the Holy Spirit. The oil carries God's grace both to renew the body and to cleanse the spirit. The service follows the apostolic tradition mentioned in the Gospels. "…Let him call for the elders of the church, and let them pray over him, anointing him with oil in the name of the Lord; and the prayer of faith will save the sick man, and the Lord will raise him up; and if he has committed sins, he will be forgiven." James 5:14-15

The service is composed of Psalms from the Old Testament, hymns of direct supplication to God, and prayers to saints to intercede for the petitioner. In addition, there are seven readings from the Gospels preceded by seven other New Testament writings, notably the epistles of St. Paul and St. James. After each set of scriptural readings, a prayer is offered on behalf of the penitent by the priest asking for forgiveness and the sanctification of the oil.

At the end of the service, the priest puts holy oil on the forehead, cheeks, chin, and hands of the parishioner in the form of a cross, saying: "O Holy Father, physician of our souls and bodies, heal your servant [name] from every physical and emotional affliction."

Holy unction is a sacrament of great comfort to the faithful. It provides uplift and asks for patience to accept the will of God whatever the physical outcome. HOWEVER, IT SHOULD NOT BE USED AS A SUBSTITUTE FOR MEDICAL TREATMENT.

HOLY WEDNESDAY SERVICE

On Holy Wednesday of Holy Week, sick and healthy alike attend church to receive the sacrament of holy unction. Holy Week is a time of repentance, confession, and forgiveness. Parishoners must prepare themselves, ideally through confession, to receive the oil with a clean heart. At the end of the service, each parishioner walks to the front of the church, and the priest puts a small amount of holy oil on his or her head and hands as described above. The dispensing cotton swabs are collected in the back of the church to be disposed of in a proper manner. Extra holy oil is usually available to take home. This can be used right away or kept in the home *ikonostási* for use at any time.

PRIVATE SERVICE

When a person is very ill — physically, mentally, or both — a private service can be held at any time at home, church, or hospital. If possible, the recipient should prepare with confession, repentance, and fasting (health permitting) to receive the sacrament with a pure heart and faith in the power of God to heal. The private service is conducted by one or more priests. In an earlier time, seven priests participated, but this requirement has been dropped for practical reasons.

Have ready for the priest on a table:

- An icon (preferably Christ or the Virgin Mary)
- A Bible
- A bowl containing five cups of flour
- Seven candles placed in the bowl of flour
- A lighted wick floating in olive oil
- Small measure of wine
- Incense
- Cotton balls or swabs

A shorter version of the Holy Wednesday service is performed; a candle is lit after each Gospel reading. The oil with the floating wick becomes holy oil, symbolizing the grace of God, and is used by the priest for anointing. You may want to thank the priest for his services with a small gift or remuneration.

After the service, the candles and floating wick should continue to burn until consumed. Dispose of the cotton properly by burying it or its ashes where no one will step on them. Do not put it in the garbage. Traditionally *prósforo* (bread for the holy communion) should be made from the flour and taken to church the following Sunday along with a list of names of living family members (including the sick individual) that you want remembered in the Divine Liturgy. If you ask the priest, he will save a portion of the *prósforo* for you. (See *Religious Breads* for recipe)

Greek Orthodox Clergy

HOLY ORDERS

Occasionally Americans see Orthodox holy men in full black rega-
lia: a tall hat with veil, long beard, and flowing black robes. The
effect is startling. As the figure floats among those in Western
dress, an air of mysticism surrounds him. While few Orthodox
priests in America today dress like this, they still have a spiritual
aura and are respected by their people. As guardians and teachers
of the Orthodox Christian faith, their induction into the priesthood
is one of the most sacred rites of the church, bestowed by holy
sacrament.

THE SACRAMENT OF HOLY ORDERS

The vital work of the church was begun by Christ who appointed
twelve apostles to assist in the ministry of Christianity. Fifty days
after his Resurrection, the apostles received the Holy Spirit at
Pentecost to continue Christ's work. They in turn anointed others.
This continuous line of holy men anointed by other holy men is
known as the apostolic succession, a direct link with the original
apostles, and one of the most important concepts in Orthodox
priesthood. The sacrament of holy orders repeats this tradition.

Ordination in the service of God can be on various levels in the
Orthodox church, major and minor. Members of a major order —
bishop, priest, and deacon — are ordained during a Divine Liturgy
by a bishop. During the service, a priest leads the candidate
around the altar three times while hymns are sung. The candidate
then kneels and rests his head on the altar. The bishop puts his
stole and right hand over the candidate's head as the candidate
receives the Holy Spirit. The entire congregation witnesses the
ordination and proclaims its consent by shouting in unison, *Áxios!*
(Worthy! — pron. *Áksios*) The bishop bestows sacred vestments
on the new priest, who then receives communion and recites a
special prayer.

Minor orders, including subdeacons, readers, chanters, and aco-
lytes (altar boys), are ordained by a bishop during a worship
service.

The elaborate ceremonial vestments worn by the church hierarchy
lend dignity and solemnity to Orthodox services. The striking tall

hat, a *kalimáfchion*, can be worn by all priests. Unmarried priests and bishops wear a veil over it making the hat an *epáno-kalimáfchion*. The tall hats, a carry-over from Byzantine society where they were worn by the clergy and laymen, are worn mainly by bishops in the United States, but are very common in Greece.

THE PRIESTHOOD

QUALIFICATIONS

Candidates for holy orders must have a firm faith, exemplary conduct, and theological training commensurate with their duties. Ordained positions are for males only. If priests and deacons marry, they must do so before being ordained. Only unmarried priests may become bishops.

Priests who have their own parishes must be well educated. In addition to an undergraduate degree, a graduate degree from an approved theological school is desired. It is the principle of the Greek Orthodox Archdiocese of North and South America that its priests graduate from an Orthodox theological school, and the vast majority of its priests have done so. In the United States there is one Greek Orthodox theological school, Holy Cross Greek Orthodox School of Theology, in Brookline, Massachusetts, under the Archdiocese. There are three other Orthodox theological schools: The Carpatho-Russian seminary, also under the jurisdiction of the Archdiocese, and two others affiliated with the Orthodox Church in America.

RESPONSIBILITIES

Many demands are made on the local priest, who serves as a celebrator, educator, counselor, and administrator. As a representative of Christ, his religious responsibilities include preserving the correct faith, administering sacraments, conducting services, and educating his people about Orthodox tradition and living as good Christians. Parishioners look to him for advice and counsel about their daily lives. In addition, he must possess administrative, management, and political skills if his church is to run smoothly and successfully.

PRIESTS AND LAITY

RELATIONSHIP WITH PRIEST

Because of the emphasis on family in Orthodoxy, the priest becomes well acquainted with his parishioners and their personal lives. Parishioners invite him to their homes for special celebrations, such as the blessing at Epiphany or an engagement, and for parties or a simple dinner. Ideally the priest becomes a spiritual father, an old Orthodox tradition.

Traditionally, people stand when the priest enters a room, and kiss his right hand when greeting or receiving something from him. It is through his hands the sacraments are received. It has become customary for parishioners to give the priest remuneration or a small gift for personal services such as conducting a wedding, funeral, house blessing, etc.

PROPER FORMS OF ADDRESS

The following forms should be used when addressing the clergy. Use the title in third-person situations such as addressing a letter or listing in a printed program. Use the salutation when speaking to the individual or as a greeting in a letter.[1]

His All Holiness [first name]
Archbishop of Constantinople and Ecumenical Patriarch
    Salutation: Your Holiness

His Eminence Archbishop [first name]
Primate of the Greek Orthodox Archdiocese of America
    Salutation: Your Eminence

His Excellency Metropolitan [first name] of New Jersey
    Salutation: Your Excellency

His Grace Bishop [first name] of [name of diocese]
    Salutation: Your Grace

The Very Reverend [first and last name] — (unmarried priest)
    Salutation: Father [first or last name] (formal)
                Father (informal)

The Reverend [first and last name] — (married priest)
    Salutation: Father [first or last name] (formal)
                Father (informal)

The Reverend Deacon [first and last name]
    Salutation: Deacon [first or last name] (formal)
                Father (informal)

Since the Greek word for "priest" is *"presvýteros,"* his wife is called *"presvytéra."*

THE ROLE OF WOMEN IN THE CHURCH

Women have a limited official role in the Orthodox church. Their greatest limitation is exclusion from the priesthood. The church reinforces this position with various arguments. Since Jesus was a man, the priest should also be a man — the image or icon of Christ. Therefore when conducting the Divine Liturgy, culminating with communion, the priest must symbolically represent Jesus offering the Last Supper to his apostles. In addition, Christ chose men, not women, to be his disciples, establishing the tradition known as apostolic succession.

Advocates for changing this position argue that the essential icon image of Christ is his humanness, not his maleness. God became human to show that both men and women could be saved and return to the divine image within them. Challengers also point out that Christ did not ordain his apostles. This was done at Pentecost by the Holy Spirit. Women were present at the time, and the Holy Spirit continues to descend on male and females alike. The Orthodox church recognizes a number of women saints as apostles, including the "apostle to the apostles," Mary Magdalene. (See Eva Catafygiotu Topping, *Holy Mothers of Orthodoxy: Women and the Church*[2])

The role of women has been limited in other ways also. Despite extensive participation by women in the first century as deacons, apostles, evangelists, and teachers, in the second century the church officially adopted policies that forbade women from preaching and teaching. However, they served as deaconesses from the first to the twelfth century, reading prayers of blessing, assisting in the liturgy, and anointing the sick according to Matushka Ellen Gvosdev in *The Female Diaconate*.[3] The Orthodox service book still contains the service for the ordination of women to the diaconate.

Orthodox women today are raising questions about the traditional role and status of women in the church in writings and confer-

Holy Orders

ences. Three international Orthodox women's conferences have been held in: Romania, 1976; Rhodes, 1988; and Crete, 1990.[4]

Monastic Orders

The monks and nuns of the Orthodox church take special vows and occupy a unique position within the church. Each monk and nun strives to achieve union with God through prayer, fasting, poverty, and celibacy, undistracted by the temptations of the secular world.

St. Anthony, the father of Orthodox monastic life, lived in the third and fourth centuries. He is typical of the anchorite monk who lives alone but comes together with others for work and worship. The cenobitic monks reside and worship in organized monasteries as defined by St. Basil. Solitary monks (eremites or hesychasts) live completely alone in isolation. The largest and most famous Orthodox center of monasticism is at Mt. Athos, Greece, with twenty active monasteries. The six monasteries of Meteora in Thessaly, Greece, sit on top of spectacularly high rocks.

---

1. Source of titles: Chief Secretariat Office of the Greek Orthodox Archdiocese of North and South America.

2. Eva Catafygiotu Topping, "Orthodox Women and the Iconic Image of Christ," 125, and "Orthodox Eve and the Royal Priesthood," 103, in *Holy Mothers of Orthodoxy: Women and the Church* (Minneapolis: Light and Life Publishing Company, 1987).

3. Matushka Ellen Gvosdev, *The Female Diaconate: An Historical Perspective* (Minneapolis: Light and Life Publishing Company, 1991).

4. World Council of Churches, "Report on the Consultation of Orthodox Women, 11-17 September 1976, Agapia, Roumania" (Geneva, Switzerland: World Council of Churches, 1977). World Council of Churches, "The Place of Women in the Orthodox Church and the Question of the Ordination of Women, Rhodes, Greece, 30 October-7 November 1988, Rhodes, Greece" (Istanbul: The Ecumenical Patriarachate, 1988) (available through World Council of Churches). World Council of Churches, "Church and Culture: Second International Orthodox Women's Consultation, 16-24 January 1990, Orthodox Academy of Crete" (Geneva, Switzerland: World Council of Churches).

St. George

❧ *Saints*

Icons of saints with penetrating eyes and flowing robes dominate the interior of Orthodox churches. Infants receive the names of saints at their baptisms, and festivals celebrate saints' feast days. To the Greek Orthodox, saints are extended family with which to share worship, holidays, and intimate moments.

SAINTS AS MODELS AND PROTECTORS

Saints serve as examples of the heights each individual can reach. They are human beings who have achieved a goal that seemed unattainable, people who tried to imitate the life of Christ. Just as Christ was not held back by adversity and hurdles but continued walking the road set by God, so the saints accepted with patience all adversities to reach their goal, union with Christ (*théosis*). For this the saints not only receive honor and recognition in the Christian community but serve as models to a Christian person.

Saints also protect and assist the faithful like extended family. Just as you might turn to a family member for help and guidance, you may pray to a saint for assistance. The saint intercedes on your behalf with God, acting as a petitioner and a defender. This tradition comes from the Orthodox belief that everyone, here and in heaven, is a vital part of the family of God.

CHOOSING SAINTS

Generally, there are three main categories of Orthodox saints: martyrs who died for Christianity; ascetics such as nuns and monks; and men and women who were major figures in church history. Today, an Orthodox saint is chosen by a special committee that studies, searches, prays for guidance, checks every detail of a candidate's life, and looks for signs of holiness after death. Then the Ecumenical Patriarchate in Constantinople issues a special letter to recognize the person, making him or her a saint.

One of the most recent saints is St. Nektarios, who died in 1920 and was canonized in 1961. A noted writer and educator, he founded the Convent of the Holy Trinity for nuns on the Greek island of Aegina. His shrine there at St. Nektarios chapel at the convent is the object of many pilgrimages for healing and miracles. When near his tomb, believers smell a beautiful fragrance, a sign of his holiness.

Another sign of saintliness is the preservation of the body after death without embalming. For example, the body of St. Spyridon who lived in the fourth century is still intact without artificial means in St. Spyridon Cathedral in Corfu, Greece. Nuns and monks are usually buried in the ground in a shroud only, and their condition is revealed after exhumation in three years.

Patron Saints

A patron saint is someone with special significance for you, your family, organization, cause, or city. For a family, it is often the saint for whom the head of the house is named. An organization may choose a saint who is helpful to its cause. For example, St. Basil Academy, a residential childcare center in New York, is so named because St. Basil founded the world's first orphanage and was famous for his philanthropic work with poor children.

The Orthodox believe that saints can intercede with God for general and specific concerns. Sometimes God works through them to perform miracles, especially healing. The faithful may pray directly to a specific patron saint for help in a specific situation.

ILLNESSES	SAINTS
Birthmarks	St. Symeon
Childbirth	St. Eleftherios
Eye disease	St. Paraskevi
Headaches	St. Paraskevi
Illness (general)	Ss. Cosmas and Damian (best known)
	St. Nektarios
	St. Panteleimon
	St. Spyridon the Miracle Worker
Retarded and incurable children	St. Marina

SPECIAL SITUATIONS

Children	St. Basil the Great
	St. Nicholas
	St. Stelianos
Crops	St. Demetrios the Great
Education	The Three Hierarchs:
	• St. Basil the Great
	• St. Gregory the Theologian
	• St. John Chrysostom
Godparents	St. John the Baptist
Lost property	St. Phanourios
Orphans	St. Basil the Great
Peace	St. Irene
Pious parents	Ss. Joachim and Anna
Poor	St. Basil the Great
	St. George the Great
Rain, thunder and lightning	St. Elias the Prophet
Roads	St. Barbara
Sailors	St. Nicholas
Scholars	St. Katherine
Shepherds	St. Demetrios the Great
	St. George the Great
Warriors	St. George the Great
	St. Procopius
	St. Theodore Tyron
	St. Theodore Stratilates

INTERACTING WITH SAINTS

TÁMA (VOW)

A *táma* is a combined prayer and vow to a saint. As you pray for help, you promise to give or do something. For example, you may ask for protection during a storm or for the cure of an illness. In turn you vow, for example, to give money to the church or help someone in need. (See *Birth* and *Special Blessings, Prayers, and Appeals.*)

WAYS TO HONOR SAINTS

The Orthodox honor their saints through prayers, icons, and special observances.

Prayers and Prayer Services

Saints are praised and prayed to frequently. A prayer service *(paráklisis)* for a specific saint may be offered, particularly those known to perform miracles, such as St. Paraskevi for healing eyes. Make arrangements with your priest. The two most popular services, the Great Paraklisis and the Small Paraklisis, honor the Virgin Mary, during the first fifteen days of August. (See *Special Blessings, Prayers, and Appeals*)

Veneration of Icons

Saints are represented on icons that are venerated and handled with great respect. (See *Icons* and *The Church of the Home*)

Feast Days

Both the church and individuals honor the saints on their feast days. Celebrations include going to a church service, attending a name day party, baking bread for communion or for an *artoklasía* service, baking sweets, attending a festival, or observing regional customs.

Relics in Church Altars

Relics of a saint (vestments and/or remains) are usually buried in the altar of each Orthodox church. During the consecration of a church, a bishop conducts an elaborate service to sanctify the altar where the Eucharist is performed. The bishop places in a small crypt, usually in the center of the altar, a box made of gold or silver containing relics of a saint and then seals it. This tradition derives from the practice of using tombs of the early Christian martyrs as eucharistic tables.

Roadside Shrines in Greece

While traveling in Greece, you may notice shrines the size of birdhouses that contain icons, incense, and *kandíli.* These are usually erected by the side of a road where a life has been spared during an accident. The shrine honors a saint who may have helped save an individual. It may also be erected in memory of someone who died. You are welcome to stop at the shrine, venerate the icons, and light the *kandíli.*

Naming after Saints

The church encourages its parishioners to name their children after an Orthodox saint, a significant feast day, or a Christian symbol, such as the cross (*stavrós*). The patron saint provides the individual a role model and protector for life. (See *Selecting a Name*)

WELL-KNOWN SAINTS OF THE GREEK ORTHODOX CHURCH

Listed below are some of the most celebrated saints for whom Greek Americans are named. The brief list includes basic information each individual should know about his or her patron saint. The name day is the one most frequently celebrated. Some of the information may conflict with what you have heard because historical records for early Christians are not completely accurate or consistent. The dates of death and some of the information on relics come from the writings of George Poulos, author of numerous books on Orthodox saints.[1]

Only proper names are listed even though nicknames are very common. For example, "Tasios" and "Stacy" are short for "Anastasios." Note that three times as many male saints as female saints are listed. A woman's name is frequently a feminization of a male saint's name, such as "Demetra" for "Demetrios." For more information about female saints see *Saints and Sisterhood: The Lives of Forty-eight Holy Women* by Eva Catafygiotu Topping.[2]

St. Alexander
Name Day: August 30

Alexander lived in the third and fourth centuries and is known for his successful opposition to Arios, a man who heretically preached that Christ was inferior to God the Father.

Greek: Alexandra (f) and Alexandros (m)
English: Alexandra (f) and Alexander (m)

Anastasios
Name Day: Easter (moveable)

Anastasios means "one who shall rise again" or "of the Resurrection," referring to the church's most important feast day, Easter. Numerous saints (male and female) are named after this great event, but the name day most commonly celebrated is Easter.

Greek: Anastasia (f) and Anastasios (m)
English: Anastasia (f) and Anastasios (m)

St. Andrew the Apostle (*Protóklitos*)
Name Day: November 30

St. Andrew (*Protóklitos* — first chosen) was the first apostle selected by Christ. A vigorous orator, he converted thousands to Christianity in Greece, Asia Minor, and Byzantium and was crucified upside down on an X-cross in Patras in the first century. Patron saint of Patras, Greece.

Relics: Mt. Athos; Church of St. Andrew, Patras, Greece
Greek: Andreana (f) and Andreas (m)
English: Andrea (f) and Andrew (m)

St. Anna
Name Day: December 9

St. Anna is the mother of the Virgin Mary. This date honors her conception, but she is also honored with her husband, St. Joachim, on September 9. Together they are known as the saints of pious education for the religious instruction they provided their daughter.

Relics: Mt. Athos; Island of Patmos; Tomb in the Garden of Gethsemane in Jerusalem
Greek: Anna (f) (no masculine)
English: Anna (f) (no masculine)

St. Anthony the Great

Name Day: January 17

St. Anthony is considered the father of monastic life. He sold everything he owned and lived alone in the Egyptian desert until many followers settled nearby and emulated his example of asceticism. He formed the first monastery and died at the age of 105 in 356 A.D.

Greek: Antonia (f) and Antonios (m)

English: Antonia (f) and Anthony (m)

St. Athanasios the Great

Name Day: January 18

St. Athanasios, Patriarch of Alexandria, was influential in defining the early doctrines of the Christian faith, especially the belief that the Father, Son, and Holy Spirit are of one essence. Although exiled ten times for his beliefs, he died peacefully in 373 A. D.

Relics: Mt. Athos; St. John Monastery, near Dimitsana (Northwest of Tripoli, Peloponnesus)

Greek: Athanasia (f) and Athanasios (m)

English: Athanasia (f); Athan and Arthur (m)

St. Barbara

Name Day: December 4

St. Barbara was an intelligent, beautiful woman who was kept in seclusion in a tower by her father. When he discovered her conversion to Christianity, she was violently tortured, but Christ appeared to her in jail and healed her wounds. Refusing to accept the Roman pagan idols, she was subsequently beheaded by her father in the third century. St. Barbara is the patron saint of roads.

Relics: Rousanou Monastery, Meteora; Kechrovounion, Tinos

Greek: Barbara (f) (no masculine)

English: Barbara (f) (no masculine)

St. Bartholomew the Apostle
Name Day: June 11

St. Bartholomew was one of the twelve apostles who preached the gospel in Asia in the first century and was martyred in Urbanopolis. Although he has not been one of the most celebrated saints, nor has his name been commonly given, he is included here as the patron saint of His All Holiness Bartholomew I, Archbishop of Constantinople and Ecumenical Patriarch elected in 1991.

Relics: Mt. Athos; St. Bessarion Monastery, Pyli (Thessaly)
Greek: Vartholomeos (m) (no feminine)
English: Bartholomew (m) (no feminine)

St. Basil the Great
Name Day: January 1

One of the greatest church fathers, St. Basil the Great is renowned for his many accomplishments: He formulated the rules for monastic life; wrote the Divine Liturgy (St. John Chrysostom's is a shortened version); established institutions to care for the sick, orphans, poor, and the aged; and was a brilliant church orator. His official church title was Bishop of Caesarea, a city in ancient Cappadocia. He was born in 330 and died in 379. Basil is a patron saint of education (with St. Gregory the Theologian and St. John Chrysostom), children, orphans, and the poor. Vasilopita (bread for St. Basil) is cut each January 1 in his honor.

Relics: Mt. Athos; Koimisis Church, Nea Philadelphia, Athens; Barlaam Monastery, Meteora; Elias Monastery, Santorini
Greek: Vasilia (f) and Vasilios (m)
English: Vasilia (f); William and Basil (m)

Christ (Emmanuel)
Name Day: Christmas, December 25

The Christian faith is based on the life and teachings of Jesus Christ, the Son of God. The name "Emmanuel" means "God is with us."

Greek: Christina and Emmanuela (f); Christos and Emmanuel (m)
English: Christine and Emmanuela (f); Chris and Emmanuel (m)

Saints Constantine and Helen
Name Day: May 21

St. Constantine the Great was the first Roman Emperor to be converted to Christianity after seeing a cross in the sky saying, "In this sign you shall conquer." His Edict of Milan in 313 sanctioned religious tolerance, ending the persecutions of Christians. In 330 he moved the capital from Rome, renamed it Constantinople, and established the Byzantine empire. He convened the First Ecumenical Council that laid the basis for Christianity's beliefs with the first seven articles of the Nicene Creed. Although he died in 337, and his mother, St. Helen, died in 338, they share the same feast day.

Relics: Mt. Athos; Panagia Tourliane Monastery, Mykonos; St. John of Ipselou Monastery, Mitilini
Greek: Konstantina (f) and Konstantinos (m)
English: Constance (f) and Constantine (m)

St. Helen, the mother of St. Constantine, made a pilgrimage to Jerusalem where she discovered, under a sweet basil plant, the cross on which Christ was crucified. She erected a shrine there and churches over Christ's tomb, his birthplace, the mountain of Ascension (Mt. of Olives), and a monastery at Mt. Sinai. She is considered one of the most important female saints in the church. She was born in 255 and died in 328.

Greek: Eleni (f) (no masculine)
English: Helen and Elaine (f) (no masculine)

St. Demetrios the Great
Name Day: October 26

St. Demetrios, an officer in the Roman army, was put into prison for converting soldiers to Christianity in Thessaloniki in the early fourth century. He urged his friend, Nestor, to fight a famous gladiator and prove that, through prayer, the power of God could make him victorious. When Nestor killed the gladiator, the emperor was so angry, he ordered both Nestor and Demetrios executed. For many in Greece, October 26 also signifies the end of summer when the shepherds come down from the hills for the winter. St. Demetrios is the patron saint of shepherds, crops, and the city of Thessaloniki.

Relics: Mt. Athos; St. Demetrios Church, Thessaloniki; procession and celebration in Thessaloniki on October 26
Greek: Demetra (f) and Demetrios (m)
English: Demetra (f); Demetri and James (m)

St. Elias (Elijah) the Prophet
Name Day: July 20

Elias lived in the ninth century B.C. and was one of the greatest prophets of the Old Testament. He is most renowned for convincing the Israelites to stop worshiping the God of nature, Baal, and return to one true God. He was taken to heaven in a chariot, and thunder and lightning are said to be St. Elias traveling across the sky in his chariot. He is the patron saint of rain, thunder, and lightning.

Pilgrimages: Chapels on mountain tops throughout Greece, especially at Mt. Taygetus near Sparta.

Greek: Elias (m) (no feminine)

English: Elias and Louis (m) (no feminine)

Evangelismos (Annunciation)
Name Day: March 25

On March 25 the church celebrates the Evangelismos, the Annunciation to the Virgin Mary that she will be the Mother of God. Many men and women are named for this event and most celebrate their name day on this date.

Greek: Evangelia (f) and Evangelos (m)

English: Evangeline (f); Evan and Angelo (m)

St. George the Great
Name Day: April 23 (If during Holy Week, celebrate the first Monday after Easter.)

This saint, one of the most popular, dared to be a Christian in the Roman army. A popular myth says he slew a dragon just before a princess was about to be sacrificed to it — thus St. George is frequently depicted on a horse with a lance and dragon. He is seen as a defender of good over evil. St. George was tortured and beheaded in 303. He is famous for healing and is the patron saint of the poor, shepherds, and warriors.

Relics: Mt. Athos; Church of the Metamorphosis, Plaka, Athens; Benaki Museum

Greek: Georgia (f) and Georgios (m)

English: Georgia (f) and George (m)

St. Gregory the Theologian

Name Day: January 25

St. Gregory is one of the great church fathers who built the foundations of the Orthodox faith. While Patriarch of Constantinople, he presided over the Second Ecumenical Council in which the Nicene Creed was completed. He was born in 329 and died in 390. He is known as the patron saint of education along with St. Basil the Great and St. John Chrysostom.

Relics: Mt. Athos; Church of Evangelismos, Peristeri, Athens; St. Stephen Monastery, Meteora

Greek: Gregoria (f) and Gregorios (m)

English: Gregoria (f) and Gregory (m)

St. Helen (see Saints Constantine and Helen)

St. John the Baptist

Name Day: January 7

St. John, an ascetic and great prophet, baptized Christ and became one of the most revered saints in the Greek Orthodox church. He was later beheaded by Herod in the first century to satisfy the request of his stepdaughter, Salome, and wife Herodias. Because he baptized Christ, he is the patron saint of godparents.

Relics: St. Demetrios Church, Neo Phaleron, Piraeus; Benaki Museum, Athens; Topkapi Museum, Constantinople

Greek: Ioanna (f) and Ioannis (m)

English: Joanna (f) and John (m)

St. Katherine

Name Day: November 25

St. Katherine is renowned for her intellect, wisdom, and per-suasive oratory. A princess in Alexandria and highly educated in the classics and Christian theology, she was ordered at age eighteen by Emperor Maxentius to worship the Olympian gods. She refused to do so and at her trial debated at least fifty philosophers, converting all of them to Christianity. Placed in jail, she converted the empress and many soldiers. Tortured on a wheel, she was released by an angel, but was eventually beheaded in 311. St. Katherine is the patron saint of scholars.

Relics: St. Nicholas Church, Kato Palesia, Athens; Zerbitsa Monastery, Sparta; St. Katherine Monastery at Mt. Sinai, Egypt

Greek: Ekaterini (f) (no masculine)

English: Katherine (f) (no masculine)

Mary (Panayia)

Name Day: August 15

The Virgin Mary is the mother of Jesus Christ and the most highly honored and beloved saint. She has four names in the Greek Orthodox church: Theotokos (Mother of God), Panayia (All Holy), Aiparthenos (Ever Virgin), and Despina (Our Lady). August 15 is one of the most important church holidays.

Pilgrimage sites:

- Mary's tomb at the foot of the Mount of Olives, Jerusalem
- Miraculous icon at the Church of the Evangelistria on the island of Tinos

Greek: Maria, Panayiota, and Despina (f); Panayiotis (m)

English: Mary and Maria (f); Panayiotis (m) and Peter (popular but incorrect)

Saints Michael and Gabriel (the Archangels)

Name Day: Nov. 8

Saints Michael and Gabriel are the two archangels of God. St. Michael is popularly believed to conduct souls to God after death. St. Gabriel announced the Virgin birth to the Theotokos. Gabriel is not a common Greek name.

Pilgrimage: Miraculous icon at the Panormitis Monastery on the Dodecanese island of Simi

Greek: Michailia (f) and Mihael (m)

English: Michele (f) and Michael (m)

St. Nicholas

Name Day: December 6

Bishop of Myra in Lycia (now southeast Turkey) in the fourth century, St. Nicholas was tortured and imprisoned for his faith. But with the ascendancy of Constantine and the toleration of Christianity, he attended the First Ecumenical Council. He was admired for his love of giving presents to poor children and families. In northern Europe, Santa Claus became the name for St. Nicholas. St. Basil is also known for giving gifts; it is on St. Basil's name day in Greece, not Christmas, when gifts are given to children. St. Nicholas is the patron saint of children and sailors.

Relics: Mt Athos; Barlaam Monastery, Meteora; St. Nicholas Monastery, Vlasia (Peloponnesus)

Greek: Nicoleta (f) and Nikolaos (m)

English: Nicole (f) and Nicholas (m)

St. Paul

Name Day: June 29

St. Paul was the greatest missionary of the church. Formerly a fervent Jew named Saul, he was converted to Christianity by a blinding light on the road to Damascus and proceeded to convert thousands to Christ. His extensive writings (almost half of the New Testament) have greatly influenced Christian thought. He is considered by some to be the single most influential Christian after Christ himself. A "pillar of the church," he was beheaded in Rome circa 67.

Relics: St. John Monastery, Patmos; Taxiarchon Monastery, Digiatia (Peloponnesus)

Greek: Pavlos (m) (no feminine)

English: Paula (f) and Paul (m)

St. Peter the Apostle

Name Day: June 29

St. Peter is considered the leader of Christ's apostles. He conducted an extensive ministry and founded the church in Antioch and Rome. He is popularly known as "the rock" for the firm foundation he gave Christianity. He fearlessly proclaimed God's word and baptized 3,000 people on Pentecost.

Relics: Mt. Athos; St. Nicholas Church, Chalandri, Athens; Eisodia Monastery, Oblon (Peloponnesus)

Greek: Petroula (f) and Petros (m)

English: Petroula (f) and Peter (m)

St. Sophia

Name Day: September 17

St. Sophia had three daughters, Faith, Hope (Elpitha), and Love (Agape). In the second century, her daughters, ages nine, ten and twelve, were thrown into a boiling vat of tar and asphalt by the Emperior Hadrian. The emperor then had them beheaded. The mother prayed for her own death, died, and was buried next to her daughters. Women named Elpitha and Agape also celebrate this name day. (Churches named St. Sophia [Holy Wisdom] celebrate their feast day the Monday after Pentecost, not on September 17).

Greek: Sophia (f) (no masculine)

English: Sophia (f) (no masculine)

St. Spyridon the Miracle Worker

Name Day: December 12

St. Spyridon was a simple shepherd from Cyprus who had no formal education. He memorized the Bible, however, and became a bishop who attended the First Ecumenical Council. Many miracles have been attributed to him, including healing the Emperor Constantine. A patron saint of illness, it is believed that he often leaves the church at night to perform miracles for those who invoke his name. It is said that the shoes by his casket are periodically worn out from his travels and have to be changed each year. He died in the mid-fourth century.

Relics: St. Spyridon Cathedral, Kerkyra, Corfu. Casket opened by special request, and pieces of his slippers may be purchased. Procession and celebration on December 12.

Greek: Spiridoula (f); Spyridon and Spiros (m)

English: Spiridoula (f); Spyridon and Spiros (m)

Stavros

Name Day: September 14 (The Exaltation of the Holy Cross)

"Stavrós" means "cross," the most important symbol in all of Christianity. Many people are named after this symbol and celebrate their name day in commemoration of St. Helen's discovery on September 14, 325, of the true cross on which Christ was crucified. The return of the captured cross from the Persians to Constantinople in the seventh century is also remembered at this time.

Relics: To prevent its capture again, the cross was split and taken to Mt. Athos, Rome, Alexandria, Constantinople, and Antioch. Other churches claim splinters also.

Greek: Stavroula (f) and Stavros (m)

English: Stavroula (f) and Stavros (m)

St. Stephen the Protomartyr

Name Day: December 27

St. Stephen the Protomartyr, the first Christian martyr and deacon, was stoned to death in the year 36 in Jerusalem. He was one of seven assistants to the apostles in their ministry.

Relics: Mt. Athos; Kykko Monastery, Cyprus; St. Stephen Monastery, Meteora

Greek: Stephania (f) and Stephanos (m)

English: Stephanie (f) and Stephen (m)

St. Theodore

Name Day: Third Saturday of Souls (first Saturday of Lent — moveable)

The church honors two Theodores on this Saturday along with the miracle of the *kóllyva* (boiled wheat). Theodore Tyron and Theodore Stratilates both appeared in a vision to a Patriarch in the fourth century, warning him of contamination of the food for Lent and urging the Christians to eat boiled wheat instead. (See *Easter Season*) Some individuals celebrate the fixed name days: Theodore Tyron (February 17) or Theodore Stratilates (February 8).

Relics: Meteora Monastery, Meteora; St. Bessarion, Pyli (Thessaly); Nea Moni Monastery, Chios

Greek: Theodora (f) and Theodoros (m)

English: Theodora (f) and Theodore (m)

All Saints Day

Date: Sunday after Pentecost (moveable)

If you are unable to find the name day for a specific saint, celebrate on All Saints Day when every saint in the church is honored.

---

1.   George Poulos, *Orthodox Saints: Spiritual Profiles for Modern Man,* 4 vols., (Brookline, Mass.: Holy Cross Orthodox Press, 1976-82), and *Lives of the Saints and Major Feast Days* (1981; reprint, Brookline, Mass.: Greek Orthodox Archdiocese of North and South America, 1989).

2.   Eva Catafygiotu Topping, *Saints and Sisterhood: The Lives of Forty-eight Holy Women* (Minneapolis: Light and Life Publishing Company, 1990).

⚜ *Name Days*

Many Greek Americans describe with nostalgia the old days when family members and friends gathered together to celebrate a name day. Along with Easter and Christmas, name days were among the most joyous occasions in the family, especially the name day of the male head of the family. The name day, not the birthday, was remembered.

Name day celebrations gave the immigrants a continuity with the customs of Greece. A typical party in Greece, even today, is an open house with different kinds of food and drink, especially brandy. An invitation is not required. For example, on St. Basil's name day (January 1) every household with a member named Basil, celebrates. One simply drops by different homes to wish the honoree, *"Chrónia pollá"* ("Many years").

Such spontaneous visits are the exception in America. If a name day party is held here, guests attend by invitation only. Perhaps a greater appreciation of the name day's significance will revive the joyous tradition of celebrating name days.

Chrónia Pollá

RELIGIOUS SIGNIFICANCE

A person's name day is the feast day of the saint for whom he or she was named. In most cases the feast day is the anniversary of the saint's death. This tradition began during the first century when Christians prayed to God in the catacombs on the anniversary of the martyr's death, thanking God for the martyr's example and asking him through the saint's intercessions to guide and direct their lives. Frescoes depicting such gatherings still exist in some of the catacombs. According to the church, saints come to earth on their name days.

A common bond exists among people with the same name and guardianship by the same saint. The people are *synonómati*, sharer of the same first name.

CELEBRATING IN AMERICA

WHEN TO CELEBRATE

The Greek Orthodox church lists the feast days of thousands of saints, and saints with the same name may celebrate on different days. How do you know which day to observe? Most people remember the name day of the person for whom they were named. For example, a *yiayiá* and her granddaughter with the same name would remember the same day.

If your family does not keep this tradition, check the alphabetical listing in *Saints* or the chronological listing below. If your saint is not listed, talk with your priest or check an Orthodox calendar and reference books. Be careful when selecting the date. Over the years, social and church tradition favor one saint over another. For example, there are approximately fifty saints named "John," but most people with that name celebrate January 7, the Feast Day of St. John the Baptist. You can, however, choose another St. John, such as one from your region of Greece, and be perfectly in order with the church.

Women named after male saints usually celebrate on the male name days. Women named "Georgia" and "Alexandra" remember April 23 and August 30, respectively. However, there was a St.

Georgia (August 11) and a St. Alexandra (April 21). Those name days could be used instead, and there are hundreds of women saints from whom to choose.

Sometimes there are different celebration days for the same saint. For example, the majority of Orthodox remember the Virgin Mary on August 15 (The Dormition of the Mother of God), but a few choose to celebrate her name day on September 8 (The Nativity of the Mother of God).

If determining the name day becomes too complicated or the information cannot be found, celebrate on All Saints Day — a time when every saint in the Greek Orthodox church is honored. This is a moveable date, the Sunday after Pentecost.

WHAT TO SAY

Wish the celebrant either: *"Chrónia pollá"* ("Many years") or *"Ke tou chrónou"* ("And to next year").

WAYS TO CELEBRATE

Attend Church

Divine Liturgies are celebrated for the well-known saints. A church will always hold a service for its patron saint, and you are welcome to attend those services. If a special service is not conducted nearby, attend church on the nearest Sunday to the name day and take communion.

Make a Phone Call

Today most name days are remembered with a simple phone call and a wish of *"Chrónia pollá"* or *"Ke tou chrónou."*

Have a Party

Parties are usually by invitation and range from an open house with appetizers and sweets to a sit-down dinner.

Bake Bread or Sweets

Make bread for communion or the *artoklasía* service. (See *Religious Breads* for details and recipes.) Some people also make sweets for the church coffee hour following services.

Take your Godchild to Church

If it is your godchild's name day, attend church together and discuss the life of the saint.

Attend a Church Festival or Celebration

A church may hold a Greek festival in honor of its name day. This is a replica of the festival (*paniyíri*) that most small villages in Greece hold on a name day. Typically there is an abundance of Greek food and dancing. Many churches also give dances or dinners.

Decorate Icons

Some parishioners place a single flower or small bouquet by the saint's icon at church and at home.

CELEBRATING IN GREECE

PILGRIMAGE TO CHURCH

Many Greeks and Greek Americans make pilgrimages to churches in Greece where the relics of saints are kept. Relics (the body, bones, or vestments of saints) are believed to emit God's grace and have healing powers. Pilgrimages may also be made to locations where a miracle involving the saint is said to have taken place. (See *Visiting Greece*)

ATTEND A *PANIYÍRI*

Find a village, town or church celebrating its name day with a *paniyíri*. The festival usually lasts three days in the *platía* (town square) with Greek food, music, and dancing at its best! Many who have moved away from the village come back at this time as a homecoming. Sometimes major cities will also hold special celebrations. For example, Thessaloniki, the second largest city in Greece, honors its patron saint, St. Demetrios, on his feast day, October 26, with a procession of his relics through the streets. A similar celebration takes place for St. Spyridon on December 12 in Corfu.

GREEK SECULAR CUSTOMS

Many secular customs are observed on saints' name days. For example, shepherds traditionally break winter camp on St. George's day. In the villages of northern Greece on January 18, St. Athanasios Day, no work is done because it is considered bad luck. On July 17, St. Marina's Day, at Metrae, Thrace, the villagers cut the first bunch of grapes of the season.

POPULAR NAME DAYS

People usually celebrate the following name days (see "When to Celebrate" above):

September 14	Stavroula/Stavros [from *stavrós* (cross) — Exaltation of the Holy Cross]
September 17	Sophia (St. Sophia)
October 26	Demetra/Demetri and James (St. Demetrios the Great)
November 8	Michele/Michael (Saints Michael and Gabriel the Archangels)
November 9	Nektarios (St. Nektarios)
November 25	Katherine (St. Katherine)
November 30	Andrea/Andrew (St. Andrew the Apostle)
December 4	Barbara (St. Barbara)
December 6	Nicole/Nicholas (St. Nicholas)
December 9	Anna (St. Anna)
December 12	Spiridoula/Spyridon and Spiros (St. Spyridon the Miracle Worker)
December 25	Christine and Emmanuela/Chris and Emmanuel (The Nativity of Jesus Christ)
December 27	Stephen (St. Stephen the Protomartyr)

January 1	Vasilia/Basil and William (St. Basil the Great)
January 6	Photini/Photios [from *ta phóta* (the light) — Epiphany]
January 7	Joanna/John (St. John the Baptist)
January 17	Antonia/Anthony (St. Anthony the Great)
January 18	Athanasia/Athan and Arthur (St. Athanasios the Great)
January 25	Gregory (St. Gregory the Theologian)
First Saturday of Lent	Theodora/Theodore (St. Theodore)
March 25	Evangeline/Angelo (from Evangelismos [Annunciation])
Easter	Anastasia/Anastasios (from Anastasi [Resurrection])
April 23	Georgia/George (St. George the Great — if during Lent, celebrated Monday after Easter)
May 21	Constance/Constantine (Constantine the Great) Helen (St. Helen)
June 11	Bartholomew (St. Bartholomew the Apostle)
Sunday after Pentecost	All Saints Day
June 29	Paula/Paul and Peter (Saints Peter and Paul)
July 20	Elias and Louis (Elias the Prophet)
July 26	Paraskevi (St. Paraskevi)
August 15	Mary, Maria, Panayiota, Despina/Panayiotis (Virgin Mary)
August 30	Alexandra/Alexander (St. Alexander)

The Mother of God and Jesus Christ
(Wall painting from St. George's Chapel,
Monastery of St. Paul, Mt. Athos, 16th Century)

⚜ *Icons*

The pensive faces and flat bodies of Orthodox icons, flickering in candlelight, have an unreal quality compelling the viewer to contemplate the world of the divine. They inspire ritualistic customs: kissing, decorating, and honoring. Their presence and inspiration are an integral part of Orthodox worship.

MEANING AND PURPOSE

Mystical Byzantine icons contrast with the religious art of the Western renaissance that depicts important Biblical characters and scenes with great realism. The contrast comes from the different theological traditions of the Latin West and the Orthodox East. Catholics stress that God became man, and the Orthodox emphasize that man is to become like God (*théosis*).

It is this profound concept of the sacred image of God within humans that underlies the meaning and purpose of an icon, which means "image." Icons are sacred images of extraordinary human beings who have become godlike and achieved divinity through grace. An icon is a window to the spiritual world, revealing the heavenly possibilities for each viewer on earth and providing models to imitate. The unearthly appearance of the icon subjects is intentional, pushing the viewer beyond the real world. As such, they play a critical role in worship and Orthodox theology. Most icons depict individual saints, but they may also represent significant events such as the Annunciation and the Nativity of Christ.

HISTORICAL CONTROVERSIES

Icons appeared during the time of Christ, but it took 800 years to define their role in church tradition. Controversy often raged over the depiction of the divine. In keeping with Old Testament tradition, the depiction of God was forbidden. How should Christ be shown? Was he God (and forbidden), or was he human? The controversy was not resolved until 692 when the church agreed upon the dual nature of Christ. The Quinisext Council declared that Christ was both divine and human and should be depicted as a human, not symbolically as a lamb or fish. This canon became the theoretical basis for Orthodox liturgical art. Art must reflect divine revelation and the kingdom of God.

The popularity of icons greatly increased. Some factions of the church believed icons were worshiped like idols, a practice forbidden by the Bible. In addition some still could not accept the depiction of the divine Christ. The iconoclasts (image breakers) triumphed when the Imperial Edict of 726 prohibited religious images, and many icons were destroyed. For 157 years icons were banned, except for a brief time of restoration. But in 843 through the efforts of Empress Theodora, a church council condemned iconoclasm for the last time. On the first Sunday of Great Lent there was a great procession to St. Sophia Cathedral in Constantinople bringing back the icons. The return of the icons is still commemorated in the church on the first Sunday of Lent (Sunday of Orthodoxy) with a procession of icons.

CREATING AND RESTORING

ICONOGRAPHERS

Iconographers translate revealed scripture and divine truths into visual images, writing — not painting — the icon with consecrated brushes, paints, and materials. Ideally, they should be pious individuals trained by holy fathers. Monks and nuns, therefore, have traditionally been the primary source of icons. Most iconographers outside of monasteries today have commercialized the sacred art of iconography.

Iconographers should pray, fast, and avoid worldly excitement during their work. Individual interpretation should be kept to a minimum as their task is to pass on tradition by replicating previous icons within proscribed limits. Works should remain anonymous, but if signed, be inscribed with the words, "By the hand of [name]."

MEDIA

Theology and history dictate that icons be two dimensional. Three-dimensional art (sculpture) is not allowed to avoid the appearance of an idol and sensual realism. Icons may be executed in a variety of media such as wall frescoes, moveable paintings on wood and canvas, mosaics, on eggs (Russian) and lacquer boxes (Slavic), etc. In the United States, large mosaics are being installed in churches, particularly in the dome and altar area, in a revival of the Byzantine mosaic tradition like that at St. Sophia Cathedral in Constantinople. The stained glass windows in some Orthodox churches are not traditional.

Techniques for small, moveable icons also vary. The classic medium for an icon on wood is egg tempera which gives a unique richness, depth, and softness to the icon. Oil and acrylic also are common. Sometimes silver pounded in the form of a picture covers all of the icon except specific body parts, usually the head and hands. This gilding tradition originated with the custom of giving precious metal to a saint to fulfill a *táma* (see *Special Blessings, Prayers, and Appeals*). The least expensive icons are paper reproductions laminated on wood.

CHARACTERISTICS

Certain characteristics give icons their unique, mystical look. Subjects appear flat and may have exaggerated features such as large eyes to reveal the soul and high foreheads to emphasize the spirit. An unrealistic appearance reveals the divine, spiritual nature the saints have achieved. Inverse perspective may be employed where certain subjects thrust themselves forward on the viewer, emphasizing their importance. This contrasts with the linear perspective of realism that shows vanishing points and three dimensions. Certain colors are symbolic. For example, gold, a primary background color, represents the divine light of God's world.

There are strict formal rules of composition. Fixed patterns in a repetitive design and craftsmanship must be exact. Oral tradition, descriptions in scripture, church writings, canons, and manuals prescribe how icons should look. Depictions of saints generally appear a certain way: the Virgin Mary with the Christ Child, Saints Cosmas and Damian together with medical instruments, and Mary Magdalene with a red Easter egg and myrrh bottle.

INSCRIPTIONS

The saint's name and/or initials seen in the upper corners of the icon tell the viewer who or what they are seeing. For example, the icon of Christ is always shown with "IC" (Jesus) in the upper left corner and "XC" (Christ) in the upper right. Or there may be a brief title of an event like Metamorphosis, Greek for Transfiguration.

STYLISTIC HISTORY

Despite the conformity and anonymity in iconography mandated by the church, artistic styles have changed through the centuries ranging from realistic to the mystical. With the fall of Constantinople in 1453, regional styles gained prominence with the rise of such centers as Crete, Cyprus, the Balkans, Mt. Athos, and Russia. In Russia, Theophanes the Greek and his pupil, Andrei Rublev, at the Novgorod school produced some of the most famous icons in the world during the late fourteenth and fifteenth centuries.

In the twentieth century, iconography took a dramatic turn back toward the strict religious Byzantine tradition, led by Photios Kontoglou in Greece and Leonid Ouspensky, a Russian in Paris. (This revival is now favored in America also.) Kontoglou returned to the original intent of the church fathers and established strict rules and standards for iconographers. Ouspensky and Vladimir Lossky wrote the definitive books on icons, *The Meaning of Icons* and *Theology of the Icon*.[1] An American professor, John Yiannias, in "Orthodox Art and Architecture" in *A Companion to the Greek Orthodox Church*, suggests outstanding examples of Byzantine icons that can be seen in Greece, Turkey, Italy, Cyprus, Egypt, Russia, Yugoslavia, Bulgaria, and Rumania.[2]

RESTORATION

The restoration of a historic icon should be done by an experienced iconographer. The process may be too complicated for an artist who is not an icon specialist. Contact a reputable icon dealer for references.

VENERATION

The Orthodox draw a clear line between venerating and worshiping icons. Worship would constitute idolatry, whereas veneration is respect and reverence for the subject of the icon, such as the person of Christ or St. Sophia. Icons help the petitioner visualize the living saint in heaven. It is that represented person toward whom appeals and thanksgiving are directed, not the icon itself. For example, when taking a journey, people customarily kiss an icon and ask the saint's assistance in safe travel.

In the church the most common form of veneration is to light a candle, bow slightly as you make the sign of the cross, and kiss the icon. The icons in the narthex are always venerated. If no service is in progress, you also may venerate any of the icons in the *ikonostásion.*

Icons relating to special feast days are placed in the narthex or sometimes at the front of the nave. For example, an icon of the Annunciation will be displayed on March 25. The church usually decorates these icons with fresh flowers. Parishioners also may bring a single flower or tiny bouquet and place it by the icon. The Sunday of Orthodoxy commemorates the restoration of the icons to the church in 843 with a procession around the church.

MIRACLES

Through the centuries many miracles have been attributed to the power of personal and famous icons. The first icon is said to be that of Christ himself when he placed a linen cloth on his face, and his image immediately transferred. The holy cloth was taken to King Abgar of Edessa who was healed by its miraculous power.

HEALING ICONS

During an illness, believers often bring icons into a sick person's room. Harry Mark Petrakis, in *Stelmark: A Family Recollection* describes the role of icons during his mother's struggle with typhoid fever when she was two years old.

[The doctor] offered scant hope that the child would survive. My grandparents prayed to my mother's patron saint
and placed small icons in the four corners of the child's
sick room... An icon of St. Luke in a nearby monastery was
reported to have supernatural powers... They carried the
icon back to my mother's room... my grandfather raised
my mother in his arms. "Come, child, kiss the icon and it
will make you well." My mother claims to this day she
remembers those words spoken to her, and the cool feel of
the icon under her lips. Afterwards, miraculously, she
recovered.[3]

ACQUIRING AND SELLING

INHERITANCE AND GIFTS

Orthodox families treasure their icons. With love and reverence
they are passed on to other family members, usually after someone dies. It is common, for example, for the icon of the patron
saint of a deceased grandmother to be given to her granddaughter
with the same name. People also give icons to newborns and the
afflicted.

CONSIDERATIONS FOR PURCHASE

Identify the Occasion

Before buying an icon, clearly define why you are purchasing it.
Is it a gift of a patron saint for a newborn or a name day? Is it for
your home *ikonostási*? Is it an aid for a specific cause? Does it
simply appeal to you?

Learn about the Saint

Research the life of the saint, including how the saint is traditionally depicted. For example, Saints Constantine and Helen are
always shown together. If St. Helen is shown alone, this is
incorrect. Depictions can vary, however, and still be correct. For
example, St. George most often rides a horse while slaying a
dragon, but he may also appear alone holding a spear.

Train your Eye

Observe a variety of icons in churches, on the covers of the Sunday bulletin, in books, etc. Which ones conform to Orthodox theology and Byzantine tradition as described above?

Determine your Budget

In a religious sense, a "value" cannot be placed on an icon. Its value comes from its purpose, meaning, and sentimentality. In this sense, many icons are priceless. Nevertheless, you may find yourself in the market for icons, and prices vary greatly. The least expensive and most readily available icons are mass-produced photographs of historic icons, without backing or laminated on wood. Hand-painted icons of acrylic or oil are generally moderately priced. Somewhat more expensive are icons painted in the traditional medium of egg tempera. The price of icons that are covered with precious metal varies, depending on the quality of the particular covering —for example, brass and silver plate versus sterling silver and gold. In general, the most expensive icons are antiques more than one hundred years old and made with egg tempera or with precious metals. These icons are rare, and when found, can cost thousands of dollars.

BUYING IN THE UNITED STATES

Mail Order

Contact the following distributors for their icon catalogues: Holy Cross Orthodox Bookstore, 50 Goddard Avenue, Brookline, MA 02146; Holy Transfiguration Monastery, 278 Warren Street, Brookline, MA 02146; Light and Life Publishing Company, 4836 Park Glen Road, Minneapolis, MN 55416.

Bazaars, Conventions, and Shops

For hands-on shopping, look for moderately priced icons at church bazaars, Greek-American conventions, and in Greek specialty stores. For expensive antique icons, some may be found on rare occasions at an auction house, through an antique dealer, or through a general art dealer. The most dependable sources are antique icon dealers, only a small number of whom are in the United States. A reputable icon dealer will be willing to provide you with a list of client references and provide a written guarantee of the icon's authenticity. Good dealers can be trusted; however, you may also want to confirm authenticity of the icon by having it professionally appraised. Look for a museum staffed with people who are knowledgeable about icons. Fake antiques have become a problem.

Commission

Commissioning an icon requires research, time, patience, and money. Of utmost importance are the religious qualities an icon projects and the iconographer's method. Are they in keeping with the meaning and purpose of icons discussed here? Theoretically the iconographer remains anonymous and icons are not purchased because of the iconographer's reputation. As a practical matter, however, your priest may be able to help you locate a trustworthy iconographer. Another source is exhibits of icons at church festivals and Greek-American conventions.

BUYING IN GREECE

In Greece, a wide variety of icons are available on the street, in shops, churches, and especially monasteries. Most of the religious stores are located on Mitropolis Street behind the Mitropolis Cathedral in Athens. Check also with the Byzantine Museum on Sophias Street in Athens and ask your family and friends who live in Greece.

There is usually no problem in taking new icons out of the country. Some icons are stamped, "Approved for Export." Historic icons are another matter. It is illegal to remove these from Greece without an export permit. Be aware that even old family icons could be seized by customs officers. See *Visiting Greece* for detailed customs information.

BLESSING BEFORE USE

Be sure that each icon is blessed by the church. When you purchase one, ask if it has been consecrated. Many are, especially if they were prepared at a monastery. If the icon has not been blessed or you are uncertain, take it to your church and ask your priest to consecrate it by keeping it in the altar area for forty days and saying a special blessing.

SELLING

The church considers it sacrilegious to buy and sell icons for purposes of investment alone; icons should be part of worship, not a financial portfolio. (Of course, if the funds are needed for an emergency, this is understood.) When this is not the case, but you want to sell an icon, consider donating the money realized for a worthy cause. If it is an historic icon, you may want to sell it directly to or put it on consignment with a good dealer. Another option is to sell it through a reputable auction house.

---

1   Read Leonid Ouspensky, trans. E. Meyendorff, *Theology of the Icon* (Crestwood, N.Y.: St. Vladimir's Seminary Press, 1978) and Leonid Ouspensky and Vladimir Lossky, *The Meaning of Icons,* rev. ed. (Crestwood, N.Y.: St. Vladimir's Seminary Press, 1982).

2   John Yiannias, "Orthodox Art and Architecture," in *A Companion to the Greek Orthodox Church,* ed. Fotios K. Litsas (New York: Department of Communication, The Greek Orthodox Archdiocese of North and South America, 1984), 104-105.

3   Harry Mark Petrakis, *Stelmark: A Family Recollection* (New York: David McKay Company, 1970), 17-18.

Home Ikonostási

❧ *The Church of the Home*

Many Greek-American homes contain a little corner of serenity and holiness to house the family's icons and religious effects. A soft light bathes the holy items, inviting the making of the sign of the cross or the murmur of a prayer. This is the *ikonostási*, a family altar that is the physical center of the church of the home.

The concept of the church of the home (*kat' íkon ekklisía*) is an old Orthodox tradition. The name, coined by St. Paul in the first century, refers to the gathering of Christians in a private home in the days when there were no churches. Today the term refers to the spiritual atmosphere created by a positive Christian way of living and respect for the following traditions.

THE *IKONOSTÁSI*

CONTENTS

The *ikonostási*, the physical religious center of the house, contains the following items:

- Icon of Christ
- Icon of the Virgin Mary
- Icon of the family patron saint
- Optional: Other icons such as those of saints of family members
- A cross
- A prayer book
- The Bible
- Seasonal items from church holidays:
    - First piece cut from the Vasilopita at New Year's
    - Holy water from the Epiphany church service
    - Palms from the Palm Sunday service
    - Holy oil from the holy unction service on Holy Wednesday
    - Flowers from special services: Good Friday, etc.
    - Easter egg
- Seal (*sfrayítha*) for communion bread
- Censer (*thimiató*) with incense and charcoal pellets
- Light or candle (*kandíli*)

Icon of the Family Patron Saint

Generally the patron saint of the family is the saint for whom the head of the family is named. It could also be a saint of special significance such as the patron saint from your region of Greece, for instance St. Michael for individuals from the island of Simi.

Vasilopita

Each family cuts a Vasilopita (bread for St. Basil) on New Year's Day in honor of St. Basil's name day. The first piece is always cut for Christ, wrapped in foil, and put at the *ikonostási.* (See *New Year*)

Easter Egg

Many people save either the first egg removed from the dye on Good Thursday (the egg of the Virgin Mary) or an egg from the Easter midnight service. The eggs are said to have protective power against the evil eye. (Yes! It will miraculously last all year — the inside evaporates.)

Seal (*Sfrayítha*) for Communion Bread

The church encourages members to make *prósforo*, the bread for communion. The seal (*sfrayítha*) imprints a religious design on the dough before baking (see *Religious Breads*).

Censer (*Thimiató*)

The *thimiató* (pron. *THimiató*) is a small metal container used for burning incense on charcoal pellets during prayers at the *ikonostási.* It may be carried from room to room as prayers are being said to bless the house (see "Censing the Home" below).

Light or Candle (*Kandíli*)

A lit candle, symbolic of the light of Jesus, should constantly be burning as a reminder that Christ is in the home. The traditional *kandíli* is an enclosed glass holder suspended by a chain with a wick attached to cork floating in oil. A wax candle may be used, but it cannot burn continuously and must be watched closely. Electric candles or lights, while not as aesthetically pleasing, are convenient and safe — accounting for their great popularity.

Disposal of Seasonal Items

Seasonal items from the previous year such as the Vasilopita, palms from Palm Sunday, flowers from special services, and the Easter egg should be disposed of on Holy Thursday by burning them in a metal container or foil. Bury the holy remains outside the house in a place where no one will walk.

LOCATION AND ARRANGEMENT

If possible, locate the *ikonostási* on an east wall of the house so that you face east while praying. According to Orthodox belief, Christ, the light of the world, will come again from the East. Choose a relatively private area conducive to prayer but accessible to all of the family. Some people prefer an upstairs hallway; others select the parents' bedroom. The choice is yours.

There are many ways to arrange the *ikonostási*. The items may go into a glass-enclosed cabinet, on open shelves, and/or hung on the walls above a small table.

USING THE *IKONOSTÁSI*

The *ikonostási* is your family's place of worship. Traditionally the *kandíli* is kept lit, but some prefer to light it only during special occasions such as:

- Daily prayer — individually and as a family.
- On Sunday. Since the church day begins at sunset the night before, light the *kandíli* on Saturday evening.
- Prayers for illness, thanksgiving, etc.
- Forty days of mourning.
- Major holiday seasons, such as Christmas and Easter. At Easter light the *kandíli* with the flame brought home from the midnight service.
- Any other special occasions, such as name days, the birth of a baby, etc.

CASE FOR MARRIAGE CROWNS (*STEPHANOTHÍKI*)

The case for the marriage crowns (*stephanothíki* — pron. *stephanoTHíki*) preserves and displays the marriage crowns, a symbol that the husband and wife are the king and queen of their own kingdom. The case is usually placed by the *ikonostási*. Sometimes a case is not used, and the crowns are put with the other *ikonostási* effects.

ICONS

Icons are revered and treasured in the Greek-American home. Small or large, old or new, elaborate or simple, they remind the faithful of the holy presence of God and the saints. (See *Icons*)

WHERE TO DISPLAY

In addition to icons at the *ikonostási*, it is common to have icons in other parts of the house. For example, you may want to put an icon of each family member's saint in their respective bedrooms.

SPIRITUAL USE

The Orthodox use icons as a part of personal worship in times of crisis, celebration, and regular devotion. For example, icons may be decorated with flowers on a feast day or brought into a sick person's room to invoke a saint's help.

CENSING THE HOME

Incense contributes to the mystery of the Orthodox church service. The fragrant smoke symbolically carries prayers to God, an ancient tradition described in the Old Testament: "Let my prayer be counted as incense before Thee, and the lifting up of my hands as an evening sacrifice." Ps. 141:2

Censer

You may want to duplicate this church tradition in your home. In addition to burning incense at the *ikonostási*, you can say prayers throughout the house, using the censer (see *illustration*). Light the censer by igniting a charcoal pellet in the bottom of the censer with a match. Add the incense and when it becomes fragrant and smoky, lift the censer, making the sign of the cross with it. Go through the house asking for God's blessing and mercy, especially at each family member's bedroom. A common prayer for the front door is, "May only good things come through my front door." Censing can be done at any time, the beginning of the Sabbath on Saturday evening, when making a prayer, when someone is ill, or before a name day or a feast day. The very devout cense twice a day, in the morning and before going to bed at night.

Spiritual Atmosphere

The *ikonostási* acts as the physical religious center of the church of the home, providing a place of worship and prayer. It is only a part of the Christian atmosphere of the entire household. The home, along with the church, must nurture religious values. You lay a solid Christian foundation through positive examples of worship and conduct.

❧ *Special Blessings, Prayers and Appeals*

The Orthodox acknowledge God's presence and importance in all aspect of their lives, turning to him for protection and strength. The church recognizes this need, providing various blessings, prayers, and appeals for many situations: a new home or business, an illness, times of trouble, and thanksgiving. Devout Greek Americans frequently involve their church and priest in the matters of everyday life.

SPECIAL BLESSINGS

Recognizing the benefits of God's watchful presence, many call upon their priest to bless and say prayers in various situations: communion for the sick; the beginning of church school; a time of thanksgiving; installation of officers; adoption of a child; blessing of homes, icons, cars, anniversaries, medals, or any object the petitioner wishes. A few of these blessings are detailed below.

NEW HOME

Whenever you move into a new residence, it is advisable to have the priest come and give a special blessing. The service includes sprinkling the entire house with holy water and reciting prayers asking God to "keep safe also from harm them who now desire to dwell here. . . and bless this their home and dwelling, and preserve their life free from all adversity."[1]

Prepare for the service by cleaning the house and having all the rooms open and lit. The service should be conducted by the family *ikonostási* on a small table upon which a clean bowl of water, candle, icon, and incense burner have been placed. The priest sanctifies the water (*ayiasmós*) by dipping a cross and a small bunch of flowers, preferably basil, in it three times while singing the hymn, "Lord Save your People." Each person kisses the cross and receives a sprinkling of water. If possible, have the entire family at home to walk in a procession led by the priest through the house as he blesses each room. Save the holy water for the next morning and have each family member drink a little before eating or drinking. Thank the priest with a small gift or remuneration. The same procedure is followed at the beginning of each year (see *Epiphany*).

VEHICLE

The blessing for a vehicle asks God to "send down upon it Thy guardian Angel, that all who desire to journey therein may be safely preserved and shielded from every evil end."[2] Popular customs include putting a blessed icon or medal somewhere in the car.

ICON

Religious Medal

Icons must always be blessed to be complete. If purchased at a monastery, an icon will have been blessed already. However, if you are unsure of its origin, take it to church, and the priest will keep it on the altar for forty days, blessing it with this prayer: "Bless and make holy this icon unto Your glory, in honor and remembrance of Your Saint (name); and grant that this sanctification will be to all who venerate this icon of Saint (name), and send up their prayer unto You standing before it."[3]

SPECIAL PRAYERS

PARÁKLISIS AND AGRYPNÍA

Paráklisis are prayers of supplication asking a saint, especially the Virgin Mary, for assistance in praying to God for strength, healing, and guidance. The Great and Small Paraklisis are offered the first two weeks of August before The Dormition of the Mother of God on August 15. You may also ask your priest to conduct a private *paráklisi* in your home or at the church for illness or other difficulties. This intimate approach can be helpful and comforting. For a large group concerned about a common problem such as a lost child or extrordinary illness, prayers may be said at an extended night vigil (*agrypnía*).

DISPELLING THE EVIL EYE

The church acknowledges the evil eye (*vaskanía*) as legitimate and believes in the power of Christ and the cross to dispel it. The evil eye stems from a consuming jealousy that creates a powerful evil. The envious person may knowingly or unknowingly bring bad luck, illness, or even death to the envied person. Young children up to adolescence are especially vulnerable making parents wary of such phrases as, "What a smart little girl." Effects of the evil eye can vary in severity: lethargy, illness, misfortune in life. If you suspect the presence of the evil eye, talk with your priest. He can say a prayer to dispel it. This redress differs from an exorcism performed by a specially trained priest in rare, extreme circumstances. For popular folk remedies see *Superstitions*.

Special Appeals

TÁMA

A *táma* combines prayer and a vow to a saint while appealing for help and assistance. The petitioner vows to give or do something as he or she prays to a saint in times of need. Sometimes the petitioner fasts before making the *táma*.

A *táma* is personal and private. A father while praying for the safe birth of his child might promise to give money to a church in the name of St. Eleftherios. Someone may ask St. Nektarios to heal her cancer and volunteer to make hospital visits or donate something to the church. In Tinos, Greece, a typical pledge to the Virgin Mary is to crawl from the boat dock to the Church of the Evangelistria on hands and knees carrying olive oil on your back! It is also a common custom to promise a gift of precious metal. Jewelry and money are traditional. Originally people covered icons with metal to fulfill a *táma*, but this rarely happens today. In Greece the object of the request may be replicated in metal. For example, if a ship is in danger during a storm, a *táma* asking for the ship's safekeeping could be fulfilled by bringing a miniature silver boat to be hung in a church. Many churches in Greece have hundreds of metal objects hung from their ceilings. A small metal rectangle called a *táma* or *aphiéroma* embossed with a facsimile of a leg, a house, a baby, etc., may be used and is placed on the altar or in front of the church icons either before or after fulfillment (see *illustration*).

You must always satisfy a *táma* regardless of the outcome. Sometimes the *táma* is fulfilled in anticipation of the favor. Ignoring the *táma*, however, invites a lifetime of question and possible distress. The Greeks have an expression emphasizing this belief, "Do not make a pledge to a saint or to a small child unless you are sure you will fulfill it."

Some people travel extraordinary distances to the most famous church of the saint to make the *táma*. When the wish has been granted, they travel back — sometimes years later — to fulfill it. This, however, is not necessary. A *táma* can be made and satisfied any time, anywhere.

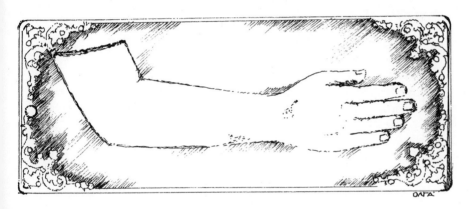

Táma

PHANOUROPITA

If you have lost something, try baking Phanouropita (cake for St. Phanourios — pron. *Phanourópita*) St. Phanourios, the patron saint of lost articles, helps people find anything from a missing piece of jewelry to good health and happiness. *"Phanoúrios"* comes from the Greek word, *"phaneróno"* (I reveal). During the baking of the cake, say a prayer for St. Phanourios' help and for the soul of his mother, a troubled woman. Share the cake with seven or more people, but do not reveal what you are trying to find.

Phanouropita

1 cup sugar

1 cup vegetable oil

2 cups orange juice

$\frac{3}{4}$ cup light or dark raisins

$\frac{3}{4}$ cup chopped walnuts

1 teaspoon baking soda

1 teaspoon vanilla

4 cups flour

Beat sugar and oil together until creamy yellow. Dissolve baking soda in orange juice and pour slowly into sugar mixture. Add other ingredients and pour into a 9" x 13" greased pan. Bake at 350°F for 45-50 minutes or until an inserted toothpick pulls out cleanly. Cut into squares for serving.

1. N. M. Vaporis, ed., *An Orthodox Prayer Book* (Brookline, Mass.: Holy Cross Orthodox Press, 1977), 154.

2. Ibid. 155.

3. Ibid. 153.

❧ *Religious Breads*

The church invites parishioners to prepare bread for several of its church services: communion and the *artoklasía*. The communion bread *(prósforo)* becomes the Body of Christ for your fellow church members at the Divine Liturgy. The loaves of bread for the *artoklasía* service commemorate Christ's miracle of feeding thousands of people with five loaves of bread.

PRÓSFORO (COMMUNION BREAD)

Communion is the most important rite of the Orthodox church. During this sacrament, wine and bread become the Blood and Body of Christ. The *prósforo*, meaning "offering," becomes the Body of Jesus, the bread of life. You are encouraged to bring the *prósforo* and red wine to church for this holy sacrament.

WHEN TO BRING TO CHURCH

The *prósforo* can be made for any number of occasions: a Divine Liturgy (particularly if you and your family take communion that day), name day, memorial, feast day, etc. Ask the priest if you may provide the bread and what time he will need it. It must arrive before *órthros*, the service in which the priest divides the bread for the Divine Liturgy.

THE RELIGIOUS SEAL (*SFRAYÍTHA*)

A religious seal (*sfrayítha*) stamps a special design on the *prósforo* before baking (see *illustration*). During preparation of the Eucharist, the priest conducts the *proskomithí* in which he first cuts out the center of the stamped design that says *"IC, XC, NIKA"* ("Jesus Christ Conquers"). It becomes the Body of Christ (the Lamb). Then the large triangle on the left is cut in honor of the Virgin Mary. The nine small triangles on the right are cut to commemorate the angels, prophets, apostles, holy fathers and prelates, martyrs, ascetics, holy unmercenaries, Joachim and Anna, and all saints, including the saint of the day's liturgy. The last cuts are tiny squares to remember specific names of the living and the dead.

The *sfrayítha* has two sides. One side features the full seal described above, and the other side has a smaller circle with the letters, "*IC XC NIKA*" (see *illustration*). When a large number of people are expected for communion, prepare extra bread, making imprints with the small seal around the large circle or on separate loaves.

Purchase the seal at a Greek specialty store or order from a catalogue and keep it in your home *ikonostási*.

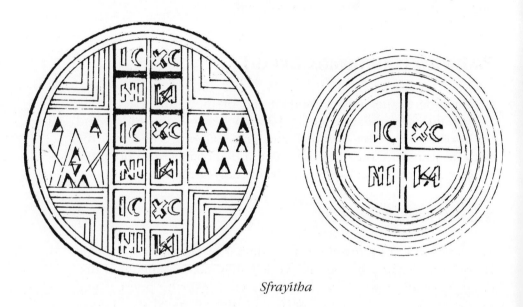

Sfrayítha

LIST OF LIVING AND DECEASED

Take the *prósforo* to church with a list of names for the priest to mention during the Divine Liturgy. Put the first names of the living in one column of your note (including those who have baked the bread, and others you want remembered) and the names of any deceased in another column. The priest cuts the *prósforo* in their honor and recites their names during the service.

PRÓSFORO

½ cup lukewarm water	4 cups bread flour
1 teaspoon sugar	½ teaspoon salt
1 package dry yeast	*sfrayítha* (seal)
1 cup water	

Dissolve the yeast in ½ cup lukewarm water with sugar and let rise until bubbly. Mix liquid ingredients. Slowly add 3 cups flour, while continuing to mix. Work the sticky dough until it forms a loose ball. Turn out on a floured surface and add additional flour until a stiff dough is formed. Knead a few minutes. Make two balls, and place one on top of the other in a cake pan that has been floured, not greased. (The double layer represents the dual nature of Christ.) Press out to edge of pan. Sprinkle the top lightly with flour. Place the *sfrayítha* in the center and press down as far as possible. Remove seal and make holes about an inch apart with a toothpick around the edge of the design. Cover the bread with a dry cloth, and let rise in a warm place until double in size. Open the holes with a toothpick again. Before baking make the sign of the cross over the bread and say the "Lord's Prayer" and/or a short prayer for those for whom you are baking the bread. Bake at 375°F for about 35 minutes. Reduce oven to 250°F and bake another 30 minutes or until hollow when tapped.

BREAD FOR *ARTOKLASÍA* SERVICE

THE *ARTOKLASÍA* SERVICE

The service of *artoklasía* (breaking of bread) is both a gesture of thanksgiving for God's blessings and a commemoration of the miracle of Christ's multiplying five loaves of bread to feed five thousand.

Five loaves of bread are brought to church, blessed, and distributed to the congregation in a short service of blessings and prayers for health and prosperity. Bread, wine, olive oil, wheat, and candles grace the service table. The priest blesses the food, considered the basic elements necessary for life by the Greek Orthodox:

Lord, Jesus Christ our God, You blessed the five loaves in the wilderness and from them five thousand men were filled. Bless now these loaves (the wine and oil) and multiply them in this holy church, this city, in the homes of those who celebrate today, and in your whole word. And sanctify Your faithful servants who partake of them.[1]

The congregation shares the bread, and the church keeps the remaining items. A church may hold an annual *artoklasía* service on its name day. Individuals or organizations may also sponsor an *artoklasía* on special occasions such as Greek Letters Day to honor the Three Hierarchs of Education.

ITEMS FOR THE SERVICE

Prior to the Divine Liturgy bring the following items for the sexton or priest to arrange on a small table at the front of the church:

- Five loaves of bread
  (see recipe below)
- One bottle of sweet red
  wine, such as mavrodaphne
- One small bottle of olive oil
- One small jar of wheat
- List of living persons to
  be commemorated

Bread for *Artoklasía*

5 packages dry yeast	3½ cups milk
½ cup warm water	1 teaspoon *machlépi*
1 tablespoon sugar	½ teaspoon *masticha*
1 cup butter	4 eggs
2½ cups sugar	5 lbs. bread flour (15 cups)

Dissolve yeast in ½ cup warm water with 1 tablespoon sugar and let stand for 5 minutes. In a pot warm the butter, sugar, and milk to dissolve. Add *machlépi* and *masticha* and cool. Beat the eggs and add them and the yeast to butter mixture. Slowly add ⅔ of the flour with other ingredients. Work the sticky dough until it forms a loose ball. Turn out on a floured surface and work in additional flour until a stiff dough is formed. Knead a few minutes. Shape into five round loaves, place in greased pans, cover with a dry cloth, and let double in a warm place. Before baking, brush with water. Make the sign of the cross and say a prayer for those you are honoring with the bread. Bake at 350°F for 35 minutes. Reduce heat to 250°F and bake another 35 minutes or until hollow when tapped. (See "Easter Bread" concerning spices)

(Lenten bread: Eliminate the butter, milk, and eggs; substitute 2 teaspoons salt and about 6 cups of water. Grease pans with vegetable shortening.)

---

1. Members of the Faculty of Hellenic College/Holy Cross Greek Orthodox School of Theology, trans. *The Divine Liturgy of Saint John Chrysostom* (Brookline, Mass.: Holy Cross Orthodox Press, 1985), 56.

❧ *Fasting*

The word "Byzantine" accurately describes fasting *(nistía)* in the Greek Orthodox church, since the complexity can confuse even the most devout with its required days, food prohibitions, and exceptions. Strict fasting in the Orthodox church is so demanding that only a minority of Orthodox believers practice it to the letter.

Few topics generate more opinions from a group of Greek Americans than the subject of fasting. Through the centuries priests and laypeople have developed their own customs. Each has his own rules from the church and from his mother or *yiayiá*. For example, one family always ate fried potatoes cooked in olive oil at noon the Saturday before taking communion; family members did not feel prepared unless they had done this. Your family may have similar customs that are meaningful for you.

The customs below may not conform to your traditions because practices vary greatly. Try to remember that the focus should always be on the purpose of fasting, not the regulations themselves.

PURPOSE

Fasting is a form of self-control over temptations, impatience, sin, and material urges, such as food. Its purpose is to discipline and cleanse the soul and body regularly. A change in diet signals a change in errant ways and assists the penitent in achieving higher and loftier goals as stated in one of Orthodoxy's Lenten hymns: "…the casting off of evil, the bridling of the tongue, the cutting off of anger, the cessation of lusts, evil talking, lies, and cursings. The stopping of these is the fast true and acceptable."

DEMEANOR

Fasting should be done privately without boasting, in keeping with the Biblical teaching:

And when you fast, do not look dismal, like the hypocrites, for they disfigure their faces that their fasting may be seen by men. Truly, I say to you, they have received their reward. But when you fast, anoint your head and wash your face, that your fasting may not be seen by men but by your Father who is in secret; and your Father who sees in secret will reward you. Matt. 6:16-28

DIETARY RESTRICTIONS

Most confusion over fasting comes from what should or should not be eaten. The canons and rules concerning this are complicated and in some cases obsolete.

Different levels of fasting are practiced: severe, strict, and moderate. Severe fasting permits no eating or drinking. Strict fasting (called *xeropháyi* — dry eating) prohibits meat, fish (with backbone), animal products (cheese, milk, butter, eggs, lard), olive oil, and alcohol (wine in moderation allowed). Shellfish, fruit, vegetables, bread, legumes, and vegetable margarine/oil may be eaten.

The very observant comply with strict fasting rules on the days specified below in "Days to Observe." In general, however, people follow a strict fast a few times a year: during the weekdays of the first week of Great Lent, Holy Week, January 5 (the day before Epiphany), and the first fifteen days of August before The Dormition of the Mother of God. In practice, most Orthodox do moderate fasting where they give up some foods, especially meat, on the specified days.

Before evening liturgies, the church authorities suggest no food or water for a minimum of six hours prior to the service.

DAYS TO OBSERVE

The observant Orthodox fasts on Wednesdays and Fridays throughout the entire year. Christ was betrayed by Judas on Wednesday, a day to evaluate one's commitment to Christ. On Fridays the crucifixion of Christ is remembered. Such regular fasting focuses the individual on a Christian lifestyle.

The church specifies four major fasting periods of varying length: Great Lent (49 days), Holy Apostles Lent (length varies), Dormition of the Mother of God Lent (14 days), and Christmas Lent (40 days). The longest fasts imitate Christ's fast for forty days in the wilderness in which he overcame temptation by the devil. These and individual fasting days are specified in "Days to Observe" below. A Lenten period is called "Tessarakosti" (formal) and "Sarakosti" (informal). Before a fasting period, people wish each other, *"Kali Sarakosti."*

The fasting periods and individual fast days listed below are reprinted from the *Yearbook 1993* published by the Greek Orthodox Archdiocese of North and South America.[1] For a more detailed listing, see a book of Lenten services called *The Lenten Triodion* by Mother Mary and Kallistos Ware.[2]

The following are fast days and seasons:
1. The day before Epiphany — January 5
2. The second Wednesday and Friday of the Triodion
3. The last week before Great Lent, although dairy products may be eaten even on Wednesday and Friday
4. Great Lent
5. Holy Week
6. Holy Apostles Lent — Monday after the week following Pentecost through June 28
7. Dormition of the Mother of God Lent — August 1-14
8. Beheading of St. John the Baptist — August 29
9. Exaltation of the Holy Cross — September 14
10. Christmas Lent — November 15-December 24
11. All Wednesdays and Fridays, except those noted below

The following are fast days on which fish is permitted:
1. Annunciation Day — March 25.
2. Palm Sunday
3. Transfiguration — August 6

The following days are completely fast-free:
1. The first week of the Triodion, including Wednesday and Friday
2. Easter Week (Bright Week)
3. The week following Pentecost
4. December 25 through January 4

CHURCH FLEXIBILITY

While fasting serves a vital purpose in the Orthodox lifestyle, the church today shows flexibility and understanding on the issue. All of the canons are not followed. For example, Canon LXIV of the Holy Apostles suggests that any holy men who do not fast for Lent or on Wednesdays and Fridays be deposed and that laymen should be excommunicated.

This canon is not adhered to today, and the church fathers themselves question strict observance of every rule. St. John Chrysostom, one of the most important church fathers from the fourth century, defended himself after being criticized for giving communion to people who had already eaten: "...consider Christ Himself, who gave the Communion to the Apostles right after supper." (Concord to Canon XXIX of the Sixth Ecumenical Synod)

---

1. Greek Orthodox Archdiocese of North and South America, *Yearbook 1993*, 90-91.

2. Mother Mary and Kallistos Ware, *The Lenten Triodion* (London: Faber and Faber, 1978), 35-37.

⚜ *Death and Mourning*

The death of a beloved family member or friend is difficult to accept. The pain and sense of loss can overwhelm even the most positive and optimistic. However, the Orthodox church through its beliefs and rituals offers the bereaved a solid structure to deal with grief and the reality of death.

ORTHODOX BELIEFS OF DEATH AND AFTERLIFE

The Orthodox belief in eternal life provides the base for many traditions relating to death and mourning. For example, cremation is forbidden by the church because it is believed that the physical body is eternal and will be reunited with the soul during the Last Judgment. Therefore, the body is not to be destroyed. The church discourages the practice of excessive wailing during a funeral because it contradicts the positive side of death: the deceased is alive with God. Also, memorial prayers seeking God's mercy for the departed are said by the living. This tradition comes from the belief that all Christians, living and dead, are united together in one church, and there is interaction between the two worlds. Finally the traditional memorial dish, *kóllyva*, made of boiled wheat mixed with sugar and other spices, symbolizes the eternal cycle: people, like wheat, must be buried to grow and have new life.

Traditions also are patterned after Christ's life. It is believed that the soul of the deceased stays on earth for forty days just as Christ did before he ascended to heaven. Hence the official mourning period is forty days. Through these rituals the church tries to help the parishioners to achieve *théosis*, becoming like God, even in death.

LAST COMMUNION

If death appears imminent, call a priest to administer communion. However, communion can only be given to an aware, conscious person. If possible, have the person prepare for the sacrament with confession.

IMMEDIATELY AFTER DEATH

TRISAGION SERVICE

After a person dies, call the priest immediately to say the Trisagion service over the deceased. The title "Trisagion" (three Holies — pron. *trisáyion*) comes from the repetition three times of the opening phrase of the service, "Holy God, Holy Mighty, Holy and Immortal, have mercy on us." This service may be repeated for a loved one in church or at the grave throughout the first year: at the time of death, the third day, the ninth day, the fortieth day, six months, one year, and any time one feels the need.

OFFERING SYMPATHY

See *As the Greeks Say* for commonly expressed sentiments to the family and other mourners.

Sympathy can be offered in many ways: Visiting the home with food for the family; attending the viewing, funeral, and after meal; sending a sympathy card, flowers, or contribution. Many families now request that contributions be made in memory of the deceased. This is in keeping with the longstanding Greek tradition of giving to the poor or doing good works when someone dies. St. John Chrysostom said, "Do you wish to honor the departed? Honor him by giving alms and by doing works of benefaction." Specifics about sending contributions and flowers should be published in the notice of death. Flowers may also be sent to the home any time during the forty-day mourning period.

Customarily close friends and family visit the grieving family throughout the forty-day mourning period. Guests are served brandy, coffee, and small, hard toast called *paximáthia*. Always call first. If the family does not want visitors, respect their wishes.

When discussing someone's death, people use a phrase to ward off a similar fate, *"Ékso apó ethó ke makriá"* ("Out of here and far away"). In Greece, you sometimes hear the phrase, "His thread is cut," referring to the ancient myth that the three "Fates" spun, measured, and cut a person's life in the form of a thread.

MOURNING CLOTHES AND DEMEANOR

The church's official mourning period lasts forty days, and the family should dress in dark clothing during that time. Women generally wear all black with little or no makeup and jewelry. People also combine black with white, the latter a symbol of new life. Close family members should conduct themselves with decorum: no dancing, loud partying, or celebrating. Some continue this during the first year.

Years ago in Greece social custom dictated that widows wear black the rest of their lives, and daughters for three years. Today, such extremes are rarely observed. A widow may wear black for a year at the most, but this is up to each individual. At one time the widow(er) wore the wedding band of the deceased mate along with his or hers on the right-hand ring finger, the finger used for the wedding ring in Greece. Other expressions of grief included soaping or covering mirrors, and men not shaving or cutting their hair for forty days. In Greece today black banners are hung on the front door or on the balcony of an apartment.

VIEWING, FUNERAL, BURIAL, AND *MAKARÍA*

ELIGIBILITY FOR ORTHODOX FUNERAL

Any person baptized in the Orthodox church is entitled to a funeral service, with some exceptions. Individuals who are in severe violation of canon law may have a prayer said after death but not a complete service. Severe violations include marriage outside of the Orthodox church, cremation, or suicide (unless caused by certified insanity). A recent ruling of the Ecumenical Patriarchate allows the local bishop to use his discretion in deciding cases where mercy should be shown. If, for example, there have been signs of remorse given publicly or in confession to the priest, these severe rules may be bent.

SELECTING A FUNERAL HOME

The funeral home helps with many details of the funeral, including a checklist of things to do, and official papers and documents required by the government, such as the death certificate. If a funeral home in the community is Greek-owned or -managed, that can be helpful in integrating Greek traditions.

SCHEDULING

Contact a priest immediately to make arrangements. His schedule and the church calendar must be taken into consideration. In the United States, a viewing is usually held at a funeral home for several hours during an afternoon and again in the evening. (All-night vigils in a home are rarely practiced as they were in Greece.) Funeral services can be held on any day except Sunday. Exceptions can be made with the approval of the Diocesan Bishop. Since embalming is tacitly accepted in the church, the body does not have to be buried within a twenty-four-hour period, and the funeral is often delayed to accommodate those coming from out of town. The interment and meal usually follow immediately after the funeral.

NOTICE OF DEATH AND OBITUARY

In small Greek villages, the slow, somber ringing of church bells alerts the community to a death. Residents run to the center of town, and the word is passed by mouth. However, in the United States it is customary to put a notice of death in the newspaper. The funeral home assists you with this task. The paid notice is usually short including date and place of death, names of the immediate family, times and places of the viewing, funeral and burial, and information regarding flowers or contributions.

An obituary is a longer article describing more about the deceased's life, accomplishments, cause of death, and surviving family. Such biographical information can be submitted to the paper(s), but each newspaper has its own policy regarding publication.

BURIAL SITE

The body should be buried under ground with the eyes of the deceased looking East for the Second Coming of Christ. The ground must be consecrated (blessed) by a priest, usually at the time of the burial. The site does not have to be in an Orthodox cemetery or section. However, some churches in large Greek-American communities buy land within a cemetery, designating it for burial of their fellow Orthodox. Orthodox theology emphasizes the unity of its members in life and in death, and an Orthodox section keeps the community together. In Greece the deceased are not embalmed, but exhumed after three years, and the bones of the family are kept together. This is not possible in the United States, where exhuming is prohibited by law except in extraordinary cases.

SELECTING A GRAVE MARKER

You may want to inquire about the kind of headstones permitted at the cemetery. Some cemeteries only allow stones set flush to the ground for ease of maintenance. Others allow upright monuments but charge a high fee that includes perpetual maintenance. Decide on the style you would like and select the burial site accordingly. The marker is usually selected after the funeral. A Greek or Byzantine cross is frequently engraved on the marker.

PREPARING THE BODY

Religious beliefs govern preparation of the body for burial. In keeping with the Orthodox goal of *théosis* (man becoming like God), an Orthodox should be buried like Christ according to the Old Testament tradition. "...for out of [the ground] you were taken; you are dust, and to dust you shall return." Gen. 3:19

Cremation

The church forbids cremation because the body is expected to be rejoined with the soul at the Last Judgment. No funeral service or burial rites can be held for a cremated person. However, a prayer can be said at the wake if the priest or bishop so decide. Exceptions to cremation are made if state laws prohibit burial (as in Japan) or the community's health is at risk from disease.

Embalming

The church accepts this practice since most funeral homes require that a body for public viewing be embalmed.

CLOTHING FOR THE DECEASED

The family usually selects a favorite article of clothing for the deceased. At one time, if the departed was young and single, a *stéphano* would be placed on the head. The family dressed the man as a groom and the woman in white as a bride. If the widow(er) is old, the ring is removed from the deceased and worn by the living spouse. Some people tape a paper icon by the deceased's heart.

In some areas people put a sheet-like shroud called a *sávano* on the body under the outer clothing. Although seldom practiced, this tradition emulate's Christ burial in white linen. In Mitilini, they use the departed's white baptismal sheet. An ancient pagan tradition is to put a coin between the deceased lips or on the eyelids to pay Charon (the ferryman to Hades) for his future services. This is rarely done in the United States and Greece.

TRANSFER OF THE DECEASED TO GREECE

The funeral home can handle the transfer of remains to Greece. The body must be embalmed. The local Greek consulate will tell you the necessary requirements, including copies of the death certificate, certification from the city health department that the deceased did not die of a communicable disease, and proof from the funeral home that proper hygienic regulations have been met.

CASKET

Style

In accordance with the Orthodox belief that the human body returns to dust, a wooden casket is preferable to a metal one so that the body can decompose more quickly. This is especially important in Greece where relatives exhume the body after three years to wash and store the bones (see "Third-Year Anniversary" below).

Additions

For the viewing and funeral, place an icon in a corner of the casket by the deceased's head or in the hands of the deceased for guests to kiss. Choose a saint with meaning for the deceased, either the namesake or someone who has been particularly important. The icon can be buried with the deceased, but this is not necessary.

Burying the *stéphana* (marriage crowns) with the deceased is an optional social custom. If the departed has been married, the *stéphana* are sometimes put into the casket for burial with the deceased spouse. Or cut the ribbon that joins the two *stéphana* and bury one crown with each of them.

Sometimes a white sheet is put in the casket to pull over the departed's face at the end of the funeral service. This is an optional social tradition also.

Open Casket

Whenever possible, the casket should be left open for the viewing and the funeral to acknowledge the reality of death. In addition, the funeral service concludes with a "last kiss" by each visitor.

OPTIONAL: ICON CARDS

The funeral home can prepare icon cards for distribution to guests at the viewing and funeral. Choose a Byzantine icon with special meaning for the deceased, if possible the patron saint. The card may include any of the following information: the deceased's name, dates of birth and death, a prayer, pallbearers, etc.

FUNERAL CLOTHING

The immediate family should dress in black for the viewing and funeral. If possible, close male relatives wear black ties. Guests are not required to wear black but should dress conservatively. Black and white are also acceptable. Black signifies mourning, and white symbolizes new life. At one time men wore black arm bands, but this is done infrequently today (see "Mourning Clothes and Demeanor" above).

SELECTING PALLBEARERS AND USHERS

Select six to eight pallbearers to escort the casket into the church. They should be individuals who have been especially meaningful to the deceased, such as grandsons and nephews. Children and spouses should never serve.

VIEWING

In Greece it is customary to have a twenty-four-hour vigil by the body. In the United States, however, most Greek Americans hold a viewing of the deceased at a funeral home for several hours one afternoon and evening. At the viewing, friends and family join together to comfort each other in their time of sorrow.

Visitors at the viewing should sign the guest book, pick up an icon card if available, and pay their respects to the deceased by going to the casket, saying a short prayer and kissing the icon or the deceased. If the priest is scheduled to come, stay for the Trisagion service. The short service pleads for the forgiveness of sins and the repose of the deceased's soul in heaven. Visitors express their condolences to the family.

Today's subdued service contrasts with some wakes and funerals held primarily in Greece years ago. These were dominated by women wailing funeral dirges (*mirolóyia* — words of fate) for the deceased.[1] However, the church discourages loud moaning and muttering because such despair contradicts the positive Christian message of life after death.

The church also discounts the superstition of keeping newlyweds and pregnant women from the viewing and funeral because it is considered bad luck. This custom has no religious basis.

FUNERAL SERVICE (*KITHÍA*)

The Orthodox funeral service emphasizes the reality of death and the new life of the deceased. It is a positive service featuring prayers for forgiveness and repose of the departed's soul. Some priests wear white to symbolize new life.

Before the service at the church, the priest repeats the Trisagion service at the funeral home. The deceased and the family then go to church where the priest begins the service by meeting the family, friends, and casket at the front door of the church. Chanting, he leads them into the sanctuary for the service. Guests who have waited outside enter the church, signing a guest book in the narthex. The family sits in the front row before the icon of Christ in the *ikonostásion*. The open casket is arranged so that the eyes of the deceased look east towards the altar, the direction from which Christ will rise again.

The priest leads the bereaved in hymns, scriptures, readings, and prayers, asking God to give rest to the departed's soul and forgive all sins.

The priest then invites the visitors to "Come and kiss the one that was with us a short time ago." Starting from the rear of the church, guests go row by row, to the casket. Except for the immediate family and exceptionally close friends, mourners kiss the icon in the casket. They pass by the family expressing their sympathy. Then the entire family gathers around the casket for the last kiss and the concluding ritual.

To conclude the priest sprinkles oil on the body in the form of a cross, saying, "Wash me with hyssop [a plant in the mint family], and I shall be pure, cleanse me and I shall be whiter than snow." The casket is closed and the service ends.

The priest may make brief remarks about the individual. Remarks by the family and friends may be done only with the permission of the authorities, and no music except for chanting is allowed. The body is carried out first and normally taken immediately to the cemetery for burial.

In some Greek villages, pottery will be thrown out of the windows as the body is taken to the cemetery. The breaking of pottery symbolizes that something has ended.

BURIAL (*ENDAPHIASMÓS*)

The funeral home transports the body and the immediate family to the cemetery. The priest says the Trisagion service for the last time and sprinkles dirt on the closed casket in the form of a cross with the words, "The earth is the Lord's and the fullness thereof, the world and those who dwell therein; you are earth and to earth

*Death and
Mourning*

shall you return." This seals the grave. Sometimes each guest puts a flower on the casket. In America people usually leave and do not watch the lowering of the casket into the ground. If the family has prepared a *makaría* (see below), the priest announces the time and location after the prayers are completed.

MAKARÍA

Mourners share a somber meal called a *makaría* to bless the deceased. It provides an opportunity for relatives and friends to refresh themselves and remember their loved one in an informal setting.

Time and Location

The family usually holds a *makaría* after the funeral, but sometimes after the forty-day memorial. The meal is a social custom that has come to be expected but is not required by the church; some people do not hold one. It can be held at a home, in the church hall, or in a restaurant, depending on the circumstances. Sometimes the Philoptochos Society (the women's philanthropic organization) of the church caters such occasions.

Menus

Menus for the *makaría* range from simple to elaborate according to the family's circumstances. The simplest menu traditionally includes brandy, coffee, and *paximáthia*. The brandy is always served to the guests as they arrive. *Paximáthia* (pron. *paksimáthia*) are traditional because they are dry, like bones, and not too sweet (see recipe below). Sweets are considered a sign of celebration. *Baklavá*, for example, would be inappropriate.

A moderate menu includes the above, plus sandwiches. A typical full meal consists of brandy, fish, salad, rice or potatoes, green beans, cheese, olives, rolls, wine, coffee, and *paximáthia*. Fish, the symbol of Christianity, is the most traditional entree, but this varies according to regional custom.

ACKNOWLEDGMENTS

Thank you notes for help, flowers, donations, and expressions of sympathy should be sent.

MEMORIAL SERVICES

PURPOSE AND ORTHODOX THEOLOGY

The Orthodox believe that intercessions on behalf of the dead are possible through the fervent prayers of those remaining on earth. Individuals who die go to a state of blessedness or damnation, but the Last Judgment is to be made at the Second Coming of Christ. Through the memorial prayers the living seek mercy and forgiveness for all of the deceased's transgressions.

While the Orthodox hold memorial services at many different times, the most widely observed service is the forty-day memorial based on the last days of Christ. After his Resurrection, Christ remained on earth for forty days: "To [the apostles] he presented himself alive after his passion by many proofs appearing to them during forty days, and speaking of the kingdom of God." Acts 1:3

Likewise, it is popularly believed that the deceased also remain on earth for forty days, patterning their death and leave-taking after him. After forty days, the soul of the deceased departs, and the official mourning period is over.

MEMORIAL SERVICE (*MNIMÓSINO*)

The memorial (*mnimósino* — calling to mind) recalls the deceased to God, the heavenly host, family, and friends. The service begins with an appeal to God to restore the departed to the divine image in which he or she was created. The priest asks God to forgive every sin and give rest to the deceased. In the service Christ, the Virgin Mary, and the saints, including the Old Testament patriarchs Abraham, Isaac and Jacob, and Christ's friend Lazarus, are asked to intercede for forgiveness and repose of the soul. The service ends with the well-known refrain, "Eonia i Mnimi."[2]:

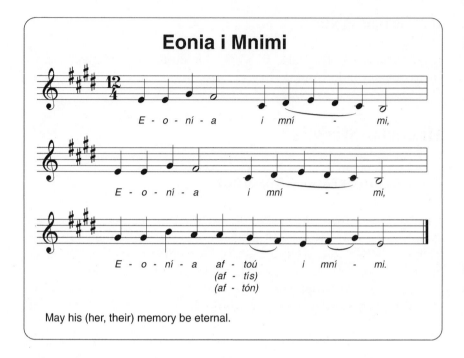

May his (her, their) memory be eternal.

Family and friends comfort the mourning family with similar words: *"Eonía i mními"* ["Eternal be (his/her) memory"]. (See *As the Greeks Say* for additional sentiments.)

It is traditional for the family to sit in the front row of the church before the icon of Christ during the service. The family provides a wheat dish called *kóllyva,* a symbolic custom based on two scriptures concerning eternal life:

> But someone will ask: "How are the dead raised? With what kind of body do they come?" You foolish man? What you sow does not come to life unless it dies: And what you sow is not the body which is to be, but a bare kernel, perhaps of wheat or of some other grain. But God gives it a body as he has chosen, and each kind of seed its own body. 1 Cor. 15:35-38

> Truly, truly, I say to you, unless a grain of wheat falls into the earth and dies, it remains alone; but if it dies, it bears much fruit. John: 12:24

The Christian message of everlasting life and hope is symbolically represented by the white mound of *kóllyva* on a tray bearing a

Death and
Mourning

cross and the deceased's initials in Greek (see *illustration*). The
tray rests on a small table with candles in front of the church
ikonostásion during the memorial service. After church the
family shares the *kóllyva* with the rest of the congregation.
(See recipe below.) If you are unable to make the *kóllyva*,
contact your church for the name of an individual or an
organization that will make the preparations.

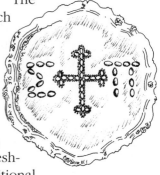

Additional tributes on that day may include making the *prósforo*,
donating altar flowers and/or candles, and bringing refresh-
ments for the coffee hour after church, such as the traditional
paximáthia. If possible, relatives visit the grave site that day.

Kóllyva

MEMORIAL DATES

The most common times to offer individual memorials are the
fortieth day following the death, at six-months, the first-year anniversary, the third-year anniversary, and Saturday of Souls (see
below). You may hold more memorials if you wish. Most individual memorial services are held on Sundays after the Divine
Liturgy, except on any of the feast days of the Lord, August 15,
Pentecost Sunday, or from the Saturday of Lazarus (one week
before Easter) through the Sunday of St. Thomas (one week after
Easter).

DURING THE FIRST YEAR

Memorial prayers may be said at the following times:

Immediately after Death

If possible, have the priest say the Trisagion service immediately over the deceased.

Third Day after Death

The priest says the Trisagion service for the deceased as a
reminder that Christ remained dead for three days. In America
this most likely will occur at either the viewing or funeral.

145

Ninth Day after Death

The Trisagion service is said on the ninth day to recognize that the spirit of the deceased has now joined the nine choirs of holy angels. In some regions in Greece *kóllyva* made on this day is taken to the church for a blessing, divided into nine portions, and distributed to nine people to eat.

Fortieth Day after Death (Saránta)

The forty-day memorial must be observed and should be offered while the deceased's soul is still on earth, even if this means holding it a few days before the forty days have passed. The official mourning period ends after the forty days.

Six-Month Anniversary

Repeat "Memorial Service" above.

First-Year Anniversary

Repeat "Memorial Service" above.

THIRD-YEAR ANNIVERSARY

Repeat "Memorial Service" above.

In Greece, families traditionally exhume the bodies of their deceased after three years. The deceased are not embalmed and by then only bones remain. This is a church custom with Biblical underpinnings:

The hand of the Lord was upon me, and he brought me out by the spirit of the Lord, and set me down in the midst of the valley; it was full of bones. And he led me round among them; and behold there were many upon the valley; and lo, they were very dry. And he said to me, "Son of Man, can these bones live?" And I answered, 'O Lord God, thou knowest.' Ezek. 37:1-3

The family members wash the bones in water mixed with wine or vinegar and place them in a special container. In some villages the container is placed in the narthex for a number of days for sanctification before being reburied or placed in a building called the *kimitírion* (sleeping place). If possible the bones are stored with those of other family members.

The tradition may be an ancient one. The bones in the tomb of Philip of Macedon, father of Alexander the Great, at Verginia are stained with wine.

OTHER YEARLY ANNIVERSARIES

Many people hold memorials on other yearly anniversaries also, such as the tenth or twentieth. This is optional. You can also remember a loved one each year during the Saturday of Souls service described below.

SATURDAY OF SOULS (PSYCHOSAVATO)

Traditionally, the Orthodox remember the dead on a Saturday, the day Christ lay in his tomb. Four times a year parishioners assemble to pray for all their deceased loved ones. These general memorial services, known as Saturday of Souls (Psychosavato — pron. *Psychosávato*) take place the two Saturdays that precede the beginning of Great Lent, the First Saturday of Great Lent, and the Saturday before the Feast of Pentecost. There is a popular belief that departed souls come back to earth at Easter and return the day after Pentecost.

If you would like to offer prayers for the deceased, write their first name(s) on a slip of paper, and the priest will read the list toward the end of the service. Submit names only once for the first three consecutive Saturdays as the names are read even if you are not present. Put the list in an envelope with a small remuneration for the priest. You may want to bring a small bowl or platter of *kóllyva*. (See below) A few parishioners also bake *prósforo*.

Following the service all the *kóllyva* is combined, symbolizing the mixing of souls in heaven. Parishioners share the *kóllyva* and greet each other with, *"O Theós na tous anapáfsi"* ("May God forgive the souls of the dead.")

OTHER WAYS TO REMEMBER THE DECEASED

- Visit the grave site.
- Light a candle in the narthex at any time or donate candles for the altar and holy *proskomithí* table where the bread and wine are prepared for communion.

- Donate altar flowers
- Submit names for the Epitaphios service on Good Friday.
- Remember the deceased's name day by:
  - Making the altar bread (*prósforo*) for communion or bread for an *artoklasía* service, giving the priest the name of the deceased to be read during the service
  - Making sweets to share with the congregation at the coffee hour
  - Offering a memorial

Special Situations

TRANSPLANTS AND DONATION OF ORGANS AND BODY

The Orthodox church believes the body to be the temple of the Holy Spirit and therefore its integrity should be maintained. However, the church does not oppose transplants now, and in many cases endorses and encourages the decision. In some cases organ donation is quietly accepted because many Orthodox also are beneficiaries of the new scientific and medical advances. In dealing with the question of organ donation in the "Tell Me Father" column of the *Orthodox Observer,* George Papaioannou strongly recommends, "…we should support and encourage people to sign up as organ donors. Consult your parish priest; discuss it with your family; and after prayerful evaluation, please sign up."[3]

Because there is no similar recent ruling regarding body donation for research, this is still officially prohibited. Any Orthodox Christian who wants to make such an arrangement should discuss it with his priest before deciding to do so.

AUTOPSY

A medical examiner is allowed to proceed with an autopsy in questionable circumstances of death, and for medical and scientific reasons.

RECIPES

---⧫⧫⧫---

KÓLLYVA
(FOR INDIVIDUAL MEMORIAL)

Start preparation of *kóllyva* two days in advance and assemble the day of the memorial.

4 cups (2 pounds) shelled wheat
½ cup granulated sugar
1½ cups finely chopped walnuts
1½ cups slivered almonds
1 cup pine nuts
2 cups white raisins
2 teaspoons cinnamon
2 teaspoons coriander
2 teaspoons cumin
2½ cups powdered sugar
2 cups finely ground zwieback toast
Optional: Seeds of one pomegranate and 1 cup chopped fresh parsley

Decoration: Whole blanched almonds without skins, white candied almonds, large silver dragees, white paper doilies

Distribution: Small plastic bags and spoons

Cover the wheat with 2 quarts of water and soak overnight. Drain and rinse. Cover with 4 quarts of water in a large heavy pot and bring to a boil. Reduce heat and simmer uncovered several hours, keeping the wheat covered with water and stirring occasionally, until wheat becomes puffy and tender. (Cooking time varies with time of soaking.) Drain in a colander, rinse, and drain again. Spread the wheat out on a smooth dish towel to dry overnight. (If desired, burn a *kandíli* beside the wheat as it dries.)

Prepare all other ingredients but do not assemble until the day of the memorial to prevent mush-like texture.

On the day of the memorial light a censer and *kandíli* while making the *kóllyva*. Cover a large tray approximately 20" x 13" with wax paper and then paper doilies that extend over the edge about an inch and a half. Combine all the ingredients except the powdered sugar, zwieback crumbs, and decorations. Put combined mixture on a tray and mold into a heaping mound toward the center, pressing it smooth. Spread crumbs evenly over the top, making sure the wheat is thoroughly covered, and press down. (This layer keeps the wheat mixture from bleeding through to the top layer of powdered sugar.) Sift powdered sugar over the mound and press smooth with wax paper.

Make a cross in the center with large silver dragees. With blanched almonds form the initial of the first name of the deceased on the left side of the cross, and the initial of the last name on the right, preferably using Greek letters (see *Pronunciation Guide*). Decorate the edges as desired.

Take the *kóllyva* to church where it will be placed on a small table by the icon of Christ at the *ikonostásion*. If the table does not have candles, put one or three in the *kóllyva* to be lit during the memorial service. After the service put about ¼ cup of *kóllyva* in small plastic bags for distribution to parishioners. Eat with spoon or fingers. In Greece relatives take *kóllyva* to the grave site and distribute to passers-by.

The ingredients have symbolic meaning: wheat for everlasting life, raisins for sweetness, pomegranate seeds for plenty, powdered sugar for the sweetness of heaven, and parsley for the green of the earth.

━━━►►◦◄━━━

KÓLLYVA
(FOR SATURDAY OF SOULS)

Make one-fourth of the above recipe. (Note that the cooking time for the wheat may be reduced.) Put the *kóllyva* in a bowl or on a small plate. Decorate the top with a cross and border design, not initials of the deceased since *kóllyva* for Saturday of Souls is generally made for more than one person.

Put a candle in the center of the *kóllyva*. Take it to church where it will be placed on the memorial table with the *kóllyva* from other parishioners. At the end of the service, all the plates of *kóllyva* are combined in a large bowl and distributed. In Greece parishioners pinch *kóllyva* from each other's dish, mixing it by hand.

PAXIMÁTHIA

(Allow two days to prepare)

2 cups warm water	1 cup vegetable shortening
1 teaspoon sugar	5 teaspoons anise seed
5 packages dry yeast	1 teaspoon *mastícha*
5 pounds flour (15 cups)	½ cup sugar
½ teaspoon salt	1 quart water

Dissolve yeast and 1 teaspoon sugar in water and let sit until foamy. Combine the yeast and all ingredients except flour. Slowly add 10 cups of flour. Work the sticky dough until it forms a loose ball. Put on a floured surface and add additional flour until a stiff dough is formed. Knead several minutes. Place in a large bowl greased with shortening. Cover with a cloth for an hour, kneading for a few minutes every 15-20 minutes (minimum of 3 times). Remove from bowl and place dough on floured surface. Cut dough into 10 portions. Cover again and let sit for 15 minutes. Form 10 oblong pieces approximately 1" high and 1½" wide. Place on baking sheets, leaving adequate space between loaves for dough to rise. Cut half way through each oblong with a sharp knife at ½" intervals. Let loaves rise until double in size. (Do not cover in summer; in winter cover with clean cloth and plastic over cloth.) Bake at 375°F on middle oven rack about 25 minutes or until golden brown. Remove loaves to racks to cool overnight. The next day, cut each loaf into pieces and place each piece flat on baking sheet. Bake at 350°F until slightly brown and then turn over to brown other side. Makes appoximately 14 dozen.

---

1. The *mirolóyia* (words of fate) is an ancient funeral dirge that originated in pagan times. One of the earliest examples is the lament of Hector's body by his wife, Andromache, in *The Iliad*. The *mirolóyia* is a long extemporaneous poem about the deceased's life sung by female relatives and friends over the body during the wake, funeral, and burial.

2. "Eonia i Mnimi" adapted from Nick and Connie Maragos, eds., *Sharing in Song,* 4.

3. George Papaioannou, "Tell Me Father," *Orthodox Observer,* 11 February 1987.

PART TWO

Greek Customs of Everyday Life

⚜ *Greek-American Values*

Greek Americans are proud of their individuality. After all, their ancestors were the first in Western civilization to elevate and glorify the individual. Yet Greek Americans maintain a common identity. They share values deeply rooted in Greek Orthodoxy, in a classical heritage from Greece, and in a dynamic American society. Each individual finds a personal balance of those influences — some people are more Greek; some are more American — thereby defying sociologists who try to profile a typical Greek American. Each, however, is influenced in some way by the following common values.

FAMILY

Most Greek Americans hold religion and family in the highest esteem. Closely linked, the two mutually reinforce each other as the Greek Orthodox church emphasizes the family, and the family emphasizes the church. In 1972 Archbishop Iakovos of the Greek Orthodox Archdiocese of North and South America explained the connection in an encyclical letter concerning National Family Week:

> Home and family life [are] the bedrock of our Greek Ortho-
> dox life-style. The spirit that binds us together as a people
> finds its deepest roots in the home where the tenderest
> values of human existence, love, compassion, forbearance,
> and mutual helpfulness thrive in abundance... Marriage is
> holy. The home is sacred. Birth is a miracle. In these we
> find the very meaning of life itself.

The ideal family is close knit and loving with a sense of mutual obligation among generations. Parents feel great love for their children and willingly sacrifice for their children's well-being and education. Deference to authority is important, and children are taught to respect their parents and other elders. Many children stay home until married. Sometimes aging parents move into a child's home. However, these last two traditions are being modified as Greek Americans become more assimilated, mobile, and affluent.

The church advocates the traditional patriarchal family consisting of father, mother, and children, an ideal strongly recommended by St. Paul in the first century. In the marriage ceremony, the wife accepts the husband as head of the house. "Wives, be subject to your husbands as to the Lord; for the man is the head of the woman..." The husband is a strong authority figure and sometimes a strict disciplinarian. Some people view this patriarchal approach as chauvinistic, while others argue that the wife does not take second place in the family. In many ways she is the cornerstone of the family, and is charged with the most important responsibility: keeping and maintaining intact the fabric of the family. Greek Americans view mothers with feelings of respect and reverence because of women's central role. Until recently, the wife assumed almost complete responsibility for housework and child rearing even if she worked outside the home. Earlier generations referred to her as the "good mistress of the house" (*kalí nikokirá*). The husband was known as the "master of the house" (*nikokíris*) which lead to interesting personal dynamics. A popular old folk saying captures the situation: "The husband is the head, but the wife is the neck that decides which way the head will turn!"

Greek Americans highly value family honor and community approval. The imprudent acts of one family member can affect the entire family's reputation; therefore each person is responsible for maintaining both personal honor and family honor. Greek Americans' concern for protecting the family reputation is one of the main reasons they are seldom involved in criminal activity.

Of course, it is difficult to maintain these values in a modern society. In fact, earlier generations feared the negative influence of other nationalities on their children. Non-Greeks were referred to as *xeni* (foreigners or strangers — pron. *kséni*). Great efforts were made to preserve the language, traditions, and purity of the family. Marriages between Greeks and non-Greeks were discouraged, even by the church. However with the defection of young people from the church and a decline in the marriage rate, in 1948 the church reversed its policy.[1]

Today six out of ten marriages are interfaith.[2] It is popularly believed that many of those families have adopted Orthodoxy and other Greek values.

The Greek-American family is subject to the same strains that weaken the American family. But the Greek love of family, nurtured for so many centuries, stands as a bulwark to many assaults, and there is hope that family values will prevail.

RELIGION

Greek Orthodoxy provides a spiritual base for Greek people and affects their life style and outlook. Much of their social life consists of celebrations that are religious in nature, such as marriages, baptisms, and holidays. In a crisis, God and the saints are often their refuge. In general, Greek people's optimism stems from their positive Christian outlook. Yet religion is treated as a natural part of an everyday life filled with many secular interests.

Many Greek Americans attend church to fulfill not only religious, but also social and cultural needs. Their approach to church contrasts with the situation in Greece where family and friends are accessible on a daily basis. In America, the church plays a more comprehensive role. Early Greek immigrants, isolated from their loved ones, turned to the church to serve all their needs, which is not as true today with second and third generations. However, even for those generations, the church remains not only a house of worship, but often the primary place to be with other Greek people and to enjoy various religious and secular events.

A close relationship between the church and Greek culture has existed since the beginning of Christianity. The New Testament was written in Greek. Much of Christian doctrine was formulated by church fathers trained and inspired by the philosophy and spirit of ancient Greece. Concepts regarding the origin of the soul, individual redemption, a human's personal relationship with God, and the ideal spiritual world are Greek in origin. The relationship between being Greek and being Christian is so deeply rooted in the Greek psyche that centuries later during the 400-year-rule of Greece by the Ottoman Empire, attempts by the conquerors to uproot this unity of religion and culture failed. The church assumed responsibility in maintaining Greek culture. Hidden or secret schools (*krifã scholiã*) conducted by the church at night in basements, monasteries, and caves have become legendary.

When transplanted to America, the Greek Orthodox church continued to safeguard religion, language, and culture. The more Americanized second and third generations, however, have pressured the church to downplay the Greek language and culture. The church hierarchy stiffly resists these pressures, and each parish and its priest makes its own accommodation on these issues. Some parishes are more "Greek" than others, but all value and respect this cultural component of Orthodoxy.

In 1993 estimates range from 520,000 to one million Greek Orthodox in the United States. The conservative number includes the approximately 128,000 paid family memberships in the 500 parishes of the Greek Orthodox Archdiocese of North and South America. The one-million figure includes those people who are baptized and consider themselves Orthodox but do not maintain official membership by paying annual church dues.

ETHNIC PRIDE

Greek Americans have cherished their Greek heritage since the first Greek immigrants arrived in the United States. Just as their Byzantine ancestors developed the early Christian faith, their Greek ancestors developed models and standards of thought and conduct acknowledged as the basis of Western civilization. The architects, philosophers, mathematicians, poets, dramatists, politicians, scientists, and historians of classical Greece remain some of the most influential men of recorded time.

To be Greek *and* American creates a special pride of its own. The world looks to America as a model of democracy and to ancient Greece as democracy's birthplace. Pride comes from knowing that the founders of the United States reached back over 2,000 years to the Greeks for their inspiration and wisdom concerning the relationship of government to its people.

Parents make a special effort to educate their children about their heritage, sending them to Greek language classes, dressing them in national costumes for programs and parades, attending Greek festivals, and visiting Greece. Increased travel and cultural exchanges over the past twenty-five to thirty years have tightened the link between Greece and America.

Greek Americans are concerned about contemporary Greece and help with a variety of causes from improvements of family homes to restoration of antiquities. Their interest also extends to politics, as they press for the rights of Greece in the world arena.

Greek Americans point with pride to any success of other Greek Americans. The emergence of some national leaders of Greek descent has stimulated the interest of the younger generation, which feels proud to be of the same ethnic background. Scholars, musicians, and business leaders are applauded for their success, which reflects well on everyone in the group. Always ethnically conscious, they continuously scan names in newspapers, books, movie credits, and other public sources, noting with delight when the name is Greek.

More than one million Americans claim Greek ancestry. According to the 1990 census the United States has 1,110,373 Greek Americans,[3] including 177,398 who were born in Greece.[4]

EDUCATION

Greek Americans highly value education for themselves and their children. Through knowledge people find their place in, and shape civilization. Ancient Greeks articulated this universal truth centuries ago. Their methods of observing, analyzing, questioning, and synthesizing provided the model for Western education still used today. Plato founded the first institution of higher learning, the Academy. The Orthodox church continued this tradition by emphasizing religious and secular education. On Greek Letters Day, January 30, the church honors the patron saints of education, the Three Hierarchs: St. Basil the Great, St. Gregory the Theologian, and St. John Chrysostom.

These saints serve as models of intellectual excellence. Ancient Greeks believed that one of the best ways to learn is by imitating an ideal model. Even during the most difficult circumstances, such as the Ottoman oppression, Greeks continued to educate themselves and their children by attending the *krifá scholiá*.

When they arrived in America, most Greek immigrants did not have the luxury of educating themselves. Their poor English skills and the necessity of earning a living meant working long hours in semiskilled jobs with no opportunity to go to school. However, they understood the importance of education and knew that dignity and freedom came from educational excellence. They were determined to educate their children. In fact the word "education" *("paedia")* comes from the ancient Greek word for "child."

Greek-American parents sacrificed greatly to send their children to institutions of higher learning. Those children lived up to their parents' expectations, often moving, in one generation, from laborers to professionals such as doctors, lawyers, scientists, engineers, business people, professors, and heads of universities and colleges.

PERSONAL HONOR — *PHILÓTIMO*

Greek Americans highly value personal honor, or *philótimo* (love of honor). *Philótimo* stems from a respect for oneself, and from it flow many other positive attributes: dignity, generosity, hospitality, consideration and love of others, and a sense of right and wrong.

Individuals are judged as having *philótimo* (or not) by their willingness to be loving and caring toward other people, even strangers. A person who lacks those qualities, therefore, lacks a basic, if not the most basic, human value. No matter how intelligent or how wealthy, an individual without *philótimo* will not have the respect of others. Conversely, a poor person (or family) with *philótimo* is held in high regard in the community.

Hospitality — *Philoxenía*

Greek hospitality dates back to ancient times. In the city-states it was expected that travelers would receive the same consideration accorded to members of the house itself. Even enemies, such as a Spartan in Athens, were entitled to hospitality, known as *philoxenía* (friendship to strangers — pron. *philoksenía*).

In *Report to Greco*, the Greek author, Nikos Kazantzakis, writes that his grandfather in Crete, "...took his lantern each evening and made the rounds of the village to see if any stranger had come. He would take him home, feed him, give him a bed for the night, and then in the morning see him off with a cup of wine and a slice of bread."[5]

Unfortunately, changes in American and Greek society preclude such blind faith in strangers today. To Greek Americans, *philoxenía* means hospitality and generosity among acquaintances, friends, and newcomers. Greek Americans graciously extend their hospitality with warmth and sincerity. Great effort is put into making guests feel welcome and at home.

Greek-American Work Ethic

Most Greek immigrants moved to the United States for economic reasons. For generations America has opened its doors to people from around the world, offered economic opportunity, and promised material success for individuals willing to work hard. The relationship between economic success, hard work, and the individual was stated by Max Weber, a German economist and sociologist, who in 1904 linked the success of capitalism to the Protestant work ethic and individualism. The three ingredients were interdependent. As noted by George Papaioannou in his book *The Odyssey of Hellenism In America*, such an economic and social system was ideally suited to the Greek immigrant who came from a culture that had emphasized and prized the individual for centuries.[6] Greek immigrants adapted naturally, and each person worked long hours to achieve success. This work ethic is a key value for Greek Americans and one of the reasons for their success.

For decades most Greek immigrants were employed in mass industries such as the textile mills of New England, railroad construction in the West, and steel mills. Many immigrants became entrepreneurs, running businesses such as restaurants, shoe repair shops, boats to collect sponges, dry cleaning stores, theaters, and florist shops. Charles Moskos in *Greek Americans: Struggle and Success* states that by the end of World War I a substantial middle class existed[7] and after World War II a professional class emerged.[8] Many professionals learned the value of hard work while helping in their parents' business. They passed that work ethic on to their children.

---

1. Athenagoras, "An Encyclical on Marriages and Family," 27 September, 1948.

2. "Future Theological Agenda of the Archdiocese — Conclusion," *Orthodox Observer,* March 1991.

3. U.S. Bureau of the Census, *1990 Detailed Ancestry Groups for States,* CP-S-1-2, 3.

4. U.S. Bureau of the Census, *1990 Foreign-born Population in the United States,* CPH-L-98, 19.

5. Nikos Kazantzakis, *Report to Greco,* trans. P. A. Bien (1965; reprint, New York: Bantam Books, 1966), 171-172.

6. George Papaioannou, *The Odyssey of Hellenism in America* (Thessaloniki, Greece: Patriarchal Institute for Patristic Studies, 1985), 69.

7. Charles C. Moskos, *Greek Americans: Struggle and Success,* 17.

8. Ibid. 52.

✤ *Birth of Children*

The Greek family welcomes a new baby with tremendous joy — children are prized, pampered, and most of all, loved. Familiar terms of endearment such as *"petháki mou"* ("my little child"), *"angeloúthi mou"* ("my angel") and *"hrisó mou"* ("my golden one") are used constantly by doting relatives and friends to convey affection and tenderness. A new child is considered a blessing that bonds the family together.

In fact, the central role of children is clear from the beginning of marriage. During the Greek Orthodox wedding ceremony, the priest often refers to procreation and implores God to let the couple "rejoice with the sight of sons and daughters" and "behold their children's children like newly-planted olive trees around their table." Such emphasis on family is a basic Greek value giving rise to many customs and traditions.

BEFORE THE BABY ARRIVES

THE EXPECTANT MOTHER

It is customary to wish an expectant mother, *"Kalí leftheriá"* (Safe delivery — literally, "good liberation!") Similarly, any prayers or promises for the health of the mother and child often are directed to St. Eleftherios, the patron saint of childbirth. In some parts of Greece, it is believed that an expectant mother will have an easier delivery if she is touched with *váya*, a cluster of bay or myrtle leaves blessed by the priest on Palm Sunday.

CHOOSING A NAME

Originally, the godparent selected the child's name and gave it at baptism. In the United States today, the parents select the name before the child is born since the hospital requires the name for the birth certificate. However, the godparent still gives the baptismal name to the child at the baptism ceremony. If the godparent has been selected before birth, discuss the name selection together out of courtesy. (See *Selecting a Name*)

THE BABY SHOWER

The baby shower is an American custom that has been adopted by many Greek Americans. Guests, generally female friends and relatives, bring gifts for the expected baby.

MALE AND FEMALE CHILDREN

In the Greek family, a desire still lingers for the birth of at least one male, primarily to carry on the grandfather's name. The historically negative reaction to females has been eased with the ending of the dowry practice. That custom required the bride to bring money and property into the marriage. Girls meant burden and expense; boys meant income. At one time girls were so unwelcome that a popular wish for a married woman was "May you have male children and female sheep!" This attitude no longer prevails, and daughters are equally loved. In some families the pressure to produce a son still exists, although this is not an exclusively Greek phenomenon.

TÁMA (VOW) FOR CONCEPTION AND DELIVERY

Sometimes a couple may have difficulty conceiving a child and bringing it to term. In such cases a common practice is to pray to a saint for assistance, making a *táma* (vow) to give or do something. Vows might include naming the child after the saint, giving a precious object or money to the church, or performing a good work (see *Special Blessings, Prayers, and Appeals*).

WELCOMING THE NEWBORN

WHAT TO SAY

When the baby arrives, parents and other family members — grandparents, sisters, brothers, aunts, and uncles — happily congratulate each other with, *"Na mas zísi"* ("May he/she live for us"). Acquaintances say, *"Na sas zísi"* ("May he/she live for you") or *"Na zísi"* ("May he/she live").

CIRCUMCISION

Circumcision is not a religious practice of Orthodoxy. The church does not oppose it, however, and leaves the decision to circumcise up to the parents and their physician.

SPECIAL PRAYERS AND BLESSINGS

First-day Prayer

You may wish to ask your priest to visit the hospital or home soon after birth to offer the first-day prayer for mother and child. However, this has become less common in America because of time, distance, and the needs of larger parishes.

On the island of Sifnos, Greece, the priest blesses water in the home, and visitors must first wash their hands with the holy water before holding the baby.

Eighth-day Prayer

There is an official prayer for the newborn on the eighth day after birth that comes from the Jewish tradition of giving the name and performing a male child's circumcision on that day. For Christians, a prayer of birth is given instead. Few Greek Americans observe the eighth-day prayer. For those who do, the priest may go to the home or the newborn may be brought to the church by the intended godparent, a relative, or a friend since the mother may not enter church for forty days. The baby may be named on the eighth day, but most children receive their names during the baptismal ceremony.

Forty-day Blessing (see below)

TRADITIONAL SWEETS

After the baby's birth, you may want to serve traditional sweets typical of your family's region of Greece to visitors who come to the home during the forty-day period. On the island of Kastelorizo, guests receive *yennitoúria,* a small potpourri of walnuts, raisins, and dried fruit wrapped in tulle tied with a little ribbon and a saint's medal. *Loukoumáthes,* deep-fried pastry puffs, symbolize sweetness and joy on the island of Mitilini.

GIFTS FOR THE NEWBORN

Silver or Gold

A beautiful custom followed in Greece and America is to *asimósi to pethí* (to silver the child). When you visit a baby for first time, bring a silver coin or a gift made of silver and place it in the baby's crib. Silver is the most common precious metal. In Mitilini, when the relatives come on the third day to watch the midwife bathe the baby for the first time, they place gold coins on a pillow by the child's crib. In Crete, visitors customarily put a gold coin, small crosses, or zodiac signs.

Filaktó

Filaktó

This is a small religious medal or tiny cloth pouch that may be pinned to an upper-back shoulder of the baby's clothing to protect against evil. The square or triangular pouch, measuring about an inch on each side, contains sacred items such as holy flowers. Decorations sometimes include beaded edges and an embroidered cross or the "eye of God." They may be made by hand, purchased in monasteries in Greece, or sometimes obtained through a Greek specialty store. Older children and adults may also wear or carry *filaktó.*

Máti

Máti

Some children receive a *máti (matopiástra* - formal), a small pin or medallion of blue stone with a black eye in the center. The child wears the *máti,* a common folk remedy to ward off the evil eye, on the upper back.

Toys, Clothing, Icons, and Accessories

These items are also commonly given to newborns and are thoughtful and appropriate.

SUPERSTITIONS

At one time in certain regions of Greece, new parents put bread under the newborn's pillow and covered the mirrors in the house to deflect evil influences. New mothers wore only white for forty days. An even more obscure tradition appeased the "Fates" that supposedly visited a newborn on the third day. The "Fates" in the form of three women gathered around a newborn's cradle to write the child's destiny. To secure a favorable outcome, sweets were left on a table in the same room. Although most Greeks do not observe these customs, some do believe in predestination. For example, if a tragic event happens to someone, they often remark, *"Étsi ítan graftó."* ("That's the way fate was written.")

THE FORTY-DAY BLESSING (CHURCHING)

The most important custom for the newborn and the mother is the forty-day blessing (*sarantismós*), a reenactment of Mary's bringing Jesus to the temple on the fortieth day after his birth (The Presentation of Jesus Christ in the Temple). The mother brings her baby to church on the fortieth day (or the closest following Sunday) for a brief service of purification and to formally bring the baby into the church. Call your local priest to arrange a convenient time.

According to tradition, this is the first time that the new mother and the baby are allowed to enter the church. (In the past some people believed that going outside the house before the prescribed forty days would bring bad luck.)

The mother and child remain in the church narthex and do not enter the nave until the priest has offered a prayer. Then the priest carries the baby to the front of the church, followed by the mother and sometimes other participants. The priest proclaims: "The servant of God is brought within the church in the name of the Father, and the Son, and the Holy Spirit. Amen."

Male children are carried around the altar. Females must remain at the altar gates in keeping with the Orthodox practice that only males may enter the sanctuary area. (This tradition is controversial, and some change is taking place. Many priests and bishops take female children into the altar area — the new practice has not been challenged by the Greek Orthodox Archdiocese of North and South America.)

After the forty-day blessing, close family members say, *"Na mas zísi"* ("May he/she live for us") and acquaintances offer congratulations with *"Na sas zísi"* ("May he/she live for you") or *"Na zísi"* ("May he/she live"). Since the mother and child are still in delicate condition, no celebration or reception afterwards is necessary.

The prohibition of a new mother from entering the church for forty days after birth stems from the church's policy on cleanliness. According to the Old Testament, women were considered unclean after childbirth. A period of purification lasting forty days was required before entering the church, a controversial tradition today. Many women do not consider themselves "unclean" from giving birth and are pressuring the church for change.

SPECIAL SITUATIONS

BIRTHDAYS

In the United States, the one-year birthday comes after twelve months. However, in Greece a child is considered to be "walking" into the second year on the first birthday, sometimes creating confusion when Greeks and Greek Americans discuss age. In Greece, name days, not birthdays, are celebrated.

ABORTION

Abortion is forbidden by the church unless the mother's life is in danger.

ADOPTION

The church will bless the union of the parents and the new child with a special prayer to bind them together.

MISCARRIAGE

In the event of this misfortune, a special prayer can be said by the priest for the mother. As in giving birth, the mother cannot enter the church until she has received the forty-day blessing.

⚜ *Selecting a Name*

Many Greek names have a timeless quality. Maria, John, Peter, Helen, Christine, and Paul are names used again and again throughout the centuries for family and religious reasons. Both grandparents and saints can be honored when naming your children. Selecting a name is easy, and if you follow tradition to the letter, your child's godparent will even do it for you!

FAMILY CUSTOMS

In the Greek family, it is customary to give the grandchildren the first names of their grandparents. The middle name is usually the father's first name. This tradition preserves the continuity of the family, creating a link between the present generation and its ancestors and honors the grandmothers and grandfathers, who enjoy having namesakes. If you do not follow this tradition, be sure to discuss the matter with your parents to avoid any hurt feelings. To some it is an insult to neglect to name the grandchildren after them.

FIRST NAME

A child's first name is the first name of either a paternal or maternal grandparent — the custom varies from region to region. The first two methods closely follow the Greek tradition of always naming the first male after the paternal grandfather. The third method is more American.

Method A
　　First male child named after paternal grandfather
　　First female child named after paternal grandmother
　　Second male child named after maternal grandfather
　　Second female child named after maternal grandmother

Method B
　　First male child named after paternal grandfather
　　First female child named after maternal grandmother
　　Second male child named after maternal grandfather
　　Second female child named after paternal grandmother

Method C
> First child named after either paternal grandfather or grandmother
> Second child named after either maternal grandfather or grandmother
> Subsequent children's names repeat pattern of naming after paternal
> then maternal grandparents

Of course, there are exceptions to the above custom. A paternal grandfather may already have a grandchild named after him, and is willing to have the child named after the other grandfather. A promise may have been made to a saint to name the child after that saint *(na to táxis to pethí)*. The non-Orthodox grandparents in an interfaith marriage may not be as concerned about the naming tradition. And if you have more than four children or more than two of the same sex, the choice is left to you and the godparents.

MIDDLE NAME

The middle name is usually the first name of the father, used as a possessive in Greek, i.e., you are the son or daughter of your father. This name is also known as the patronymic and probably comes from the Greek law requiring the father's name for the transfer of property for both males and females. The tradition also prevents confusion among grandchildren. Two grandsons could have the same name as their grandfather: Emanuel Rouvelas. The first name of the father in the middle differentiates them. For instance, Emanuel Nicholas Rouvelas is the son of Nicholas; Emanuel Eleftherios Rouvelas is the son of Eleftherios. In America, boys customarily take the father's name as the middle name, but girls rarely do. They sometimes take a feminine middle name, or none at all. For example:

Grandfather:	Eleftherios Emanuel Rouvelas
Son:	Emanuel Eleftherios Rouvelas
Grandson:	Eleftherios Emanuel Rouvelas
Grandmother:	Mary Rouvelas
Mother:	Marilyn Sue Rouvelas
Granddaughter:	Mary Pauline Rouvelas

RELIGIOUS TRADITIONS

NAME SELECTION BY GODPARENT

Traditionally the godparent alone has the right to name the child. According to Orthodox custom, a child receives his or her name during the baptismal ceremony when the godparent tells it to the priest. Today, however, godparents and parents have modified tradition somewhat and collaborate in advance so the name will be available for the birth certificate issued at the hospital.

In Greece the child is called "baby" until baptized, and the legal name is the one given at the baptism. In America, this need not be the case. A child may have one name on the birth certificate and another on the baptismal papers. Converts to Orthodoxy take a religious baptismal name, but retain their prior legal name.

NAME OF SAINT OR BIBLICAL EVENT PREFERRED

The church prefers the baptismal name to be that of a saint in the Greek Orthodox church, a significant feast day (such as Anastasios), or symbol such as the cross. This is neither canon law nor a directive. The tradition began in the fourth century in Antioch when people began naming their children after St. Meletios, who led a model Christian life. Parents wanted their children to inherit some of his saintly, exemplary qualities. Today it is still hoped that the child's behavior will be inspired by the saint's life. The namesake also becomes the child's patron saint, providing protection from danger and acting as the child's messenger to God.

CHOOSING A SAINT

Because this custom has been in effect for centuries, the grandparent's name usually will already be the name of a saint. This simplifies the selection process, satisfying both the religious and family requirements. If a specific saint and name day are not a family tradition, determine who would be a good role model and patron saint. For example, "Joanna" is the feminine of "John," and most women celebrate the name day of St. John on January 7. But one of the myrrh-bearing women who anointed Christ after his crucifixion is St. Joanna, and her feast day is June 27. This name day could be chosen instead. More options are open to women now with the recent scholarship about female saints.

Sometimes an individual is named after the saint whose feast day is closest to the date of baptism and chrismation. A man chrismated in late October might take the name "Demetrios" for St. Demetrios whose feast day occurs on October 26. For further information see *Saints* and *Name Days* and consult with your priest.

BLENDING FAMILY AND RELIGIOUS TRADITIONS

Many Greeks have ancient or mythological names such as Sophocles, Aphrodite, or Agamemnon. When the grandparent's name is not that of a saint, conflict may arise between the wishes of the grandparent and the church. Some priests accept nonreligious names for baptism, others will not. Some priests allow combined religious and secular names, for example, "Persephone Panayiota." It is wise to discuss this question well in advance of the baptismal ceremony to prevent problems. If the name presented to the officiating priest at the time of the sacrament is not an acceptable one, the priest may demand that the parents and godparent make another selection on the spot!

CONVERTING NAMES

A "two-letter" rule has been commonly adopted in converting Greek names to English. In general, two letters are taken from the Greek name, and an English name with the same two letters is found. For instance, the "Ha" from the name "Haralambos" are the first two letters of the English name "Harry."

There are countless variations on the formal names of the saints. The endings change according to gender; names are shortened, expanded, and transformed beyond recognition. One of the most popular examples is the beloved "Panayia," one of the names for the Virgin Mary. Males are called "Panayiotis" and females, "Panayiota." Female names include Panayiotitsa, Pitsa, and Yota.

⚜ *Greek School*

Adult Greek Americans love to recount their childhood Greek school experiences with humor and affection. Like taking piano lessons, they begrudgingly went because their parents insisted. Those who attended long enough to read, write, and speak are glad they did; those who did not, regret their lack of knowledge. Most then have children who feel the same way!

HISTORIC HIDDEN SCHOOLS

For many Greek Americans, afternoons at Greek school are as much a part of the ethnic experience as eating *baklavá* or dancing a *hasápiko*. For generations, parents and the church stressed the importance of learning the language, culture, and faith at classes taught in a church after school and/or on weekends. Greek classes sponsored by the church are an old tradition dating back at least to the Turkokratia (Turkish rule), when Greece was dominated by Turkey from the fifteenth to the nineteenth centuries. The hidden schools (*krifá scholiá* – also pronounced *scholía*) in Greece and Greek communities in Turkey were located in caves and secret places where priests taught children at night, to their peril. "My Bright Shiny Moon," a child's poem memorized by thousands of Greek-American children even today, describes the experience:

Φεγγαράκι μου λαμπρό
Φέγγε μου να περπατώ
να πηγαίνω στο σχολειό
να μαθαίνω γράμματα
γράμματα σπουδάγματα,
του Θεού τα πράγματα.

"My Bright Shiny Moon"

Fengaráki mou lambró	My bright shiny moon
Fénge mou na perpató	Light my pathway
Na piyéno sto scholió	To walk to school
Na maTHéno grámmata	To learn to read and write
Grámmata spouthágmata	Letter and studies —
Tou THeoú ta prágmata	God's things!

Years later the American Greek schools also sought to preserve the language, heritage, and faith. But in the United States practical considerations mattered too. Children needed to learn to read and write Greek in case they visited Greece or went there to live some day. In addition, keeping the children "Greek" was a way for the parents to maintain the Greek heritage in an alien land.

EARLY GREEK SCHOOLS IN AMERICA

Although well meaning and adamant about their goals, the early Greek schools were far from perfect. Teachers were not adequately trained and used old-fashioned methods. Texts were slavishly copied or memorized by rote. Classrooms and materials were inadequate. The resistant pupils themselves did not make things easy. Greek school was conducted two or three times a week, and students resented the extra work and time away from other friends. Teachers were strict disciplinarians, and many a disruptive student was labeled a *zóon tis kinonías* (animal of the society). Greek-American historian Theodore Saloutos attended Greek school in the twenties and recounted it with discomfort:

> I suppose one reason I hated Greek school was because it gave me little time to play or do the things I wanted to do as a youngster. Imagine a grade school youngster coming home from the public school in late afternoon, then having to ready himself for a school he had no desire to attend, and which he attended often under protest, haunted with the thought he would be reprimanded by the teacher for coming to school unprepared, taking with him often a piece of Greek bread or some other edible to curb his growing appetite, often sitting in bleak, uncomfortable and sometimes cold surroundings totally different from what he knew in the public school, and forced to have a late supper... the Greek language school was a nightmare.[1]

Parents and teachers jokingly reminded the children that they were still better off than their forebears in the *krifá scholiá!* But the church took the complaints seriously, and in the early 1930s Archbishop Athenagoras made Greek education a top priority, urging every parish to have a Greek school whether there was a church building or not. By the 1936-37 school year, the number of Greek schools (450) and pupils (25,000) had roughly doubled since 1932-33.[2] In 1944 Athenagoras established the St. Basil Academy in New York to train new teachers. But World War II disrupted the growth, and momentum was not regained despite Archbishop Iakovos' efforts to keep education at the top of the church's agenda. In 1970 he declared the old system a failure and insisted that the latest teaching methods be employed to revitalize the program and that teachers have training and attend workshops.

GREEK SCHOOLS TODAY

Since that time, a new enthusiasm and energy has strengthened the programs. For the 1994-95 school year, there were 400 afternoon Greek schools serving 40,000 students ages six to fifteen. The Archdiocese school system also includes preschools, kindergartens, adult language classes, and twenty-four parochial day schools in the United States, Canada, and South America.[3] Of the twenty-four day schools, most are accredited to meet government standards and offer a complete education, including classes on the modern Greek language, culture, and faith. Most of the schools are sponsored and financially supported by churches. Some are independent entities.

PURPOSE AND CURRICULUM

The purpose of Greek schools has become more clearly defined through the years: to transmit the moral, cultural, and religious heritage along with Greek language skills. Each Greek-American child should develop an awareness and pride in the contributions made to the world by his or her Greek ancestors. Individuals with a basic knowledge of the language can participate more fully in the church service and contribute their talents as members of the choir. Most curricula include a broad range of subjects: language, the faith, mythology, literature, geography, Greek and Greek-American history, and contemporary Greek life.

The spoken everyday language of Greece known as demotic is now taught. This language was recognized by the Greek government in 1976 as the official language in place of a stiff, formal Greek named *katharévousa* developed from Attic Greek after independence in the nineteenth century.

STUDENT PROGRAMS

The cultural programs staged for the community by the children of the Greek school delight and please their elders. They proudly watch the young people dressed in national costumes recite poems in Greek, perform plays, and dance to Greek folk music. At Christmas, they sing the *kálanda* (carols); on Óxi Day (October 28) they remind everyone of Greece's resistance to the Germans in World War II. On Greek Independence Day (March 25) they stir patriotic feelings with recitations that celebrate the end of Turkey's rule. For months, the children rehearse diligently for these events.

The most successful Greek schools are those that are enthusiastically supported by the parents. Their active interest in the school work and progress of their children is vital. They must convince the children of the value and advantage of knowing the Greek language and heritage now and in the future.

---

1. Theodore Saloutos, "Growing Up in the Greek Community of Milwaukee," *Historical Messenger of the Milwaukee County Historical Society* 29, no. 2 (Summer, 1973), 52, quoted in Alice Scourby, *The Greek Americans,* 42.

2. Athenagoras, "Encyclical on the Greek Language Schools," 7 August, 1937, quoted in George Papaioannou, *The Odyssey of Hellenism in America,* 391.

3. Greek Orthodox Archdiocese of North and South America, *Yearbook 1995,* 82.

❧ *As the Greeks Say*

The following Greek expressions and names are commonly used and easily learned. Some of the expressions are particularly colorful. For example, people wish an engaged couple, *"Kalá stéphana"* (good crowning) in reference to the crowns put on the heads of the bride and groom during the wedding service. An expectant mother may be wished *"Kalí lefteriá,"* implying "safe delivery," but literally meaning, "good liberation." Good luck! — or as the Greeks say, *"Kalí tíchi!"*

SPECIAL OCCASIONS

Baptism
> *Na sas zísi* (May he/she live for you)
>
> *Na zísi* (May he/she live)
>
> *Na mas zísi* (May he/she live for us — said among family members only)

Birth
> See "Baptism" above

Birthday
> *Chrónia pollá* (Many years)
>
> *Ke tou chrónou* (And to next year)
>
> *Na ta katostísis* or *na ta ekatostísis* (May you live to be a hundred)

Bon appetit
> *Kalí órexi* (pron. *óreksi*)

Christmas
> *Kalá Christoúgena* (Good Christmas)

Death
> *Zoí se sas* (Life to you — said to mourning family only)
>
> *Zoí se mas* (Life to us — said among mourners)
>
> *Syllypitíria* (Condolences)
>
> *O Theós na ton/tin synchorési* (God forgive him/her)
>
> *O Theós na ton/tin anapáfsi* (God rest his/her soul)

177

Easter	*Kaló Páscha* (Happy Easter — said before Easter)
	Kalí Anástasi (Good Resurrection — said after Good Friday service)
	Christós anésti (Christ has risen — said after Anastasi service) Responses: *AliTHós anésti* (Truly he is risen) or *AliTHós o Kírios* (Truly the Lord)
Engagement	*Kalá stéphana* (Good crowning)
	Syncharitíria (Congratulations)
Evil eye	*Ptou, ptou* (Verbal substitute for spitting)
Forty-day blessing	See "Baptism" above
Funeral	See "Death" above
Good luck	*Kalí tíchi* (Good luck)
Hello/goodbye	*Yiá sou* (Hello/goodbye — informal)
	Chérete (Hello/goodbye — formal)
Independence Day	*Zíto i Ellás* (Long live Greece!) *Zíto i eleftheria* (Long live liberty!)
Lent	*Kalí Sarakostí* (Good Lent)
Marriage	*Na zísete eftychisméni* (Live happily)
	Na zísete (Long life)
	Na mas zísete (May they live for us — said among family members only)
	Syncharitíria (Congratulations)

Ke sta thiká sou (And at yours [wedding] —
said to single women and men)

Ke sta pethiá sou/sas (May your children get
married and to theirs — said to married
couples with children [formal/informal])

Memorial	*Eonía i mními* (Eternal be [his/her] memory) See also "Death" above
Misfortune	*Étsi ítan graftó* (That's the way fate was written)
Name day	*Chrónia pollá* (Many years)
	Ke tou chrónou (And to next year)
New Year	*Chrónia pollá* (Many years)
	Kalí chroniá (Good year)
Pregnant woman	*Kalí leftheriá* (Safe delivery)
Saturday of Souls	See "Memorial" above
Sneeze	*Yiá sou/sas* (To your health — formal/informal)
So so	*Étsi k' étsi* (So so)
Toasts	*Yiá sou/sas* (To your health — informal/formal)
	Is iyían (To health)
	Yiá chará (Health and joy)
To avoid a problem	*Ktípa ksílo* (Knock on wood)
Trip	*Kaló taksídi* (Good trip)
Yippee!	*Ópa!*

The following phrases are commonly used to respond in many of the above situations:

- *Efcharistó* (thank you)
- *Epísis* (and to you too)
- *Ke tou chrónou* (and to next year)

Be careful! You would not say, *"Epísis"* when someone says, *"Kalí lefteriá."*

SPECIAL PEOPLE

Greek grandparents love to be called *"yiayiá"* and *"papoú."* The terms add to the joy of grandchildren and confirm a respect for their heritage. Other common relationships are listed below.

The form used in this listing is for direct address. The first ending in a word is masculine; the ending after a slash is feminine.

Aunt	*Thía* (pron. *THía*)
Brother	*Adelphé* (pron. *athelphé*)
Child	*Pethí; petháki* (diminutive)
Countryman	*Patrióti* (from same region of Greece)
Cousin	*Eksáthelphe/eksathélphi*
Daughter	*Kóri* or *thigatéra* (pron. *THigatéra*)
Father	*Patéra; Babá* (affectionate)
Father-in-law	*Patéra* or *Babá* (Use *peTHerós* for third person)
Godfather	*Nouné* (*nounó* — popular usage)
Godmother	*Nouná*
Grandfather	*Papoú*
Grandmother	*Yiayiá*
In-law(s)	*Sympéthere/sympethéra* (pron. *sympeTHéra*) *Sympétheri* (plural)
Mother	*Mitéra; mamá* (affectionate)

Mother-in-law	*Mitéra* or *mamá* (Use *peTHerá* for third person)
Mr.	*Kírie*
Mrs.	*Kiría*
Priest	*Páter*
Priest's wife	*Presvytéra*
Relation by baptism or marriage	*Koumbáre/a*
Sister	*Adelphí* (pron. *athelphí*)
Son (my son)	*Yié mou*
Uncle	*Thíe* (pron. *THíe*)

⚜ *Food and Drink*

Delicious food is one of the great pleasures of Greek culture, and today the general public enjoys many Greek specialties. *Baklavá, moussaká, souvláki,* and the *gýro* (pron. *yíro*) have found their way into the American mainstream. For Greek Americans, food goes beyond these popular images. It is an integral, emotional part of their ethnic identity and one of their most satisfying traditions.

CUSTOMS AND TRADITIONS

An old Greek proverb says, "If the pot boils, friendship lives." Social life often revolves around the table where families bond together and friendships are solidified. Here, amid large platters of food, values are transmitted, old times recounted, politics discussed, and differences aired. Hours pass by as friends and family talk together. Sharing a meal is the most common Greek social activity.

Both the quantity and the quality of the food are important. A heavily laden table suggests well-being and generosity. Large quantities of food entice guests to eat as much as they want, and running out of food is considered a great embarrassment. Guests are continually urged to eat and to take second helpings. Increasingly, however, Greek Americans are becoming more aware of the effects of certain foods. In today's world, favorite old recipes have been modified to lower fat and cholesterol. Olive oil, a Greek mainstay, has no cholesterol and is low in saturated fat.

On religious holidays special food brings a renewed appreciation of tradition. During Lent, *fasolátha* (bean soup) reminds one of sacrifice and restraint. At Easter the traditional red eggs, Easter bread (*tsouréki*), a soup called *mayerítsa,* and roasted lamb enhance the joy of the Resurrection of Christ. Cracking red eggs symbolizes Christ's emergence from the tomb. The cutting of the New Year's Vasilopita (bread for St. Basil) and finding the lucky coin focuses everyone on the coming year. Eating and sharing *kóllyva* (boiled wheat) following a memorial service for a departed loved one reinforces the hope of afterlife. These special foods strengthen beloved Greek traditions.

ORIGINS

Greek cuisine today is a blend of old and new. The old goes back to classical Greece where sophisticated Athenians analyzed and enjoyed certain dishes. Food and dining became an art form like drama, sculpture, and architecture. Greek cuisine spread to other countries, and the Romans were known to import Greek chefs. Later there was substantial Middle Eastern influence due to Greece's proximity to the Middle East, its ties to the Byzantine Empire, and its subjugation to the Ottoman Empire for centuries. Yet, even during the occupation, much of Greek cuisine was preserved. Greek chefs fled to Orthodox monasteries to preserve their culinary traditions. They wore tall white hats to be distinguished from the priests wearing black ones — and from this began the practice of chefs' donning high white hats. It is difficult to determine exactly how many dishes are of Greek origin, since some Greek foods such as *baklavá* have Turkish names. Despite the names, however, the fact remains that many countries in the Middle East share similar foods with the Greeks.

THE GREEK TASTE

Certain ingredients and flavors distinguish Greek food. Their complexities and subtleties must be discovered at the table and in the numerous cookbooks available. Excellent books may be purchased at bookstores and through Philoptochos societies of many Greek Orthodox churches. Consult these books for a more complete discussion of ingredients, recipes, and serving suggestions. The following tips deal with some of the most popular elements of Greek cuisine.

OLIVE OIL

The foremost ingredient of Greek cooking is olive oil, a splendid greenish-gold liquid that threads its way through a variety of dishes, enhancing the flavor of vegetables, stews, and meats. It tastes best, perhaps, alone with chunks of hearty bread. Greeks love to recount the famous myth where the city of Athens conducted a contest to see which god or goddess would be its patron, depending on who gave the most valuable gift. Athena was chosen for giving the olive tree, useful for its oil, fruit, and wood.

It outranked Poseidon's gift of a spring of sea water. The finest olive oil is cold pressed extra-virgin, generally used for eating. A less refined oil may be used for cooking.

OLIVES

Greece is one of the largest olive producers in the world. Luscious black, green, or brown olives appear as a side dish on most Greek-American tables, eaten before and during meals. Different regions produce different types; some are picked earlier than others; some cracked open. The most famous is the large black Kalamata olive, but be adventurous and try some of the other kinds. Look for olives that are firm and not too salty. If you prefer, lessen the salty taste by soaking the olives in water for several days, changing it periodically; draining; drying; and adding olive oil, red wine vinegar, garlic, and oregano as a marinade.

CHEESES

Féta, *kasséri*, and *kefalotíri* are among the most popular Greek cheeses available in the United States. *Féta* (meaning "slice") remains the best known. Traditionally made by shepherds in the mountains of Greece, the most popular variety comes from the milk of sheep and is white, flaky, and slightly salty. *Féta* made from goat's milk is harder and sharper. Avoid the inferior *féta* made from cow's milk. Freshness is essential. Always ask the grocer for a little taste to make sure it has not become rubbery and tasteless. Keep the cheese fresh in the refrigerator by storing it in an airtight container completely submerged in brine made by crumbling a little cheese in water. Eat within several weeks of purchase.

SPICES, HERBS, AND FLAVORINGS

Certain spices, herbs and flavorings predominate in Greek cooking. Fresh parsley, mint, and dill are used generously, and a variety of wild oregano from Greece called *rígani* is preferred. (Basil, an herb with religious significance, is rarely used in cooking.) Generous quantities of fresh garlic season lamb, stews, and the antisocial *skorthaliá* (garlic sauce). Lemons are a key ingredient in the popular *avgolémono* (egg-lemon) sauce that can be added to a soup. Wedges of fresh lemon come with most meals.

Cinnamon appears in both tomato sauces and pastries. The most famous honey, a common sweetener, comes from thyme-covered Mt. Hymettus in Attica, Greece.

PHÍLLO

Many Greek dishes are constructed with layers of *phíllo*, paper-thin sheets of dough. A variety of fillings from spinach and cheese to egg custard and nuts are sandwiched in between the layers to make *spanakópita* (spinach pie), *galaktoboúriko* (milk custard between *phíllo*), and *baklavá*. To the novice, working with the fragile pastry sheets seems nothing short of miraculous until you see an experienced cook deftly handle the sheets, rapidly applying butter to each one. *Phíllo* (sometimes called strudel leaves) is now sold in many supermarkets in the freezer section. Try to find recently made dough. Work with it at room temperature, keeping the unused dough on the side under a slightly damp towel to prevent drying.

BEVERAGES

Wines

Greece is more famous for its god of wine, Dionysos, than the wines themselves. Recently, however, as Greece attempts to become competitive in the aggressive world of wine production, wine regions have been formed and standards set. For now, many Greek Americans buy Greek wines out of loyalty and nostalgia, especially at Easter. The most distinctive Greek wine is *retsína*, a white wine made by adding a small amount of pine resin at the beginning of fermentation. If properly made, the resin taste can be pleasing, but even many Greeks have failed to develop a taste for it. Only Greek wineries produce *retsína*, a name protected by law.

Oúzo

Oúzo is the informally adopted national drink of Greece. It is a clear, anise-flavored aperitif that tastes like licorice and is most often taken with *mezéthes* (appetizers). There are many brands of *oúzo*, but the island of Mitilini claims to be the best producer. An acquired taste for many, *oúzo* may be drunk straight or with ice. Most popular is a mix of one-part *oúzo* to two-parts water. When water is added, the *oúzo* becomes a milky white color.

Brandy

Many companies produce brandy, but Metáxa brand remains the preferred Greek brand. There are three qualities from which to choose: three, five and seven-stars (seven is the best). Brandy is served to toast a special occasion or served after dinner. Following a death it is customarily served at the *makaría* (the meal following a funeral) and to guests who visit the grieving family during the forty-day mourning period.

Coffee

Potent and strong, Greek coffee is served black with foam on the top, in a small demitasse cup called a *flintzáni*. Since sugar is brewed together with the coffee, declare your preference when you order: *skéto* (plain), *métrio* (medium), or *glikó* (sweet). Avoid drinking the thick coffee residue remaining in the bottom of the cup. One or two cups may be made at a time in a small, long-handled pot called a *bríki*. (Consult a Greek cookbook for directions.)

Reading coffee cups is a favorite pastime. After drinking, the coffee cup is turned over, and the residue forms patterns on the inside of the cup that can be read to predict the future.

A TYPICAL TABLE

Mealtime provides an opportunity for good company and good times. A wide variety of delicious foods may be presented, but certain side dishes always complement the fare. Just as Americans automatically place salt and pepper shakers on the table, Greeks put out little dishes of olives, sliced cheese, wedges of lemon, and carafes of olive oil, and red-wine vinegar.

Appetizers are called *mezéthes*. Popular ones include *tiropitákia* (little cheese pies) and *keftéthes* (meatballs), dips made of fish roe (*taramosaláta*) and eggplant (*melitzanosaláta*), and pickled vegetables. Sometimes a sampling of these little snacks make a repast known as the *mezé*, often accompanied by *oúzo*.

Meals often begin with the light and tasty *avgolémono* (egg-lemon) soup. *Pítes* (pies) made with *phíllo*, meat, vegetables and/or cheeses are standard fare. Artichoke and eggplant are among the most popular vegetables, along with roasted potatoes and the typical Greek village salad of cucumbers, tomatoes, and *féta*. Rice prepared as *piláfi* and hearty bread may accompany the meal. Chicken roasted with lemon, lamb grilled on skewers (*souvláki*), and baked fish are favorites. Lamb has a special status in Greece because of its association with the biggest holiday, Easter, when it is roasted on an outdoor spit. Other times of the year lamb makes excellent stews and casseroles.

Fruit marks the end of the meal. Elaborate sweets are served later. Standard favorites include *galaktoboúriko*, and nut cakes and tortes drenched with sweet syrup. Some sweets are associated with certain times of the year and occasions. Christmas and New Year treats include *baklavá*, *melomakárona*, *thíples*, and *kourabiéthes*. *Halvá* is served during Lent. *Baklavá* and *kourabiéthes* are popular at weddings and christenings. Sweets symbolize joy and good wishes. Greek guests customarily bring sweets when visiting someone's home to "sweeten" the friendship.

Greek food tastes best in its cultural context: after a glorious wedding, with a family gathered around the table, at a church bazaar, or at a *tavérna* by the sea. Then you experience the true Greek tradition of food. *Kalí órexi* (Bon appetit)!

❧ *Popular Music*

The many moods of Greek music fascinate the Western ear — the lamenting of the clarinet, the exuberance of the *bouzoúki*, the mystery of the minor key. To the uninitiated, the music invites images of intriguing places, food, and people. For the Greeks the sounds and rhythms express their very essence: their dreams, sorrows, joys. Add dancing and nothing more need be said. Two families whose children have just married share their happiness after the wedding by joining hands in one large circle to dance together. A proud grandfather dances alone, arms outstretched, to show his pleasure at his grandson's baptism. Through music and dancing, Greeks express *kéfi*, their pleasure and satisfaction with life.

There are three major categories of popular Greek music: *dimotiká* (pron. *thimotiká*), *laiká*, and *Evropaiká*. Understanding the categories will help you know what you are hearing, what to request, and what recordings to buy.

DIMOTIKÁ

Dimotiká are traditional rural folk songs with a non-Western sound. They are often played by a small ensemble of instruments such as the clarinet, lute, violin, dulcimer, and drum. A single voice sings the words, the rhythms have complex times like 7/8, 9/8 or 5/8, and the mode is usually in minor key. These songs go back centuries, perhaps even as far as classical Greece. Music historians, however, have been unable to establish a direct connection between folk music and that of the ancient Greeks.

Bouzoúki

The influence of both Byzantine church music and the Middle East is unmistakable. While the rhythms are not ecclesiastical, the distinct, single melodic line in minor key that dominates most folk songs resembles the monophonic Byzantine chant still heard in Orthodox churches today. The early church encouraged secular music at the feast day celebrations, and the priest would even start the first dance. The music of the Middle East has used similar instrumentation and rhythms for centuries. Greek folk songs remained a combination of Byzantine and Middle Eastern music, untouched for the most part by Western influence during the four-hundred years of domination by Turkey that ended in the nineteenth century. (The Ionian islands closest to Italy are an exception.) Common themes include love, politics, war, and lamention.

With Greek independence from Turkey in 1821, Greece became receptive to Western influences, and the tango and fox trot began making their way into *dimotiká*. Each region of Greece had its own style that still exists today. Songs of the islands are more lighthearted and relaxed than those of the mainland. The Ionian islands show Italian influence with their serenades (*kantáthes*). The Aegean islands are famous for improvisations before the main song, instrumental (*taxîm*) and vocal (*amané* — Turkish for "alas"). Cretan music is highly syncopated. On the mainland, the Peloponnese have a strong vocal tradition heard in the heroic *kléftica* songs, music composed by the resistance fighters who fought the Turks in the mountains. Thracean music has a lively tempo while that of Epirus is slower, a characteristic especially evident in its instrumental laments called *mirolóyi* (words of fate).

Patriotic songs (*patriotiká*) are a special kind of *dimotiká*. Most of these songs tell stories of heroic deeds and tragedies relating to the Ottoman occupation and to the revolution.

Dimotiká are still popular today, and their rhythms provide the base for popular folk dances like the *kalamatianós, sirtós, tsámiko, zeibékiko, hasápiko,* and *tsiftetéli* (see *Folk Dancing*). Bands today often substitute the electric guitar, electric keyboard, and a set of drums for the traditional equivalents.

Laiká

(General *Laiká, Rebétika, Elafrolaiká,* and Modern *Elafrolaiká*)

Laiká are urban songs of various styles: general *laiká, rebétika, elafrolaiká,* and modern *elafrolaiká*.

General *laiká* developed after the turn of the twentieth century. This urban folk music was greatly influenced by *rebétika,* a sound that began in the early 1900s in *cafe amans* and back city streets. Small nightspots called *cafe amán* became very popular in Asia Minor and the urban centers of Greece. A cross between a coffee house and a nightclub, the *cafes* featured Turkish-style songs played on the *bouzoúki* and *baglamá*. Beginning in 1922 a great influx of Greeks arriving from Asia Minor after the war between Turkey and Greece brought more Middle Eastern influence.

Meanwhile a new sound was emerging in the back streets of Aegean seaports such as Piraeus, home to destitute people called *rebétes*. Others were criminals who composed music while in jail. Many were refugees living on the fringe of society. They lived in an underworld where smoking hashish was commonplace and part of the music scene. Musicians there began playing a kind of soulful folk music also featuring the *bouzoúki* and *baglamá*. Similar to American blues, the close harmony, low-life lyrics, and emotionalism proved captivating. Combined with the influences of Asia Minor, a soulful folk music called *rebétika* evolved. Despite its allure, *rebétika* was not acceptable to the government nor the middle and upper classes because of its sometimes crude themes and Turkish sound. In the thirties *rebétika* began moving out of the hashish houses, resulting in classic *rebétika*. When the government closed the houses in the late thirties, many *rebétika* musicians became part of the established music scene incorporating the *bouzoúki* and *rebétika* sound into urban folk music.

After World War II, music featuring the *bouzoúki* became the rage all over Greece. Respectable composers like Mikis Theodorakis and Manos Hatzidakis began using the tantalizing sound. Popularly referred to as *bouzoúki* music, nightclubs called *bouzoúkia* flourished and continue to do so today. Most *laiká* music today features the *bouzoúki* sound.

The *bouzoúki* is now considered the premier Greek instrument. With electrification, the power and force of the *bouzoúki* evokes an extreme range of emotions. During a solo *taxím*, the *bouzoúki* takes the listener from painful loneliness to exuberant happiness. Like the violin, it possesses a haunting quality even in upbeat compositions.

A lighter *laiká*, known as *elafrolaiká*, comes from the *laiká* tradition, but the sound is softer and more modern. These are easy-listening songs popular with the general public. Modern *elafrolaiká* is far removed from general *laiká* and *elafrolaiká*. These songs have a faddish quality, absorbing the latest sounds from Europe and the United States, including the rhythms and styles of disco and rock. The beat is distinctively Western.

EVROPAIKÁ

Evropaiká has a distinct European flavor but with Greek words. After the revolution of 1821, European music gained enormous popularity. At that time, the *kantátha* (an Italian and German hybrid) and waltz were the rage. The sound remained Greek, often retaining some traditional instruments such as the clarinet and *bouzoúki*, but blending several cultures. Easy listening and fun to dance to, *evropaiká* is still popular especially with the older generation. Today's Greek singers, such as Giannis Parios, tend to revive old songs, including ballads about love, loneliness, and gambling.

GREEK MUSIC IN AMERICA

In the United States, music trends basically follow those of Greece. During the forties, some Greek-American music was heavily influenced by the big-band sound. In the fifties, two major trends emerged: the *rebétika* sound and a return to more *dimotiká* especially at baptisms, weddings, and dances. Today the Greek-American public enjoys a variety of Greek music.

At one time Greek-American musicians and composers recorded with such companies as RCA Victor, Columbia, Capital, Balkan, and Astro. Their recordings of *rebétika* before World War II are particularly valuable since recordings were restricted in Greece. They also continued to record *dimotiká* when it was considered unsophisticated by the urban population in Greece. Most recordings of Greek-American music today, however, are made in Greece.

BUYING RECORDINGS

If you are unfamiliar with Greek music, listen to it with someone who can identify the above types. Discover what you like and learn some of the key vocabulary that may appear on recording labels. Some catalogs organize the music by categories: *dimotiká*, *laiká*, and *elafrolaiká*. If you want traditional dance music, look for words such as *kalamatianós*, *sirtós*, *tsámiko*, *zeibékiko*, and *hasápiko*. You might also look for some of the well-known composers and performers who have remained popular through the years (listed below).

Finding a good selection of recordings may prove difficult. Many Greek Americans therefore buy Greek music when they visit Greece. In the United States, general music shops carry a limited selection of Greek recordings. Greek specialty stores have a wider choice, depending on the size of the Greek community. Ask to see the specialty store's mail-order catalog or obtain one through advertisements in a Greek-American newspaper. The largest mail-order company is Greek Video Records & Tapes, Inc., in Brooklyn, New York. Call 1-800-555-1212 (information) to obtain their toll-free number. The following names appear in their catalog.

WELL-KNOWN PERFORMERS AND COMPOSERS

Many Greek singers are versatile and perform in more than one category. Giorgos Dalaras, for example, sings *rebétika*, *laiká*, and *elafrolaiká*. Some have only one name.

Dimotiká

Hronis Aidonidis
Tassos Halkias
Kitsakis
Oi Konitopouleoi (family)
Yiannis Konstantinou
Giorgos Papasideri

Vasilis Saleas
Domna Samiou
Sofia Vembo *(patriotiká)*
Tacia Vera
Nikos Xilouris

Laiká

Haris Alexiou
Antipas
Grigoris Bithikotsi
George Dalaras
Litsa Diamanti
Stratos Dionisiou
Glikeria
Manos Hatzidakis (composer)
Stelios Kazantzidis
Stamatis Kokotas

Marinela
Dimitris Mitropanos
Poli Panou
Giannis Parios
Katerina Stanisi
Mikis Theodorakis (composer)
Prodomos Tsaousakis
Vasilis Tsitsanis
Markos Vamvakaris
Stavros Xarhakos (composer)

Evropaiká

Nikos Gounaris
Tonis Maroudas

Nana Mouskouri

❖ *Folk Dancing*

For centuries, infectious Greek songs with their insistent rhythms have lured listeners to dance — to celebrate happy occasions, bond together in wartime, and even express loneliness. Communal dancing appears on ancient Greek vases and in Byzantine frescoes. One dance, the *tsakónikos* from the Peloponnesus, allegedly represents the mythical king Theseus threading his escape through the labyrinth of the minotaur in Crete.

GEOGRAPHIC DIVERSITY

There are hundreds of traditional Greek folk dances. Each region boasts its own favorites and has certain characteristics. Cretan dances are proud and vigorous. The dances of the plains of Thessaly are controlled and composed, and some mountain people dance with wide steps and leaps. Even cold weather can affect dance style when heavy clothing is worn, as evident in northern Epirus. Some dances are named for their locality (*rodítikos* from Rhodes) or a profession (*hasápiko* from the word for butcher, *hasapis*). Names are also derived from a city, an event, or a special person. Many dances are related to each other, with individual variations.

Greeks and Greek Americans enjoy nonfolk dancing also, such as the tango, waltz, disco, rock, and the latest trend. The danger of forgetting the traditional dances always exists, but they continue to survive along with the modern. Greek Americans like to mix contemporary and traditional dancing when they celebrate.

DANCE TIPS

The great fun of most Greek dancing is its communal, inclusive nature. With the exception of a few solo and couples' dances, everyone joins in the serpentine lines that whirl and weave around the floor: the reluctant novice, the two-year-old, the dance expert, the irritable grouch.

Anyone can join an open-circle dance by grabbing someone's hand at the end of the dance line or by breaking into the middle. You are swooshed into the heady whirl, taking lessons on the spot just by imitating the person next to you. People tend to be patient and encouraging with beginners, pleased that you want to learn. You will be criticized more for not trying than for making mistakes.

Leaders of the line, however, are expected to know the basic steps and variations, so the front is not a comfortable position for a novice. A good leader puts on a show. Partially suspended from a handkerchief held by the next person in line, the leader performs variations on the basic steps, sometimes leaping into the air. Others in the line show their approval by shouting, *"Ópa,"* or making a hissing sound through closed teeth. After a brief time in the spotlight, the leader moves down the line, letting another dancer take over the lead.

In contrast, dances like the *zeibékiko* and the *tsiftetéli* are intended for one or two people. To be strictly traditional, no one would join in and distract from the dancer(s). At most Greek-American functions, however, many individuals and couples dance the *zeibékiko* and *tsiftetéli* while others are also on the floor. If you are uncertain, always wait and watch what others do.

At one time, certain dances like the *hasápiko* and the *zeibékiko* were reserved for men. Even the dancing styles for men and women were different. Men were open, vibrant and virile, performing leaps and turns, improvising complicated steps. Women danced modestly with eyes downcast. This, however, is not true today. Women lead lines and frequently dance a *zeibékiko*.

Appreciative spectators sometimes throw money on the floor, but it is meant for the band, not the dancers. In Greece the old practice of dashing plates to the floor has been prohibited, and in the big nightclubs, flower petals are scattered instead.

THE DANCES

The following six dances are the basics of the Greek-American dance floor. Learn these and you will rarely miss a beat. It is highly recommended that you take Greek dancing lessons from an experienced individual or perhaps a class sponsored by a church. Taking Greek dancing lessons has become a Greek-American tradition of its own! Imitating a dancer in line or watching videotapes are the next best ways of learning.

KALAMATIANÓS (OPEN CIRCLE)

If a Greek national dance was declared — unlikely, given the regional rivalries — the *kalamatianós* might be the choice. Easy and extremely popular, it is danced everywhere and has twelve basic steps in 7/8 time. Contrary to popular belief, it did not begin in the town of Kalamata (although one version did), but was derived from a very old dance, the *sirtós*.

SIRTÓS (OPEN CIRCLE)

It is believed that the *sirtós* is the oldest dance, and many dances are variations of it. In fact the ancient Greeks called all circular dances "*sirtós.*" In a *sirtós* the feet "drag" along the floor with a controlled reserve and tension even when the beat is fast. Twelve basic steps are executed in 2/4 time.

TSÁMIKO (OPEN CIRCLE)

Some describe the *tsámiko*, a stately warlike dance, as the most handsome in Greece. It originated in the Tsamouria area in Epirus and was originally danced only by men. Also called the *kléftikos*, it was danced by the *kléftes*, the fighters and rebels of the revolution of 1821. The dance showcases the leader's ability. Each area dances it a little differently.

HASÁPIKO AND *HASAPOSÉRVIKO* (OPEN LINE)

The *hasápiko* is a lively, hopping-style dance that dates back to Byzantium when it was danced exclusively by butchers in Constantinople. Influenced by *rebétika* music and enjoyed by many Greek sailors, it became the "sailors' dance." Its lively 1-2-3 kick step is danced arm-over-arm. When danced fast, the dance is called a *hasaposérviko* and resembles the Jewish hora. However, the hora moves clockwise, and the *hasaposérviko* moves counterclockwise. The *sirtáki* combines the *hasápiko* and the *hasaposérviko*, beginning slowly and ending in a frenzy.

TSIFTETÉLI (ONE OR TWO PEOPLE)

The *tsiftetéli* originated in the Middle East where it is danced by belly dancers. The undulating hips and provocative style evoke images of a harem. Greeks and Greek Americans do the dance in a restrained yet seductive way either with one person or together as a couple.

ZEIBÉKIKO (SOLO)

The *zeibékiko* is an intensely personal dance executed with great restraint and control. The dancer with lowered head and drooping outstretched arms is totally self-absorbed, performing alone on the floor. Traditionally, no one interrupts the dancer's trance-like movements. Today, however, many individuals dancing the *zeibékiko* may ocupy the dance floor at the same time. The steps are improvised, making each dance different. Sometimes the dancer performs stunts such as dancing with a glass of wine on the head, or circling a glass of wine on the floor and then picking it up by the teeth and drinking it without hands. A small table is sometimes picked up in the teeth.

Brought by Greek immigrants from Asia Minor, the *zeibékiko* flourished in the underclass world of *rebétika* before World War II and was danced originally only by men. It gained widespread popularity with both men and women, however, after the rise of *bouzoúki* music.

VIEWING TRADITIONAL FOLK DANCING

America may be one of the best places to see a variety of Greek folk dancing since people from all over Greece may come to a single Greek-American dance. In addition many churches and organizations sponsor Greek dancing classes whose participants wear authentic costumes and perform at church bazaars and special programs. Some churches hold dance competitions.

The best dancing may be seen at the annual Greek Orthodox Folk Dance Festival sponsored by the Diocese of San Francisco of the Greek Orthodox Archdiocese of America. (Locations vary each year.) Nearly 2000 dancers from seven western states perform in authentic costumes at the four-day competition. The festival celebrates and preserves the Greek folk dance heritage.

In Greece, Dora Stratou's National Dance of Greece Ensemble performs daily in their theatre on Philopappou Hill across from the Acropolis. Their show provides the most authentic traditional dancing. You may also be entertained by groups (professional or amateur) in restaurants or at special celebrations. Fortunately the traditional dances and songs are being recorded for posterity in projects headed by Simon Karas at the Society for the Dissemination of National Music in Athens and the Lyceum Club of Greek Women in Athens. Mr. Karas maintains a large collection of Greek instruments, and the Lyceum Club collects and sells folk crafts and costumes.

❧ *Proverbs and Sayings*

The Greeks are full of wisdom and humor, from the loftiest sentiments to the earthiest folk advice. Aristotle reminded his fellow
Greeks that "Dignity does not consist of possessing honors but in
deserving them." In modest contrast, an old proverb advises, "If a
dog doesn't bite, let it bark with all its might!"

The following proverbs and sayings were collected from Greek
families, friends, and written sources.[1] They represent treasures
remembered and loved.

Apó to stóma sou stou theoú to aftí.
From your mouth to God's ear.

Yírise o tétsiras ke vríke to kapáki.
The pot rolled around until it found the lid.
(That person found the right match.)

To krasí ke ta pethiá léne tin aliTHia.
Wine and children speak the truth.

Ópou akoús polá kerásia, mikra kaláTHia vásta.
When they brag of many cherries, bring along a small container.

Pan métron áriston.
Moderation in all things is excellent.

Yiátrepse ta páTHi sou keh ystera ta thiká mou.
Mend your own faults, then look at mine.

Ekí pou íse ímouna, ke ethó pou íme THa élTHis.
Where you are, I have been; and where I am, you will be.

Káne to kaló ke ríchto sto yialó.
Do a good deed and cast it to the sea.

Áplose ta póthia sou óso fTHáni to páplomá sou.
Extend your legs only as far as your coverlet reaches.
(Live within your means)

O kalós fílos, stin anángi fénete.
A true friend proves himself when needed.

Prépi na válís tin perispoméni?
Do you have to add the accent?
(Must you have the last word?)

I kalí méra apó tin avgí fénete.
A fine day from dawn shows itself.

To mílo THa pési káto apó tin miliá.
The apple will fall under the apple tree.

To éma neró then yínete.
Blood cannot become water.
(Blood is thicker than water)

Mazí miláme ke hória katalavénoume.
Together we speak but apart we understand.
(We are not communicating.)

Páre papoútsi apó ton tópo sou ke as íne baloméno.
Take a shoe from your own country or town even if it is patched.
(The known is better than the unknown.)

Pes mou piós íne o fílos sou na sou ipó piós ise.
Tell me who is your friend, and I shall tell you who you are.
(You are judged by the company you keep.)

Ótan mbis sto horó prépi na horépsis.
When you get into the dance, you must dance.
(When you get involved you, are committed to perform.)

---

1. Compiled by Helen Panarites from various sources, including
    Greek Proverbs, by Steven G. Economou, N.p., 1976.

⚜ *Superstitions*

Greeks love garlic — in sauces, dips, stews, roast lamb, and even in their pockets! A popular superstition says that garlic protects against the evil eye. If a child looks especially attractive one day, inviting the envy of others, the mother may take a little precaution by tucking a clove of garlic in the child's pocket.

Such folk superstitions are common among Greeks and many other nationalities. The superstitions below probably span thousands of years and thousands of miles. Most Greek Americans view them as fun and colorful — a form of amusement — yet many give lip service to at least a few.

Some superstitions combine both religious and superstitious beliefs. For example, there is a superstition that any part of a baptized baby's body that was not rubbed with oil during the service will smell for the rest of the person's life. The oiling of the child is religious, symbolizing God's reconciliation; but the superstition about the odor is strictly folk belief — probably!

LUCK

USING THE SAME DOOR

Use the same door when entering and leaving someone else's house. To not do so, invites bad luck on an impending matter, such as a marriage proposal or a business deal.

COIN FOR NEW VENTURES

Put a coin of precious metal in a new house, a new car, or a safe place in a newborn's crib for good fortune.

THE NEW YEAR

See *New Year*.

PREVENTING MISFORTUNE

JINXING

Do not spoil a good thing by bragging or predicting success. Overconfidence can bring failure. For example, never brag that you will get an "A" on a test before it is returned or make a million when the deal is closed. If you boast ahead of time, you may fail. Even in ancient times, myth had it that the gods chastised men if they became too over confident. When the triumphant Agamemnon returned home as a conquering hero from the Trojan war, he walked on a purple carpet reserved only for the gods. His arrogance offended them, leading to his downfall.

KNOCK ON WOOD (*KTÍPA KSÍLO*)

Knock on wood to keep a good thing from going wrong. This is a cousin to the idea of jinxing. If you must predict that something will go well, for example, "It looks like the sun will shine for the wedding," knock on wood several times to keep away the rain.

This custom may have religious origins. Many early Christians carried pieces of wood believed to be part of the original cross. When in a danger, they touched the wood, receiving God's protective power.

PREVENT THIRD MISFORTUNE

Some believe bad things happen in three's. After two bad things have occurred (such as two funerals) say, "*Na min tritósi*" ("May it not triple") to prevent a third unfortunate event.

PREDICTIONS

DREAMS

Bad dreams mean something good will happen. Good dreams means bad things are on the way. If you dream about something red, you will hear news right away. If you are barefoot in your dreams, your worries will be relieved. If a dream on Saturday night is to come true, it will happen before noon on Sunday.

READING COFFEE CUPS

This is a common form of entertainment. After finishing a cup of Greek coffee, swirl the dregs, turn the cup over into a saucer and cool. The grounds form unique patterns inside the cup that are then read by a fortune teller (*kafetzoú*).

SPIRITS

NERÁITHES

Observers in remote areas of Greece and at sea have sometimes spotted beautiful nymph-like maidens called *neráithes*.

KALIKÁNTZARI

See *Christmas*.

EVIL EYE: IDENTIFICATION AND FOLK REMEDIES

Contrary to popular opinion, the evil eye (*vaskanía*) is recognized by the church as a legitimate religious phenomenon. It is part of a larger picture of evil generated by the devil. For a more detailed description see *Special Blessings, Prayers, and Appeals.* The church helps its parishioners exorcise the evil eye with a prayer offered by the priest. Some people practice the following superstitious folk remedies, even though the church discourages their use.

IDENTIFICATION

A popular folk method for determining if someone has the evil eye is to put three drops of oil in a glass of water. If the oil stays separate from the water, you do not have it. If the oil blends with the water, you do.

PREVENTING THE EVIL EYE

Common Expressions

Ptoú, ptoú

> The most common protection against the evil eye is the simple phrase, *"Ptoú, ptoú,"* uttered immediately after receiving a compliment. A cautious Greek parent upon hearing, "Your son is so handsome," would counter with *"Ptoú, ptoú"* to keep the evil eye from harming him. Or it might be said by the person who gives the compliment. The phrase is a verbalizing of spitting to scare away evil spirits. In the Orthodox baptismal service, the godparent spits three times and denounces Satan.

Na mi se matiáso (Not to eye you)

> One way of giving a compliment without bringing on the evil eye is to end the remark with, *"Na mi se matiáso"* or *"Ptoú, ptoú, na mi se matiáso."* This lets the person know that you are not putting on the evil eye.

Skórtha sta mátia sou (Garlic in your eye!)

> A less polite response to a compliment (see "Garlic" below).

Home Precautions

Garlic

> Garlic not only makes Greek food delicious but also fights evil. Put it anywhere — in your pocket, purse, closet, or cupboard — for protection.

Dirt Behind the Ear

> A favorite trick of some people is to make the sign of the cross behind a child's ear with black soot, charcoal, or dirt from the bottom of a shoe.

Eye over Door

Some homes keep a picture of an eye over the main entryway to dispel envy brought in from the outside.

Máti

The *máti* ("eye") is a folk talisman made of blue stone, glass, or plastic with a black eye in the center. It is commonly given to newborn babies and pinned to clothing at the upper back. Adults also wear it as a pin, a necklace, on a charm bracelet, and even on the same chain as their cross. Although frequently viewed with amusement, the *máti* evokes a skeptical respect from even the most sophisticated!

Máti

Layman's Prayer (Ksemátiasma)

Another folk remedy employed by the Greeks to dispel the evil eye is a ritual prayer (*ksemátiasma*) that is passed on orally. The prayer cannot be written, or, legend says, it will lose its power. If you are a woman, you must learn it from a man; if you are a man, from a woman. It is passed on when the bearer is old as the bearer's power is lost once the prayer is revealed.

MISCELLANEOUS

DEATH

See *Death and Mourning.*

FATE (*MÍRA*)

See *Birth of Children.*

HAIR

Never cut your hair when the moon is "emptying;" you will lose your hair. Conversely, if your hair is cut while the moon is "filling," your hair will be fuller.

ITCHING HANDS

If your left hand itches, you will receive money; if your right hand itches, you will pay someone.

KNIFE

Do not hand a knife directly to someone, or you will have an argument. Lay it down, and have the person pick it up. If you hand a knife, say *"Ptoú, ptoú."*

MARRIAGE

Write the names of unmarried single women on the under hem of the wedding gown. The names will follow the bride to the altar, and the women will have good luck in finding a husband.

Before the marriage ceremony, roll a young child on the wedding bed and sprinkle the bed with *kouféta*, rice, and money to ensure the couple's fertility.

Include a small pair of scissors in the bride's bouquet to "cut" the evil eye.

Someone wishing ill will can cast *mayá* (a spell) on an engaged couple, preventing the wedding or keeping the marriage from being consummated. Consult a priest if a spell is suspected. Always cut the tips off the candles used on the wedding table during the marriage ceremony. If someone else takes them, they can put a spell on the newlyweds.

A single woman will dream of her husband-to-be if she places *kouféta* from a *bonboniéra* under her pillow. Chances of finding a husband improve if the *kouféta* comes from the wedding tray.

PURSE

Do not leave your purse on the floor, or it will never be full.

RECEIVING SOAP, KNIVES, COLOGNE, AND HANDKERCHIEFS

If you are given a handkerchief, cologne, or a knife, hand the person a penny to avoid an argument and loss of friendship. Never give a friend soap as a gift or hand it to them. It washes away the friendship.

RINGING EARS

You will hear some news.

SNEEZE

If you sneeze, you are telling the truth, or someone is talking about you.

STEPPING OVER A CHILD

Do not step over a child, or the body part you crossed will not grow. The curse can be undone by stepping back over it.

STONE OVER BACK

If you throw a black stone behind you as you leave a place, you will never return.

FOLD IN BEDSPREAD

Fold up the corner of the bedspread before going on a trip, so that you will return safely.

✤ *Community Life*

In explaining the greatness of classical Athens, the statesman Pericles said, "Here each individual is interested not only in his own affairs but in the affairs of the state as well." Pericles may have been referring specifically to government, but in fact Athenians cared about all aspects of their community.

When Greek Americans first came to the United States, they were unable to participate fully in American society because of poor English language skills, lack of education, and financial pressures. Innately political, however, they formed their own societies, organizations, and churches. The churches in particular became arenas for political views, especially concerning the politics of Greece. Slowly this has changed, and today Greek Americans are highly involved in the American community.

They have maintained, however, a broad range of Greek organizations, both religious and secular. They pool their energy, talents, and resources for wider goals, such as preserving the culture, giving scholarships to needy students, lobbying for justice in Cyprus, and helping the elderly. They particularly enjoy working together, bonded by mutual experiences, values, humor, and a strong sense of kinship. The following briefly describes the organizations and activities in the Greek-American community.

THE GREEK ORTHODOX CHURCH

With approximately 500 parishes, the Greek Orthodox Church is the largest organization in the Greek-American community. The administrative head is the Greek Orthodox Archdiocese of America (formerly of North and South America) located at 8-10 East 79th Street, New York, New York 10021.

CHURCH PROGRAMS

The church provides many opportunities for service, the foundation of its strength coming from the dedicated volunteers who give time and talent to run its programs. You may want to become involved in the following programs in which lay people typically serve:

- Parish council (governing body of each parish)
- Greek Orthodox Ladies Philoptochos Society
- YAL (Young Adult League)
- GOYA (Greek Orthodox Youth of America — ages 13-18)
- JOY (Junior Orthodox Youth — ages 7-12)
- HOPE (Hellenic Orthodox Primary Enrichment — under 7)
- Religious education (Sunday school)
- Education (day schools and Greek language classes)

The Archdiocese also sponsors a number of projects, events, and publications:

- Hellenic College/Holy Cross Greek Orthodox School of Theology (training of Orthodox priests)
- St. Basil Academy (residential childcare center for children without family support)
- St. Michael's Home for the Aged (elderly home in Yonkers, New York)
- Home and Overseas Mission (program to spread Orthodoxy worldwide)
- St. Photios National Shrine (memorial to first Greek immigrants, St. Augustine, Florida)
- Ionian Village (youth camp in Bartholomio, Greece)
- Retreat centers in Cheyenne, Wyoming; Dunlap, California; and Seattle, Washington
- Clergy-Laity Congress (biannual national church convention)
- *Orthodox Observer* (national newspaper)
- *Yearbook* (annual reference book)

LOCAL CHURCH FESTIVAL

Most church parishes sponsor a Greek festival once or twice during the year. The festival *(paniyiri)* is similar to those typically held by churches, cities, and towns in Greece to celebrate a name day. The general public is invited to eat wonderful food, dance, hear music, and browse for Greek crafts and art work. Every effort is made to be authentic, such as roasting lambs on spits over charcoal, deep frying *loukoumáthes*, and brewing fresh Greek coffee. The *paniyíri* presents Greek culture to the broader community, and gives Greek Americans a chance to touch their roots and celebrate their heritage. Generally the largest project of the year with the most volunteers and the source of substantial revenue, the church festival has become a Greek-American tradition of its own.

YEARBOOK

The Archdiocese annually publishes a useful resource book called the *Yearbook*. It contains the religious calendar and a wealth of current information about church departments, individual parishes, statistics, Greek-American secular organizations, newspapers, and radio and television programs. Your church office will have a copy, or it can be purchased from the Archdiocese at a nominal cost. (*The Encyclopedia of Associations* available at most local libraries also lists Greek-American associations.)

REGIONAL SOCIETIES (*TOPIKÁ SOMATÍA*)

If you have strong ethnic ties, you may want to join a regional society (*topiká somatía*). These groups bring together individuals from the same area of Greece. For example, former residents and their descendants from the region of Macedonia have their own club. Even Greek cities have their societies, such as The Athenian Society and the Sparta Fraternity. In an earlier time, some of these groups organized to build Greek churches in America and to raise money for modernization in their home villages. Today the number of native-born participants is smaller, and the need in Greece has dwindled. The *topiká somatía* have fewer members and provide primarily social and cultural activities. The *Yearbook* contains a large list of societies from Epirus, Macedonia, Peloponnesus, Steria Hellas, Thessaly, the islands, Cyprus, Constantinople, Asia Minor, Egypt, and elsewhere.

EDUCATIONAL, CULTURAL, AND SPECIAL INTEREST GROUPS

The Greek-American community cares deeply about preserving the Hellenic heritage at the grass-roots level. Schools have long been established to teach the Greek language and Hellenic tradition. The Archdiocese school system sponsors afternoon Greek schools, pre-schools, kindergartens, adult language classes, and parochial day schools. Private schools such as the Hellenic American Academy in Potomac, Maryland, are also available. (See "Higher Education" below for college and university programs.)

In addition, various organizations are devoted to education and cultural awareness. The largest secular organization is AHEPA (American Hellenic Educational Progressive Association) established in 1922. Its goals included helping Greek immigrants obtain American citizenship and participate in American life while promoting an appreciation of Hellenism. AHEPA has broadened its scope and become a major philanthropic organization, giving millions of dollars in scholarships, for charities, disaster relief, construction projects, and historic preservation. Its annual national convention is one of the largest Greek-American gatherings, and its annual congressional dinner the largest Greek-American political event.

Numerous intellectual societies and literary groups focus primarily on ancient and modern Hellenism, such as the Hellenic University Club, the Parnassos Society of New York, and the Athenaeum University Club in Washington, D.C. Extensive private library collections are located at Annunciation Cathedral, Baltimore, Maryland, and the Speros Basil Vryonis Center for the Study of Hellenism in Rancho Cordova, California. The International Folklore Society publishes *Laografia,* a journal documenting Greek traditions and customs (6 Golden Star, Irvine, California).

Hundreds of other groups organize according to their own special interests: doctors, dentists, business people, bankers, educators, and college students. For example, business people in Los Angeles may join a group called Axios. Professional networking is increasing nationwide with such groups as the Greek-American Women's Network based in New York City.

Educating the United States government on foreign policy relating to Greece has become more organized since the invasion of Cyprus in 1974. Foreign policy crises involving Greece act as a rallying point for Greek-American organizations, particularly when Greece is threatened by Turkey. The most prominent groups include AHEPA headquartered in Washington, D.C.; the American Hellenic Institute Public Affairs Committee in Washington, D.C.; UHAC (United Hellenic American Congress) in Chicago; the American Hellenic Alliance in Reston, Virginia; and the Pancyprian Association of America in New York.

Large community service organizations have been formed such as the Hellenic Foundation in Chicago, and HANAC (Hellenic American Neighborhood Action Committee) in New York. The Hellenic Foundation, started forty years ago, uses public, private, and church funds to deliver a wide variety of social services: senior housing, translating, emergency aid, and a senior recreation center. HANAC, funded primarily with public monies, originally started to assist Greek-American senior citizens but has expanded to a range of services similar to those of the Hellenic Foundation.

The Cyprus Children's Fund in New York City sponsors refugee children in Cyprus, and the Hellenic Cardiac Fund for Children at Children's Hospital in Boston sponsors Greek children who need medical attention in the United States.

HIGHER EDUCATION

HELLENIC, BYZANTINE, AND MODERN GREEK STUDIES

A number of American colleges and universities across the country offer programs in Hellenic, Byzantine, and Modern Greek Studies:

- Harvard University, Cambridge, Massachusetts
- Harvard University (Dumbarton Oaks), Washington, D.C. (Byzantine only)
- Hellenic College, Brookline, Massachusetts
- New York University, Alexander S. Onassis Center for Hellenic Studies in New York
- Ohio State University, Columbus, Ohio

- Princeton University, Princeton, New Jersey

- Queens College, City University of New York, Flushing, New York

- Rutgers University, New Brunswick, New Jersey

- San Francisco State University, San Francisco, California

- University of Florida, Gainesville, Florida

- Wayne State University, Detroit, Michigan

Important scholarly journals include: The *Journal of Modern Greek Studies*, the *Journal of Modern Hellenism*, the *Modern Greek Studies Yearbook*, and the *Journal of the Hellenic Diaspora*.

GREEK-AMERICAN STUDIES

The study of Greek Americans has developed over the last thirty years. The first major scholarly work, *The Greeks in the United States*, by Theodore Saloutos was published in 1964. Other important books include *Greek Americans: Struggle and Success* by Charles Moskos, *The Odyssey of Hellenism in America* by George Papaioannou, and *The Greek Americans* by Alice Scourby.[1] While no separate courses devoted entirely to Greek Americans are offered in the country, research and publication continues in such areas as labor, music, women, immigration, psychology, and regional communities.[2]

GREEK-AMERICAN LITERATURE

Some Greek-Americans have written about immigrant life, starting with a novel called *Gold in the Streets* by Mary Vardoulakis in 1945.[3] The two most prominent writers include Nicholas Gage and Harry Mark Petrakis. Gage's *A Place for Us* relates his adjustment to America after the murder of his mother in Greece, which he recounts in his famous book and movie, *Eleni*.[4] Harry Mark Petrakis's most popular novel, *A Dream of Kings* was also made into a movie. Other writings by Petrakis draw heavily on ethnic life in Chicago, especially *Stelmark: A Family Recollection*.[5] For additional writers and a description of their works see *Greek Americans* by Charles Moskos.[6]

GREEK-AMERICAN MUSEUMS

Cultural centers featuring artifacts and memorabilia relating to the Greek-American experience may be seen at the Hellenic Museum & Cultural Center, 400 North Franklin Street, Chicago, Illinois 60610; Hellenic Cultural Museum at Holy Trinity Cathedral, 279 South 300 West, Salt Lake City, Utah 84101; and St. Photios National Shrine, 41 St. George Street, St. Augustine, Florida 32085.

"GREEK TOWNS," U.S.A.

Some Greek Americans live in cities with a substantial Greek population. The three most distinct "Greek Towns" are in Astoria, New York; Chicago, Illinois; and Tarpon Springs, Florida.

ASTORIA, NEW YORK

The largest concentration of Greek Americans lives in the Astoria section of Queens, a borough of New York City. The area has a mix of apartment buildings, attached row houses, and shops, and restaurants. In warm weather, the ambiance and street scenes are typical of city life in Greece: patrons eating in outdoor restaurants and people strolling arm-in-arm. Astoria can be reached by cab or a twenty-minute subway ride across the river from Manhattan. The subway runs along 31st street, the street with the most Greek restaurants and stores. The large rectangular neighborhood is formed by Steinway and 31st streets, running east and west, and Ditmars Boulevard and Broadway, on the north and south.

The New York area remains the "capital" of Greek America, with 82,690 Greeks, including all the boroughs but not the suburbs.[7] Two major Greek-language newspapers, the *National Herald* (*Ethnikos Kiryx*) and *Proini,* are published there, and the vast majority of Greek food, music, and specialty items are distributed through New York companies. The headquarters of the Greek Orthodox church and the main cathedral, Holy Trinity, are located in the borough of Manhattan.

CHICAGO, ILLINOIS

A substantial Greek-American community of 83,865 resides in the Chicago area.[8] Most of the old original Greek Town has been displaced by the University of Illinois at Chicago, and the Greek population has dispersed widely throughout the city and suburbs. The largest concentration of Greek restaurants, nightclubs, and grocery stores may be found near the heart of downtown Chicago on Halsted Street between Monroe and Van Buren streets. Approximately six miles north lies a Greek residential area clustering around St. Demetrios Church. The neighborhood, mainly comprised of three- to four-story brick attached houses, starts on Lawrence Street at Western Avenue and extends westward. Specialty stores and restaurants featuring Greek food are scattered along a six-block stretch on Lawrence Street. Recently the neighborhood has become more diverse.

TARPON SPRINGS, FLORIDA

Tarpon Springs, a unique community in southwest Florida, is the most reminiscent of a Greek village with its outdoor tables, white stucco buildings, and tin cans of flowers. In 1905 immigrants from the Greek islands started the natural sponge industry, and a Greek community quickly developed and thrived. With the invention of synthetic sponges, however, the market changed. This, together with the red tide scourge (a disease that killed sponges) in the late 1940s, crippled the sponge economy. Today tourism is the primary industry and much of the Greek culture has been preserved. The Greek community of 2,840 (excluding those in outlying developments) comprises one-sixth of the town's population.[9] The annual celebration of Epiphany on January 6 is the principal Greek event in Tarpon Springs. (See *Epiphany*)

GREEK-AMERICAN MEDIA

The Greek-American media facilitates communication within the community. There are electronic and print media in both the Greek and English languages.

NEWSPAPERS

The *Yearbook* lists newspapers and monthly publications. The most prominent national newspapers are:

In Greek

National Herald (Ethnikos Kiryx) (daily from New York)
Proini (daily from New York)

In English and Greek

National Herald (Ethnikos Kiryx) (weekly from New York)
The Greek Star (weekly from Chicago)
Orthodox Observer (monthly from the Archdiocese in New York. Largest circulation of all Greek-American newspapers.)

In English

National Herald (Ethnikos Kiryx) (weekly from New York)
Hellenic Chronicle (weekly from Boston)
The Greek American (weekly from New York)
Hellenic Journal (biweekly from San Francisco)

MAGAZINE

The most prominent publication in English covering Greece, Greek Americans and the diaspora worldwide is:

Odyssey (bimonthly from Athens, Greece; distributed through New York City)

RADIO AND TELEVISION

Radio stations in the larger markets broadcast programs with news, announcements, and Greek music. The *Yearbook 1995* lists sixty-four shows in seventeen states.[10]

Also listed are twenty-three television programs in twelve states.[11] A national program concerning Orthodoxy and Hellenism may be viewed on cable's Faith and Values channel. The majority of the shows are produced by GOTelecom (Greek Orthodox Telecommunications), an independent company under the auspices of the Greek Orthodox Archdiocese of North and South America.

The span and influence of Greek Americans has been briefly covered here. This chapter does not do justice to their contributions in various organizations and informal endeavors. Their accomplishments testify to the ideals of Hellenism and Orthodoxy and have resulted in countless contributions to society.

1. Theodore Saloutos, *The Greeks in the United States* (Cambridge: Harvard University Press, 1964); Charles C. Moskos, *Greek Americans: Struggle and Success;* George Papaioannou, *The Odyssey of Hellenism in America;* Alice Scourby, *The Greek Americans.*

2. See Charles C. Moskos, "Modern Greek and Greek-American Studies" in *Greek Americans: Struggle and Success,* 187-193; and Dan Georgakas and Charles Moskos, *New Directions in Greek-American Studies* (New York: Pella Publishing Company, 1991).

3. Mary Vardoulakis, *Gold in the Streets* (New York: Dodd, Mead, 1945).

4. Nicholas Gage, *A Place for Us* (Boston: Houghton Mifflin Company, 1989). Nicholas Gage, *Eleni* (New York: Random House, 1983).

5. Harry Mark Petrakis, *A Dream of Kings* (New York: David McKay Company, 1966). *Stelmark: A Family Recollection* (New York: David McKay Company, 1970).

6. Charles C. Moskos, *Greek Americans: Struggle and Success,* 98-104.

7. U.S. Bureau of the Census, *1990 Census of Population and Housing,* Summary Tape File 3.

8. Ibid.

9. Ibid.

10. Greek Orthodox Archdiocese of North and South America, "Radio Programs," *Yearbook 1995,* 193-195.

11. Ibid., "Television Programs," 197-198.

GREECE

⚜ *Visiting Greece*

Images of classical antiquity, ancient gods and goddesses, intense blue skies, and whitewashed buildings lure thousands of tourists to Greece each year. For Greek Americans, the reasons for visiting go beyond those of the typical tourist. It is a chance to renew family ties and touch the roots of their rich heritage.

THEN AND NOW

Today many Greek Americans of different generations enjoy being with their families, relaxing, brushing up on language skills, visiting historic sites of their ancestors, and making religious pilgrimages. The wide use of commercial airplanes has reduced the time and expense of a once arduous trip made by a limited few. The Greek-American tradition of visiting Greece is changing.

In an earlier time, such trips could be a financial and emotional trauma for first-generation immigrants. Many who intended to stay in the United States for only a few years to earn money ended up staying for their entire lives. Some were expected to return with substantial wealth to disperse to the relatives. If they had not been back for many years, their friends and family were much older and in some cases gone. After their arrival back home, some experienced a sense of alienation because of contrasting cultures and values. Although very welcomed, in Greece they were considered Americans, and in America they were considered Greeks. Many felt caught between both countries. They did not feel they belonged in either place, despite their longing for Greece and intense feelings of exile in a foreign land (*xenitiá* — pron *ksenitiá*). Most desired to go back permanently or to visit. The Greek poet George Drosinis expressed their feelings:

> And should it be my fate —
> A black and desolate fate —
> to leave and never to return,
> I will finally ask you to forgive me.
>
> (George Drosinis, "The Soil of Greece")

Such emotionalism is generally less dramatic today, depending on each individual situation. There is better communication by telephone, trips are more frequent, and the two cultures have more in common as economic disparities have lessened. For most Greek Americans, going to Greece is a positive, rewarding experience. They feel at home in both countries.

VISITING THE FAMILY

A primary aim of the trip is visiting the family. Word of a visit spreads quickly, and relatives throw open their doors and hearts. Hospitality (*philoxenia*) remains a national characteristic, a point of honor; and a guest is well attended to, well fed, and pampered. The table is laid and many inquiries are made about other family members. Often visitors are plied with gifts: a bunch of basil, a batch of fresh figs, homemade food such as cheese and cookies, hand-crocheted doilies, and Greek recordings.

GIFTS

Customarily Greek Americans take presents to their families, ranging from inexpensive tokens to extravagant gifts, depending on the circumstances and number of relatives. Popular items include cosmetics, clothing, and money. (Children especially enjoy having a few dollars pressed into their hands.) Some Greek Americans bring substantial sums for a variety of reasons: helping family members in need, building and restoring residences, commissioning icons in a local church. This custom began when early immigrants came to the United States primarily to make money to send back to Greece. However, a trip should not be postponed or canceled because it is believed the gifts would be inadequate. Such a delay is a loss for both the families in America and Greece.

ACCOMMODATIONS

Most Greek Americans stay with their families unless they are traveling outside the area. Family always takes care of family, and failing to stay with them could embarrass your Greek relatives. While traveling there are many fine hotels, and people in small towns often take guests in their homes. If you like local color, the

Greek government has restored and developed some traditional accommodations. Contact the Greek National Tourist Organization (see "Sightseeing" below).

REUNION IN THE VILLAGE

Many Greek Americans emigrated from small villages and enjoy returning there for family reunions. The village (*horió*) is often the central meeting place for those who emigrated from Greece and for Greeks who left the village for larger cities, such as Athens and Thessaloniki, after World War II. The village remains a touchstone and has become a popular summer vacation spot for Greek city residents. Village life is simpler with its fresh air and produce, olive trees, flowers, and extended family of uncles, aunts, cousins, *yiayiá,* and *papoú.*

Many plan their visit to coincide with the *paniyíri,* the celebration of the feast day of the village's patron saint. The *paniyíri* becomes a "homecoming" with celebrations lasting for several days, including church services, music and dancing in the village square, and plenty of delicious food.

In some Greek villages, summer attracts the most visitors. In effect, traditional villages are becoming summer resorts. As a result, some villages are losing their year-round economic base and population. This phenomenon is explored in a film, *My Sweet Village*, by a brother and sister, Greek-Americans Mary and George Chochios, about their town of Vassara in the Peloponnesus.[1]

Village Life

RELAXING

The slower Greek life style appeals to many Greek Americans looking for a change from the hectic pace of the United States.

LEISURE ACTIVITIES

In addition to sightseeing, Greece offers many leisure activities such as cruises, beach lounging, tennis, hiking, festivals, health spas, and horseback riding. Information regarding these activities may be obtained from the Greek National Tourist Organization, a commercial travel agency, or a guidebook.

DAILY ROUTINE

Greeks stop their morning activity around one or two o'clock in the afternoon for a large meal and a rest. At one time everything — shops, businesses, restaurants — closed until around four o'clock in the afternoon. With the increased tourist trade, particularly in the summer, these hours are being modified. (Check with your relatives or hotel concierge.) After the afternoon meal and rest, Greeks often consume thick black coffee and a piece of pastry and begin what seems like a second day of work. Shops stay open until around eight, and dinner is late, between ten or eleven at night. In warm weather, Greeks love to eat outdoors at sidewalk tavernas and restaurants crammed with people. The favorite social activity in the evening is to sit at an outside cafe and people-watch. Those who are energetic go to nightclubs, staying until the early hours of the morning.

SPECIAL PLACES TO EAT AND CELEBRATE

Try some of the special restaurants and nightclubs with a unique Greek flair. A *psistariá* features meat roasted on spits, especially succulent pork, lamb, and chicken. A *psarotavérna* specializes in fresh fish and seafood. The most famous ones are in Piraeus in an area called Mikrolimano (formerly called Tourkolimano). If you cannot read the menu, act like the Greeks: go to the kitchen, look in the pots, and point out what you want!

For a leisurely break, enjoy coffee at a *kafenío* or *oúzo* at an *ouzerí*. Traditionally the *kafenío* has been for men only. Men would gather there to smoke, play cards, and discuss business and politics while clicking their *kombolói*, a string of worry beads worked with the fingers. The men-only rule has been modified, but in some places women still do not "violate" this male preserve. People sip *oúzo*, beer, and wine at an *ouzerí*, while nibbling on tidbits of food.

For late night fun and great music, try a *bouzoúkia*, á nightclub featuring music played on the *bouzoúki,* the predominant Greek instrument. The loud and raucous clubs are the most popular form of entertainment.

SIGHTSEEING

Greeks are justifiably proud of their rich and diverse heritage. With pride they walk the same places where democracy began and worship at churches where Christianity first flourished. World-famous historical attractions are everywhere. For an entertaining and thoughtful overview of Greek life today in its historical context, read *Hellas: A Portrait of Greece* by Nicholas Gage.[2] Also contact the head office of the Greek National Tourist Organization (GNTO) in New York City for free information on sights, leisure activities, travel tips, customs, lodging, and summer programs. The GNTO also provides maps and brochures on specific areas. Write: GNTO, Olympic Tower, 645 Fifth Avenue, Fifth Floor, New York, New York 10022. Branch offices are located in Los Angeles and Chicago. You also may want to purchase one of the many excellent commercial guidebooks that are available.

Guidebook information will not be duplicated here, but listed below are the highlights of ancient Greece, Byzantine Orthodoxy, and modern Greece — essentials to fully appreciate the Hellenic Orthodox heritage.

ANCIENT GREECE

The ancient Greeks shaped much of Western civilization contributing in every area: politics, art, architecture, philosophy, science, drama, mathematics, medicine, law, literature, and language. Prepare for your trip by reading some of the many books available, including histories and the primary works of Homer, Hippocrates, Aristotle, Socrates, Plato, Herodotus, Sophocles, and Euripides. Children can be introduced to their heritage with stories of the myths and explanations of the Greek way of life. *Book of Greek Myths* by Ingri and Edgar Parin d'Aulaire remains the most well-known source for young children.[3]

Essential ancient sites to visit:

Athens	Knossos	Sparta
Delphi	Mycenae	Santorini
Delos	Olympia	Vergina
Epidaurus		

Essential museum to visit:

The National Archeological Museum, Athens

BYZANTINE/ORTHODOX HERITAGE

The Byzantine empire spanned many countries and one thousand years from the fourth to the fifteenth centuries. Some of the most outstanding examples of Byzantine architecture and art still exist in Greece and are listed below.[4] Use a guidebook for further information and attend a service if you are visiting a church:

- *Benaki Museum.* Houses Byzantine miniatures and icons. Located at the corner of Vasilisis Sofias Avenue and Koumbari Streets, Athens.

- *Byzantine Museum.* Houses a reproduction of a Byzantine Orthodox church, icons, frescoes, and ecclesiastical vestments. Located at 22 Vasilisis Sofias Avenue, Athens.

- *Meteora Monasteries.* Six monasteries set atop mountain pinnacles of Meteora. Located approximately 200 miles northwest of Athens.

- *Mistra.* A well-preserved, deserted, Byzantine town featuring architecture and mosaics of the thirteenth to fifteenth centuries. Located approximately three miles west of Sparta.

- *Monastery of Daphni.* Superb eleventh-century architecture and mosaics. Located approximately seven miles northwest of Athens.

- *Monastery of Nea Moni.* Excellent example of eleventh-century mosaics. Located at Nea Moni Church on the Island of Chios in the Aegean.

- *Monastery of Ossios Loukas.* Outstanding eleventh-century architecture with beautiful mosaics. Located southeast of Delphi.

- *Mt. Athos.* The holy mountain of Greek Orthodoxy. Monasteries of special interest: Dionysiou, Megisti Lavra, and Stavronikita. Located on the eastern finger of the Chalkidiki peninsula southeast of Thessaloniki. Only men can visit and special permission must be obtained (see "Pilgrimages" below).

- *Thessaloniki Churches.* Outstanding fifth-century-style architecture and seventh-century mosaics at rebuilt St. Demetrios church. Fourteenth-century architecture and mosaics at the Church of the Holy Apostles.

MODERN GREECE

The following tourist attractions relating to the war of independence from the Ottoman Empire in 1821 are of special interest to Greeks and Greek Americans:

- Patras is the primary location for honoring the Greek declaration of independence in 1821 from the Ottoman Empire. The most popular site is the monastery of Ayia Lavra located one hour outside Patras. It is an accepted tradition that Bishop Germanos declared the revolution here; some historians claim the declaration was made in Patras at St. George's Square. Visit both sites along with the Psila Alonia, a large town square with a statue of the bishop.

- At Messolongi in western Greece, the great English poet Byron died in 1824 while fighting in the Greek revolution. He was buried outside of town in the Garden of Heroes. His stirring poetry helped rally world public opinion for the liberation.

> The mountains look on Marathon —
> And Marathon looks on the sea;
> And musing there an hour alone,
> I dreamed that Greece might still be free,
> For standing on the Persians' grave,
> I could not deem myself a slave.
>
> (George Gordon, Lord Byron, *Don Juan*, Canto iii)

PILGRIMAGES

Greeks and Greek Americans often make religious pilgrimages to churches for retreats, to honor saints, worship, and fulfill or make a *táma* (vow). Thousands of pilgrims visit the following sites each year where healing icons and saints' relics may be located. In some cases, you can spend the night. (See *Saints* for additional sites.)

- *Aegina.* Major site to honor St. Nektarios, a modern-day saint known for healing many ailments. St. Nektarios is buried at St. Nektarios chapel at the Convent of the Holy Trinity on Aegina, an island located south of Piraeus in the Saronic Gulf.

- *The Ionian Village, Bartholomio.* While not a pilgrimage site in a traditional sense, young Greek Americans go on retreat to the Ionian Village in Bartholomio, a small seashore town located south of Patras. Sponsored by the Greek Orthodox Archdiocese of North and South America, the Village program teaches children ages twelve to eighteen and young adults nineteen and older about Orthodoxy and Hellenism. Young people stay at camp, and take occasional trips to nearby sights.

- *Kerkyra, Corfu.* Major site to honor St. Spyridon, patron saint of numerous ailments. He is buried in St. Spyridon Cathedral in Kerkyra, the capital of Corfu, an island in the Ionian Sea, west of mainland Greece.

- *Mt. Athos.* The largest and most important community of Eastern Orthodox monks in the world. Located on Chalkidiki peninsula southeast of Thessaloniki. A limited number of men only may visit for up to four days. Men should apply three or four months in advance by sending a request to: The Ministry of Northern Greece, Directorate for Cultural Affairs, Diikitirion Square, 54623 Thessaloniki, Greece. Include in your request a declaration of intent to be a pilgrim, the date you would like to visit, a letter of recommendation from your consulate, and a copy of your passport. You will be notified in writing that your permit has been approved, but it must be picked up in person in Thessalonika.

- *Patmos.* The sacred island where St. John wrote the Book of Revelation. The monastery of St. John houses an important

Byzantine library and the relics of sixty saints. Located northwest of Rhodes in the Dodecanese Islands.

- *Simi.* Major site to honor St. Michael at the Monastery of
Panormites. A miraculous icon of St. Michael is housed at the
monastery. Located in the Dodecanese islands near Rhodes.

- *Tinos.* Major site to honor the Virgin Mary. Church of the
Evangelistra houses a miracle-working icon of the Theotokos.
An Aegean island located northwest of Mykonos.

- *Thessaloniki.* Major site to honor St. Demetrios who is buried
in St. Demetrios Church. Thessaloniki is located in northern
Greece.

SHOPPING

Information from the Greek National Tourist Organization and
commercial guide books give tips on shopping for clothing, home
furnishings, and handicrafts. The following tips relate to the customs and traditions in this book.

TRADITIONAL HANDICRAFTS IN ATHENS

Embroidery, worry beads (*kombolói*), Greek hats, copper ware,
Greek costumes (including *foustanéles*), and other interesting mer-
chandise may be purchased throughout Athens. If you have time
to browse, start at Monastiraki, the largest flea market, at Ermou
and Athinas streets near the ancient agora. Costume shops are
located on Pandrossou Street. Then walk east to Plaka with its
charming shops at the base of the Parthenon. Visit also the
National Welfare Organization, the Lyceum Club of Greek Women,
the Greek Women's Institution, and the Hellenic Artisan Trades
Cooperative. (See GNTO tour book for addresses.)

Kombolói

RELIGIOUS ITEMS

Icons and *filaktá* may be purchased at monasteries throughout
Greece. In Athens the largest selection of religious items (including icons, censers, crosses, and liturgical supplies) may be found
on Mitropolis Street behind Mitropolis Cathedral, a few streets
north of Plaka and east of Monastiraki.

CERAMICS, SCULPTURE, AND JEWELRY

Most museum shops have beautiful, authentic reproductions of these items.

EXPORTING ANTIQUES AND ARTIFACTS

Genuine antiques and artifacts (including sculpture, ceramics, icons, and furniture) are illegal to export without a permit. Be aware that Greek customs has the right to seize suspect items. To obtain a permit, submit a letter describing the object, its origin, and purpose for export, along with a photograph to the Directorate of Antique Shops and Private Collections, 13 Polygnotou Street, Athens. The letter will be reviewed by the Archaeological Council of the Ministry of Culture to decide whether to issue a permit. If a permit is denied, the state must purchase the antiquity at 50 percent of declared value. An export tax of 50 percent of declared value must be paid if a permit is issued. In effect, the laws are prohibitive, giving rise to a vigorous black market.

---

1. Mary Chiochios (producer) and George Chiochios (director and editor), *My Sweet Village* (Watertown, Mass.: Hellenic Images, 1990).

2. Nicholas Gage, *Hellas: A Portrait of Greece,* 3d. ed. (Efstathiadis Group, 1987)

3. Ingri and Edgar Parin d'Aulaire, *Book of Greek Myths* (Garden City, N.Y.: Doubleday and Company, 1962).

4. With the exception of the Byzantine and Benaki Museums, the church and monastery list was compiled from an article by John Yiannias, "Orthodox Art and Architecture," in *A Companion to the Greek Orthodox Church,* ed. Fotios K. Litsas (New York: Department of Communication, Greek Orthodox Archdiocese of North and South America, 1984), 104-105.

PART THREE

Feast Days, Fasts, and Holidays

Greeks are forever celebrating — personal occasions, feast days, festivals, and political triumphs. Life is a celebration! They offset these jubilant times with interludes of soul-searching and spiritual cleansing through fasting. The intermingling of festivities and quiet contemplation brings a balance to life expressed by the ancient Greeks: *Pan métron áriston* (Moderation in all things is excellent).

The following feast days, fasts, and secular holidays are the most significant in the Greek Orthodox church, however these occasions are not equally observed by Greek Americans. The most commonly observed are described extensively below.

Greek Americans enjoy these holidays within their own community, whereas in Greece the entire country celebrates religious holidays together. The constitution of Greece mandates Orthodoxy as the official faith of the country. This official status makes major religious observances legal holidays. The entire country stops work and spends the day in religious devotion and recreation. For example, on the first day of Lent (Clean Monday) families traditionally go picnicking and fly kites. National legal holidays in Greece are: Oxi Day, Christmas, New Year's Day, Epiphany, Annunciation/Greek Independence Day, First Day of Lent, Good Friday, Easter, May 1 (Flower Festival), and The Dormition of the Virgin Mary.

The church year begins on September 1, the day Christ began his public ministry to the world by preaching in the synagogue. The Ecumenical Patriarchate in Constantinople observes the event with great ceremony. The following calendar does not include the feast days of many popular saints, except when it is a part of a larger observance, such as St. Basil's day. For additional feast days see *Name Days*.

ANNUAL CALENDAR

AUTUMN	September 8	The Nativity of the Mother of God*
	September 14	The Exaltation of the Holy Cross*
	October 28	Oxi Day
	November 15	Christmas Lent begins, ending the eve of December 24
	November 21	The Presentation of the Mother of God in the Temple*

WINTER	December 25	Christmas — The Nativity of Jesus Christ*
	January 1	Circumcision of Jesus Christ
		Feast Day of St. Basil the Great
		New Year's Day
	January 6	Epiphany — The Baptism of Jesus Christ*
	January 7	Feast Day of St. John the Baptist
	January 30	Feast Day of the Three Hierarchs
	February 2	The Presentation of Jesus Christ in the Temple*

SPRING	†	Triodion begins three weeks before Great Lent
	†	Great Lent begins seven weeks before Easter
	March 25	The Annunciation of the Mother of God* and Greek Independence Day
	†	Palm Sunday — The Entry of Jesus Christ into Jerusalem* (one week before Easter)
	†	Holy Week (precedes Easter)
	†	Holy Pascha (Easter) — The Resurrection of Jesus Christ
	†	The Ascension of Jesus Christ*
	†	Pentecost* (Fifty days after Easter)

SUMMER	†	Holy Apostles Lent begins Monday after the week following Pentecost, ending the eve of June 28
	June 29	The Feast Day of Saints Peter and Paul
	June 30	The Feast Day of the Holy Apostles
	August 1	Dormition of the Mother of God Lent begins August 1, ending the evening of August 14
	August 6	The Transfiguration of Jesus Christ*
	August 15	The Dormition of the Mother of God*

---

* One of the Twelve Great Feast Days; eight are events in the life of Christ, and four are in the life of the Mother of God. Easter is not included. It stands alone as the most important Orthodox holiday.

† Moveable date set in relation to Easter.

❖ *Autumn*

THE NATIVITY OF THE MOTHER GOD
September 8

The church honors the Virgin Mary on the day of her birth, for it was through her that God became man. Mary's parents, Joachim and Anna, who had been married for twenty years, had no children. One day an angel appeared in a separate vision to each of them, announcing that they would have a daughter whom they should dedicate to God. Her nativity is celebrated with a Divine Liturgy and hymns composed in her honor.

THE EXALTATION OF THE HOLY CROSS
September 14

The Exaltation of the Holy Cross is one of the most revered observances in all of Orthodoxy. In 325 A.D., after the persecutions against the Christians had just ended, Christians were free to express their religious feelings and to adorn their places of worship with symbols of the faith, such as the cross. Empress Helen, a devout Christian and mother of the Emperor Constantine the Great, went to Jerusalem to undertake a mission to retrieve the cross upon which Christ had been crucified. After a futile search, the Empress was attracted by the scent of a plant called *vasilikós* (basil) in the area where Jesus had been put to death. She ordered excavation, and three crosses were unearthed. A paralyzed person was positioned on each of the crosses to determine the cross upon which Christ had died. When the person was placed on the true cross, he recovered miraculously and walked. On September 14, the event was celebrated. Patriarch Makarios, who had also witnessed the miracle at the historic site, raised the cross and blessed the people with it as they responded, "Lord, have mercy" (*"Kýrie, eléison"*).

Orthodoxy honors this event on September 14 at a special service in which the priest carries a small cross on a tray decorated with *vasilikós* in procession throughout the church (see *illustration*). *Vasilikós*, the traditional flower of the Orthodox church, is also

The Exaltation of the Holy Cross

used during the feast days of Epiphany, the Veneration of the Holy Cross, and any time the service of *ayiasmós* (blessing of the water), takes place.

The church has established September 14 as a day of fasting equal to that of Good Friday, as a reminder that Christ died on the cross; many parishioners take communion that day. The Gospel reading at the Divine Liturgy describes the Crucifixion of Christ. After the service, each parishioner receives a basil sprig.

OXI DAY
October 28

Oxi Day is a national secular holiday in Greece commemorating its resistance to Axis (Italian) forces during World War II. On October 28, 1940, Benito Mussolini, the dictator of Italy, demanded that Greece give free passage to Italian troops through Greek territory. The Greek Prime Minister, Ioannes Metaxas, responded with a resounding *"Oxi!"* (No! — pron. *Óchi*) Although outnumbered, the Greek forces fought valiantly for six months, routing the Italians, who retreated into Albania. The victory was the first Allied success against the Axis countries and aroused great ethnic pride. Winston Churchill said of the victory: "Hence we will not say that Greeks fight like heroes but that heroes fight like Greeks."

In America, Oxi Day is remembered at church with a special doxology, a service of thanksgiving and glorification held after the Divine Liturgy. Dignitaries attend, and poems are usually recited in Greek by children. The congregation stands to sing the Greek National Anthem, "Hymn to Liberty" ("Se Gnorizo Apo Tin Kopsi"). (See *Greek Independence Day* for lyrics.) In many communities a separate program also takes place where poems are recited, songs connected with the event are sung, and plays are presented. These programs may be sponsored by the Greek school of the parish or other Greek-American organizations.

Oxi, the day of defiance, is still widely celebrated on October 28 as a national holiday throughout Greece. Homes fly the Greek flag, and villages and towns are draped in blue and white bunting. Similar to Veteran's Day in America, it is a day to remember those who died in military service. Many people attend church where there is a liturgy and memorial for soldiers. A wreath is placed at the tomb of the Unknown Soldier, and military parades are common. Since most of the fighting in 1940 took place in northern Greece, Thessaloniki has the largest parade. In Athens an electric sign saying, "*Oxi*," shines over the city from Lycabettus Hill during the last few days of October.

CHRISTMAS LENT
November 15 - December 24

Christmas is preceded by a forty-day period of fasting. For the devout Greek Orthodox, Christmas Lent should be somber, unlike the Protestant pre-Christmas period of parties and excessive eating. The Orthodox way demands fasting, prayer, and alms, similar to Great Lent that precedes Easter. In practice, however, most Greek Americans do not strictly observe this fast. The Christmas Lenten period begins on November 15 and ends the eve of December 24.

THE PRESENTATION OF THE MOTHER OF GOD
IN THE TEMPLE
November 21

At the age of three, Mary's parents, Joachim and Anna, dedicated her to God and presented her to the temple. As was customary, dedicated children stayed with holy men of the temple for twelve years, receiving the finest education. At fifteen, Mary came home to her parents, and was visited soon thereafter by the Archangel Gabriel, announcing that she would be the Mother of Christ. She and her parents are honored with special church hymns and writings.

The Nativity of Jesus Christ

❧ *Winter*

Christmas, New Year, and Epiphany (Dodecameron)

December 25, January 1, and January 6

The Greek Orthodox combine the holidays of Christmas, New Year, and Epiphany into a period called the Dodecameron (twelve days — pron. *thothecámeron*). The period starts with Christmas on December 25 and ends January 6 with Epiphany. Once Christmas starts, the season is one of continuous celebration (except for one day of fasting in January), to commemorate some of the year's most important holidays.

Christmas

Christmas Lent

For the devout Orthodox, the Christmas season begins with Christmas Lent (November 15 to December 24), a subdued period observed by only a few. Most Greek Americans celebrate Christmas the American way, participating in a flurry of activities during the month of December, including decorations, Santa Claus, parties, and rich food. However, except for preparing food and purchasing a few gifts, this is not in keeping with the Orthodox tradition of fasting and reflection before the major feast day of Christmas. Many of the faithful, however, fast and take communion during the week before Christmas.

Significance and Church Services

Christmas commemorates the birth of Jesus Christ. The story of the Annunciation to the Virgin Mary, the journey with Joseph to Bethlehem, and the birth of Jesus in a stable is retold to worshipers each year. The story reminds the faithful that God sent his Son to save the world and that they, too, can find new life through Christ.

At one time the Christmas church service began at midnight, but this has changed in many American churches to attract greater participation. Now the Divine Liturgy may be offered early Christmas Eve and again on Christmas Day. In the Divine Liturgy the hymns and the Biblical readings declare the Christmas message of hope and renewal. Instead of a pastoral sermon, a message from the Archbishop of North and South America is usually read from the pulpit. Christmas pageants of the Nativity may also be presented by the children. The pageant is not typically Greek, but rather an adaptation of a European tradition.

Parishioners may sing both English and Greek carols at the end of the service. The Orthodox carols are rich in theology, and the best known religious Greek carol is "I Yennisis Sou" ("Your Birth, O Christ").[1] (See below)

Another beautiful hymn comes from *The Festal Menaion*:

Kontakion

Today the Virgin gives birth to Him who is above all being, and the earth offers a cave to Him whom no man can approach. Angels with shepherds give glory, and Magi journey with a star. For unto us is born a young Child, the pre-eternal God.[2]

I Yennisis Sou

I - yén - ni - sís sou Chri - sté o THe ós i-

món.   a - né - ti - le to   kó - smo to   fos to tis

gnó - se - os   en af - ti gar i tis   á - stris la-

trév - on - des   i - po a - sté - ros e - thi - thá - skon - do.

Se   pro - ski - nín   ton   í - li - on   tis thi - ke - o-

sí - nis   ke se yi - nó - skin ex   i - psous a-

na - to - lín.   Ky - ri - e,   thó - xa   si.

Your birth, O Christ our God, brought to the world the light of knowledge. For through it those who had adored the stars were taught by a star to worship you, the sun of righteousness, and to know you as the dawn from heaven, O Lord, glory to you.

CHRISTMAS FOOD AND FESTIVITIES

THE *KÁLANDA*

On Christmas Eve Day in Greece, young people, carrying triangles, small drums, and harmonicas, go in groups from house to house, singing the *kálanda* (carols) about the birth of Christ. (See "Kalanda Christouyennon" below) Before singing the children ask the traditional question, *"Na ta poúme?"* ("May we sing it for you?"). (The question is asked so that songs will not be sung at a house in mourning.) Some children carry small ships of cardboard, wood, or tin in honor of St. Basil who came to Greece by sea from his home in Caesarea to bring presents to the children. Decorated with the Greek flag and the word "Ellas," the ships hold the sweets and money given to each caroler at the end of the *kálanda*. Sometimes the children are welcomed into the house for treats. In America, this is becoming a popular activity for Greek school students.

SWEETS

The most traditional Christmas cookies are the white, powdery *kourabiéthes* and the rich *melomakárona*.

CHRISTMAS BREAD (CHRISTOPSOMO)

Christmas bread (Christopsomo — pron. *Christópsomo*) or *kouloúra tou Christoú* (round bread of Christ) graces the Christmas table. It is usually a round loaf often made with the same ingredients as Easter bread. Nuts and dried fruits may be added. Some families attend church on Christmas Eve and return home for a meal that begins with the cutting of the Christopsomo by the head of the household. Others wait until a main meal on Christmas Day. The head of the house makes the sign of the cross on the bread with a knife while saying, "In the name of the Father, the Son, and the Holy Spirit," and then cuts a piece for each person with a wish of *"Kalá Christoúyena"* ("Good Christmas") or *"Chrónia pollá"* ("Many years"). (See recipe below)

Kalanda Christouyennon
(Christmas Kalanda)

1. Ka - lín es - pé - ra - n ár - chon-
2. ná - te sí me-

tes, ki a - n i - ne
ron stin vi - THle-

o - ri - smós sas, Chri - stoú ti
é - m tin pó - li, i ou - ra-

THí - a yén - ni - si
ní a - gál - lon - te

na i - pó st'ar - chon - ti - kó
ke ke her' - i phí - sis

sas. 2.Chris - tós yen - ó - li.

1. Good evening, noble folk. if you so command,
   I will tell your noble household of the birth of Christ.
2. Today Christ is being born in Bethlehem,
   and the heavens rejoice along with all of nature.

241

———❦———

CHRISTOPSOMO OR *KOULOÚRA TOU CHRISTOÚ*

Make a half recipe of Easter bread (see *Easter Season*). Add:

¼ cup toasted pine nuts	1 cup golden raisins
¾ cup chopped walnuts	½ cup chopped dried apricots
or blanched almonds	

Soak dried fruit for one hour and drain. (Candied fruit may be substituted.) Follow Easter bread recipe, adding the fruit, nuts, and extra flour if needed. Shape into one ball for a greased 14" round cake pan or form two balls for two greased 8" round cake pans. Omit the red eggs and decorate with sesame seeds or sliced blanched almonds and/or a cross made of dough.

CHRISTMAS DINNER

Christmas menus vary from region to region, but turkey or pork is the most common main course.

❦

CHRISTMAS DINNER

Grape leaves, small pies, meatballs
Christopsomo and *avgolémono* soup
Roast pork or stuffed turkey
Roasted potatoes and Greek salad
Spinach and cheese pies
Fruit
Melomakárona, kourabiéthes, thíples, and *baklavá*

❦

GREETINGS

Wish someone a Merry Christmas with *"Kalá Christoúyena"* ("Good Christmas") or *"Chrónia pollá"* ("Many years") or *"Ke tou chrónou"* ("And to next year").

GIFTS

Most Greek Americans exchange gifts on Christmas Eve or Christmas Day, not at New Year's as in Greece. Greek-American youngsters look to Santa Claus, not St. Basil, for their presents.

NAME-DAY CELEBRATIONS

In Greece Christmas Day is a very popular time to hold open-house name day parties to honor persons with names such as Chris, Christos, Christine, Emmanuel, and Emmanuela. This is not widely done in the United States.

KALIKÁNTZARI SUPERSTITION

An old folk belief in Greece holds that mischievous goblins called *kalikántzari* appear during the Dodecameron. The *kalikántzari* live beneath the surface of the earth and chop away at a large tree trunk, the foundation of the earth. With their chopping they attempt to destroy God's work. They almost succeed when they hear the noise created by the birth of Christ. They come to earth on December 25 to disrupt people's lives with pranks and tricks such as spilled milk, disappearing keys, and broken glass. It is common to blame mishaps this time of the year on the *kalikántzari*.

Fire, light, and holy water protect people from the *kalikántzari*. On Christmas Eve some people in rural Greece light a fire to prevent them from coming down the chimney. This Christ log (*skarkántzalos*) burns until Epiphany. Sometimes large bonfires are built in the villages of Greece, and people carry a candle with them at night for protection. The little imps roam the earth until Epiphany when holy water cleans them away.

New Year

NEW YEAR'S EVE

CARD PARTIES

Greek Americans love to party and play cards on New Year's Eve. It is said that you sample your luck for the coming year on the last day of the old. Card playing may follow a dinner party or just be combined with coffee and sweets, especially *loukoumáthes*. Generally, just before midnight the lights are turned out and then turned on again at twelve to shouts of *"Kalí Chroniá"* ("Good year"), "Happy New Year," and *"Chrónia pollá"* ("Many years"). It is customary to cut a Vasilopita at this time.

VASILOPITA

The most popular New Year's custom is the cutting of the Vasilopita (bread for St. Basil — pron. *Vasilópita*). Everyone hopes to get the lucky coin baked inside the *píta*.

Legend of the Vasilopita

The Vasilopita commemorates a miracle performed by St. Basil while serving as a bishop. The legend varies as to how St. Basil became the guardian of the gold, silver, and jewelry of the people of Caesarea. Some say thieves had taken the valuables from the village, and they were recovered. Others say it was a tax the government asked St. Basil to collect, but then decided to cancel. In either case, St. Basil became responsible for returning the riches to the people. However, they could not agree on the rightful owners. St. Basil suggested that the women bake the valuables inside a large *píta*. When he cut the *píta*, each owner miraculously received the right valuable. Today a single coin is baked inside each loaf to honor this miracle, and the recipient has good luck for the coming year.

Cutting the Vasilopita

Greek Americans enjoy Vasilopita for most of the month of January. They cut the first *píta* at midnight on New Year's Eve and repeat the ritual at social occasions and community functions through-out the first half of January. Before the cutting, everyone sings the *kálanda* ("Kalanda Protochronias") announcing the new year and St. Basil.

A short poem popular in Constantinople may also be said by one of the children:

Pérno thíno to mahéri	I take the knife and put it
Stou Babáka mou to héri,	in my father's hand,
Yia na kópsi tin pitítsa	So he can cut the Vasilopita
Na mou thósi miá fetítsa!	and give one slice to me!

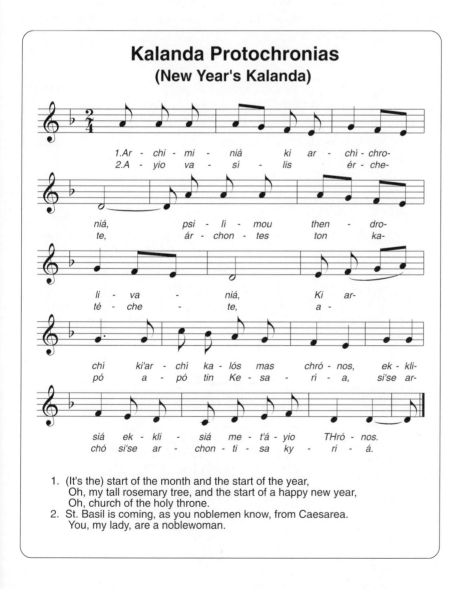

Kalanda Protochronias
(New Year's Kalanda)

1.Ar - chi - mi - niá ki ar - chí - chro-
2.A - yio va - sí - lis ér - che-

niá, psi - lí - mou then dro-
te, ár - chon - tes ton ka-

li - va - niá, Ki ar-
té - che - te, a -

chí ki'ar - chí ka - lós mas chró - nos, ek - kli-
pó a - pó tin Ke - sa - rí - a, si'se ar-

siá ek - kli - siá me - t'á - yio THró - nos.
chó si'se ar - chon - ti - sa ky - ri - á.

1. (It's the) start of the month and the start of the year,
   Oh, my tall rosemary tree, and the start of a happy new year,
   Oh, church of the holy throne.
2. St. Basil is coming, as you noblemen know, from Caesarea.
   You, my lady, are a noblewoman.

The head of the household makes the sign of the cross on the *píta* with a knife while saying, "In the name of the Father, the Son, and the Holy Spirit, Amen." Pieces are cut in a specific order. Protocol varies, but the first piece is always for Christ. It should be wrapped and placed in the home *ikonostási.* The second and third pieces are usually for the Virgin Mary and St. Basil, and the fourth for the poor. The head of the house receives the next piece and the rest of the family according to their ages, including those members who are not at home. Then pieces should be cut for guests according to their place of honor, mentioning those of highest esteem first. The person cutting the Vasilopita wishes each recipient, *"Chrónia pollá"* ("Many years") or *"Kalí chroniá"* ("Good year"), while distributing each piece. (In Greece a little Vasilopita and other food may be left out for St. Basil just as Americans leave food for Santa. St. Basil visits each house on his name day, January 1, to bring gifts to the children.)

At a public Vasilopita observance, Christ, Mary, St. Basil, and the poor are recognized before the members of the community. Then those of highest esteem are mentioned, such as the archbishop, priest's wife, presidents of the parish council and Philoptochos, and other dignitaries.

Vasilopita (Bread or Cake)

Vasilopita may be either a bread or a cake, depending on the region of Greece from which your family originated. Some regions use the recipe for Easter bread but decorate the top differently. Others make a rich, sweet cake. All versions are round and include a lucky coin. Arrange greens, nuts, and fruit (fresh and dried) around the loaf or cake.

VASILOPITA (BREAD)

Make a half recipe of Easter bread (see *Easter Season*). Shape into one ball for a greased 14" round pan or two smaller balls for two greased 8" round pans. Hide a coin somewhere in the dough. Omit the red eggs, and decorate with blanched almonds or strands of dough spelling out the year.

Vasilopita (Cake)

1 cup regular butter	1 cup milk (room temperature)
2 cups sugar	1 cup crushed almonds
7 eggs separated	1 tablespoon *machlēpi*
1 teaspoon almond extract	1 scant teaspoon *masticha*
2 teaspoon vanilla	¼ cup slivered almonds (top)
3 cups flour, sifted	1 coin
3 tablespoon baking powder	

Cream butter and sugar for ten minutes. Add egg yolks and flavorings. Add remaining ingredients, alternating milk with the flour. Fold in stiffly beaten egg whites until blended. Grease and flour a 14" round cake pan or two 8" round cake pans. Insert coin in batter and sprinkle top with crushed almonds or slivers. Bake in 350°F oven for 45 minutes. Cake is ready when an inserted toothpick removes cleanly. If more baking is required, put aluminum foil lightly over the top to prevent burning and continuing baking. Makes one large *pita* or two small.

NEW YEAR'S DAY

CHURCH SERVICES

The church celebrates two special events on January 1: The Circumcision of Christ and the Feast Day of St. Basil.

Circumcision of Christ

As a member of the Jewish religion, Christ was circumcised on the eighth day after his birth and given his name. This important event is commemorated in a church service. "And at the end of eight days, when he was circumcised, he was called Jesus, the name given him by the angel..." Luke 2:21

Feast Day of St. Basil the Great

The Orthodox observe the name day of St. Basil The Great on January 1 with a Divine Liturgy written by him. St. Basil, widely honored and revered, is one of the three great church hierarchs along with St. Gregory the Theologian and St. John Chrysostom. St. Basil lived in the fourth century working as a missionary, monk, and philanthropist. He prescribed rules of monasticism and began institutions of care for the sick, elderly, underprivileged, and orphaned. The Vasilopita, gifts, the *kálanda,* and name day parties are in his honor.

FESTIVITIES

Greetings

"Kalí chroniá" ("Good year") and *"Chrónia pollá"* ("Many years")

Name-Day Celebrations

This is a popular day to hold name-day parties for persons named Vasili, Basil, Vaso, Vasiliki, William, and Bill. It combines the joy of the new year with honoring St. Basil and his namesakes.

Traditional Food

Pork and turkey are the most popular main courses. In one region of Greece, a rooster is killed on the house's threshold to make the house strong; then *avgolémeno* soup and chicken are served. If the Vasilopita was not cut the night before, it is cut at the main meal and given to any guests who come to visit.

Superstitions

People associate luck and good fortune with the start of the new year. Some Greek Americans better their chances with a few of the following practices on New Year's day:

- Open the windows at midnight to let out the evil spirits.
- Say *"kaló potharikó"* (good omen) when the first person enters the house after midnight. Good luck for the year is related to that first person who must enter with the right foot (*póthi* or *pothári*). Many families select someone, such as the head of the house, the oldest son, or the youngest child. Families who have not been out of the house, hope someone strong and healthy will enter first, and they welcome the person with

sweets and/or money. Some people prefer an icon to enter the home first. An individual holds the icon in outstretched arms so that it crosses the threshold before anyone.

- Try to be the first to hear something good and happy.
- Eat something sweet at breakfast to sweeten the new year.
- Be happy and positive. Do not quarrel, cry, or lose anything. Whatever you do this day, it is said you will do all year.
- Set an abundant table of food to assure plenty.
- Wear new clothes, to be bright and clean all year.

Epiphany

The holiday season ends with the great feast of Epiphany or Theophania (God appears). It ranks after Easter and Christmas in importance. The faithful appreciate the customs of Epiphany, especially in receiving the blessed holy water. The events are remembered on three separate days: January 5, Eve of Theophania (Lesser Blessing of the Water); January 6, Theophania (Greater Blessing of the Water); and January 7, Feast Day of St. John the Baptist.

FASTING

For the Orthodox faithful, fasting is widely practiced the day before Theophania. Fasting prepares the body and mind to receive the holy water distributed at the church service. Since services are held on January 5 and January 6, fasting may be on January 4 or 5, depending on which service you attend. Most Greek Americans attend the service on January 6 and fast January 5.

SIGNIFICANCE AND CHURCH SERVICES

Theophania celebrates God's first public revelation of the identity of Jesus, the manifestation of the Godhead as three persons (the Father, Son, and Holy Spirit), Christ's baptism, and beginning of Christ's public ministry.

> In those days Jesus came from Nazareth of Galilee and was baptized by John in the Jordan. And when he came up out of the water, immediately he saw the heavens opened and the Spirit descending upon him like a dove; and a voice came from heaven, "Thou art my beloved Son, with whom I am well pleased." Mark 1:9-11

The special services commemorating these events on January 5 (Lesser Blessing of the Water) and January 6 (Greater Blessing of the Water) are the same despite their names.

During the service, the Holy Spirit is invoked to sanctify the water (*ayiasmós*), and the cross is dipped into it three times, symbolic of Christ's own immersion into the Jordan river. The holy water sanctifies and heals the faithful. Parishioners then come to the front of the church to be blessed by the priest, who dips a large sprig of basil or evergreen into the water and touches the parishioner's head saying, *"Chrónia pollá."* The parishioner kisses the cross and the priest's hand before receiving a small bottle of holy water to take home.

EVE OF THEOPHANIA

ATTENDING CHURCH

On January 5, parishioners may attend a Divine Liturgy and the Lesser Blessing of the Water service. Most Greek Americans fast on January 5 and attend the service on January 6.

THE *KÁLANDA*

Children in Greece also sing the *kálanda* on this day, announcing the baptism of Christ.

Epiphany has come — illumination of the world — and great rejoicing in the Lord. By Jordan River — stands our good Mary — and thus she begs St. John — "St. John Baptist — it is in your power — to baptize the child of God."[3]

EXORCISING THE *KALIKÁNTZARI*

On the eve of Theophania, young men in northern Greek villages dress in frightening masks and costumes and wear jingling bells to imitate the *kalikántzari* and scare them away. Large bonfires are also lit on the eve of Theophania to expel evil spirits.

Greek village priests often visit each home that evening, sprinkling holy water in all the rooms with a sprig of basil. This is the only method approved by the church for ridding the house of evil spirits.

THEOPHANIA: THE FEAST OF LIGHTS (TON PHOTON)

ATTENDING CHURCH

On January 6 the faithful attend a Divine Liturgy and the Great Blessing of the Water service to celebrate Theophania, also called "Ton Photon" ("Feast of Lights") with reference to the spiritual illumination of the Holy Spirit. The service commemorates the baptism of Christ and the manifestation of God in three persons as described above.

Large numbers of people attend church to be blessed and to receive holy water which they take home in small bottles provided by the church. Some parishioners bring their own bottles often made specifically for holy water. In most churches in America the blessing is held indoors, and the water is contained in a large urn. Some communities hold outdoor celebrations by a body of water.

CELEBRATING IN TARPON SPRINGS, FLORIDA

In the United States, the most famous outdoor service is conducted by the Archbishop of the Greek Orthodox Church of North and South America in Tarpon Springs, Florida. It resembles many outdoor services in Greece, including the largest one at Piraeus that is attended by the prime minister and the archbishop of Greece.

In Tarpon Springs a great procession of altar boys, children dressed as angels, young people in Greek costumes, political dignitaries, and church officials carrying large icons makes its way from the church to the bay on streets decorated with flags, pennants, and flowers. At noon the archbishop blesses the water, and a white dove is released. The archbishop throws a cross into the water while church bells ring, and boats blow their whistles. Young men dive into the water to retrieve the cross; the diver who recovers it is formally blessed back at the church and is said to have good fortune for the year. After the ceremony, a festival features traditional Greek food, dancing, and music.

HOLY WATER

BLESSING OF THE HOME

It is customary to invite your priest to bless your home with holy water within a few weeks following Theophania. Prepare by cleaning the house, opening and lighting all the rooms. Place a clean bowl of water, *kandíli*, icon, and incense burner on a small table. The priest will bless the water by dipping a cross in it and repeating a blessing. Using a basil or evergreen sprig dipped in water as a sprinkler, he will go to each room and sprinkle it in the four corners, exorcising evil spirits. Save some of the holy water in a bottle in your *ikonostási* and pour the remainder on plants.

PERSONAL USE

According to Orthodox doctrine, holy water has the power to sanctify and heal. Have each family member drink a small amount of the holy water from Epiphany and/or the home blessing. Keep the unused holy water in your home *ikonostási* for future use: times of adversity, before starting a new venture or trip, to give thanks, or when someone is ill. You may drink it and/or put it on an afflicted part of the body. To rid the house of evil spirits, it should be sprinkled in the four corners of each room, so no one will step on it. (In rural Greece the holy water is sprinkled in the fields and on the animals.)

FEAST DAY OF ST. JOHN THE BAPTIST

On January 7 the church honors St. John the Baptist. St. John's baptism of Christ has made him one of the most significant saints in Orthodoxy. The patron saint of godparents, he always stands on Christ's left side at each church *ikonostásion*.

John is one of the most popular Greek names. Most people named John (including Yianni, Joanna, Yiana) celebrate their name day on January 7. In Greece many homes are open for parties — the last festive occasion of the Dodecameron. So many families choose this name that there is an old Greek expression, *"Spíti horís Yiánni prokopí then káni."* (A home without a person named John will not succeed.)

Other Winter Feast Days

FEAST DAY OF THE THREE HIERARCHS
January 30

Three outstanding hierarchs, St. Basil the Great, St. Gregory the Theologian, and St. John Chrysostom, are honored as patron saints of education and culture on January 30. They are among the early church fathers who recognized the importance of the Greek language and culture in developing and advancing Orthodoxy.

In formulating Christianity, the church fathers questioned the compatibility of pagan classical thinking and Christianity. Should the heritage of the Greco-Roman world into which Christianity emerged be discarded and condemned? Church fathers such as St. Basil the Great, St. Gregory the Theologian, and St. John Chrysostom reasoned it should not. St. Basil advised that virtue could be found in classical thinking. One should "look for the honey and avoid the poison."[4]

These church fathers understood the importance of letters and that through the universal language of Greek, the Gospel could be spread to many. The Christian faith was developed in the Greek language and Greek thought. Instead of being discarded, ancient Greek concepts concerning the nature of the soul, man's personal relationship with God, and the ideal spiritual world, became part of Christianity.

The Greek Orthodox church still cherishes the Hellenistic influence and makes every effort to preserve it. Most Greek schools in America are sponsored by churches, and every year the Archdiocese of North and South America proclaims the week around January 30 as the week of Greek Letters. Greek school teachers are honored and recognized with a short program. Some churches hold an *artoklasía* service in honor of the Three Hierarchs.

THE PRESENTATION OF JESUS CHRIST
February 2

Forty days after the birth of Christ, his parents brought him to the temple in accordance with the Jewish custom of offering the first male child to the service of God. Christ was received by Simeon, an elderly prophet whom God had promised would not die before seeing the Messiah. Simeon's prayer is repeated during the service: "Lord, now lettest thou thy servant depart in peace, according to thy word; for mine eyes have seen thy salvation which thou hast prepared in the presence of all peoples, a light for revelation to the Gentiles, and for glory to thy people Israel." Luke:2:29-32

Today each newborn child is brought to church after forty days, reenacting the journey of Christ and the Virgin Mary. (See *Birth of Children*)

The Resurrection of Jesus Christ

❖ *Spring*

The Easter Season

Easter, the celebration of the Resurrection of Christ, is the most important Greek Orthodox holiday. The season culminates with a midnight service in a darkened church illuminated by hundreds of candles. Later the faithful feast on red Easter eggs and succulent spring lamb. Preceding this celebration is a somber period of intense self-examination for the individual, a period of rejecting an old way of life to gain a new one.

The date of Orthodox Easter changes each year, usually occurring on a date different from that of the West. (Occasionally the dates coincide.) The Orthodox calculate the date according to a canon adopted in 325: Easter is determined on the old Julian calendar as the first Sunday after the first full moon following the vernal equinox. Passover must always come before Easter.

The Orthodox use the Julian calendar only for Easter and dates dependent on it, such as Lent and Pentecost. The Julian is thirteen days behind the new Gregorian calendar on which the rest of the Greek Orthodox year is based. The fixing of the Orthodox date for Easter was a political compromise so that all Orthodox churches, including those who use the Julian year-round (Old Calendarists), could celebrate Easter on the same day.

The Easter season spans eleven weeks: The Triodion (consisting of Pre-Lent, Great Lent, and Holy Week), Easter, and Bright Week. Participation in the traditions and customs over the entire period can give your Easter celebration profound meaning.

PRE-LENT

Two conflicting messages compete during the pre-Lenten season. The church stresses themes of repentance and sacrifice, urging its parishioners to prepare for the rigors of Great Lent. Secular society, however, indulges and parties during a three-week period called carnival before the long fast of Great Lent.

CARNIVAL (*APOKRIÁ*) — A SECULAR CELEBRATION

Pre-Lenten celebration is common throughout the world. Some of the most famous festivals are carnival in Rio de Janeiro and Mardi Gras in New Orleans, Louisiana. In Greece, carnival (*apokriá* — abstinence from meat) lasts three weeks: Announcing Week (beginning of carnival), Meat Week (last week to eat meat), and Cheese Week (last week to eat dairy products).

During those three weeks in Greece there are masked balls, parades, fireworks, and plays. Masquerading is very popular, and it is common for small bands in costume, playing musical instruments, to roam the streets. Short street plays and parodies are often performed in village squares. Hundreds of children dress in their best and stroll through the parks with their parents. Zappeion Gardens in Athens is one of the most popular spots for such a stroll. Patras in the Peloponnesus is reputed to have the largest and best carnival in Greece, including a large parade with floats. A popular Cretan saying is, "In carnival even old women go wild!"

Carnival is not widely celebrated in the United States although masked balls, usually sponsored by Greek societies, are popular and enjoyed by many Greek Americans.

RELIGIOUS PREPARATION

In contrast to the secular celebrations, the church teaches its parishioners to prepare themselves for Great Lent and Easter with diet modification and themes of humility, judgment, repentance, and forgiveness. The Pre-Lenten period lasts three weeks, but includes four Sundays. Text for the following Sunday services may be found in *The Lenten Triodion* by Mother Mary and Kallistos Ware.[5]

SUNDAY #1 — THE PUBLICAN AND THE PHARISEE (LUKE 18:10-14)

The reading suggests that parishioners should emulate the humility of the publican, not the false piousness of the pharisee.

SUNDAY #2 — THE PRODIGAL SON (LUKE 15:11-32)

The reading implores the faithful to repent and return to God the Father, just as the prodigal son returned to his earthly father.

Meat Week (Kreatini)

Meat Week begins on Monday two weeks before Great Lent and is the last week to eat meat. Greek Americans do not cook special food, but in Greece roast pork is especially popular and tavernas are always packed on Tsiknopempti (Aromatic Thursday). In the villages this was the traditional week to slaughter the family pig that had been growing all year. Leftovers would be smoked and eaten after Easter.

First Saturday of Souls (Psychosavato)

The deceased are remembered at a special service called "Saturday of Souls" held four times a year: the two Saturdays prior to Great Lent, the first Saturday of Great Lent, and the Saturday before Pentecost. Orthodox believe that it is the duty of the living to remember and pray for the deceased. A general prayer is said for specific individuals and all unknown souls who have no one to pray for them. Parishioners bring small dishes of *kóllyva* to the church and submit a list of first names of deceased loved ones to the priest. For further details see *Death and Mourning*.

SUNDAY #3 — MEAT FARE SUNDAY — THE LAST JUDGMENT (MATTHEW 25: 31-46)

If strict fasting is observed, this is the last day to eat meat until Easter. The reading for the day states that an individual will be judged in heaven according to the kindnesses shown to others on earth.

Cheese Week (Tirini)

For the observant Cheese Week is the last week to eat animal products until Easter. Typical dishes include those made with milk, cheese, and eggs, such as macaroni and cheese, *tirópita* (cheese pie), and custards.

Second Saturday of Souls

See *Death and Mourning*.

**SUNDAY #4 — CHEESE FARE SUNDAY — FORGIVENESS
(MATTHEW 6:14-21).**

Animal products are eaten for the last time this day if a strict fast is going to be kept. In some parts of Greece, the custom is to eat an egg at the end of the meal and say, "With an egg I close my mouth, with an egg I shall open it again." This refers to the red Easter egg eaten after the Easter Resurrection service.

The reading emphasizes the importance of forgiving others, stating that only those who forgive will be forgiven. It also suggests that fasting should be done in a private, humble manner — an appropriate suggestion for Great Lent that begins the next day.

GREAT LENT

The Orthodox observe Great Lent (Lent) more widely than the other three Lenten periods (see *Fasting*). Great Lent precedes the most important event in the church, Christ's Resurrection. For six weeks (seven including Holy Week), the faithful modify their diet and behavior to achieve spiritual renewal. Sometimes this goal gets lost in the flurry of cooking Lenten dishes, buying new outfits, and, in America, putting together Easter baskets. While all these activities are a part of the Easter season, the most important preparation for Easter should be spiritual.

PURPOSE

Great Lent is a tremendous spiritual challenge for each individual. Three basic components are emphasized: fasting of body and soul, prayer, and philanthropy. Through self-examination, fasting, and giving to charity the old way of life can be shed. Just as Christ received new life after his death, a new life is given at Easter to those individuals who have prepared themselves. The soul must be cleansed by genuine repentance, the breaking of sinful habits, forgiveness and reconciliation. The challenge is to recover the image of God within oneself (*théosis*). Lent and Easter offer each parishioner that opportunity.

SUGGESTED READING AND TRANSLATIONS

For a deeper understanding of the season, read *Great Week and Pascha in the Greek Orthodox Church* by A.C. Calivas and *Great Lent* by Alexander Schmemann.[6]   You may want to use English translations of the Greek services while attending church. For Pre-Lent, Great Lent, and Holy Week, the classic translation is *The Lenten Triodion* by Mother Mary and Kallistos Ware. *The Services for Holy Week and Easter* by Nomikos Michael Vaporis is published by Holy Cross Orthodox Press. The Easter service and the services of the week following Easter may be found in the *Pentecostarion.*[7]   Since most churches do not supply these books, parishioners buy their own copies and bring them to church.

You may be able to buy these and other appropriate books from your church, or you can order them from Holy Cross Orthodox Bookstore and/or Light and Life Publishing Company.[8]

DEMEANOR

You can observe Lent by attending church frequently, praying, fasting, giving confession, taking communion, giving to charity, and reading religious materials. Dress should be modest, especially in church. Certain social events such as large parties and dancing should be avoided. For this reason, the Orthodox church prohibits weddings and dances during Lent.

FASTING

The purpose of fasting is to prepare for communion and rebirth at Easter. Forgoing food is a tangible symbol of controlling indulgences, both physical and mental. Fasting should not become an obsession or an end in itself, as stated in a hymn from Cheese Fare Wednesday:

> In vain do you rejoice in not eating, O soul
> For you abstain from food,
> But from passions you are not purified.
> If you have no desire for improvement,
> You will be despised as a lie in the eyes of God.[9]

Fasting during Lent varies with each individual. A few parishioners observe a strict fast for the entire Lenten season: no meat, fish, animal products, olive oil, or alcohol. A less strict approach eliminates the above foods the first week of Lent, each Wednesday and Friday, and all of Holy Week. Note that fish is permitted on two days during Lent: The Annunciation of the Mother of God (March 25) and Palm Sunday.

You can prepare interesting Lenten food (Sarakostiana) from the allowed list of legumes, vegetables, fruit, and shellfish. These include the popular *spanakórizo* (baked spinach and rice), bean soup (*fasolátha*), eggplant casserole, and Lenten *koulourákia*. The following is a typical Lenten menu.

⚜

LENTEN MENU

Taramosaláta and bread
Vegetable relish tray
Fasolátha and salad
Fruit

⚜

WEEKLY SCHEDULE

Week #1 — Clean Week (Kathara Evdomada)

Clean Monday (Kathari Deftera)

Clean Monday is the first day of Lent, and individuals wish each other *"Kalí Sarakostí"* ("Good Lent"). In the United States, fasting begins and lasts all week. Many people take communion at the Divine Liturgy of the Presanctified Gifts on either Wednesday or Friday.

In Greece, however, Clean Monday is a national holiday, traditionally observed by picnicking in the countryside or city parks. Families pack large baskets of Lenten food: shellfish, *taramosaláta*, green onions, pickled vegetables, salad, fruit, halva and *lagána*, a special bread eaten only on Clean Monday (see recipe below). Flying multicolored kites is extremely popular, and the hallmark of the day. Although meat and dairy products are not eaten on this day, many view Clean Monday as the last day of carnival because it is festive and fun.

In Athens the day is called Koulouma because the most popular picnic area used to be by the columns of the temple of Zeus. In Lefkogia, Crete, a mock funeral procession is held for the king of carnival. In Thebes a famous comic parody of a peasant wedding takes place. Two shepherds arrange the marriage of their children including negotiating the dowry. The daughter is a man dressed as a woman, and the relatives ride donkeys backward.

LAGÁNA
(BREAD FOR CLEAN MONDAY)

1 package dry yeast
1 cup warm water
1 teaspoon sugar
4 cups all-purpose flour

¼ cup vegetable shortening
2 tablespoons sesame seeds
Pinch of salt

Dissolve yeast and sugar in warm water. Mix dry ingredients with shortening. Add yeast solution and mix well, adding flour until dough pulls away from bowl. Knead for 10 minutes. Let sit for 30 minutes covered with a cloth. Knead again for 3 minutes and form into an oblong roll. Place on a 10" x 15" greased cookie sheet or large greased round baking tray. Press dough out and away from center. Brush flattened dough lightly with water. Sprinkle with sesame seeds. Let rise again, uncovered, for 45 minutes. Punch 6 holes throughout the dough to keep bread from popping as it bakes. Bake at 375°F on middle oven rack for 20 minutes. Remove immediately from pan and place on rack to cool.

Wednesday— The Liturgy of the Presanctified Gifts

The Liturgy of the Presanctified Gifts offers communion of the holy gifts (Eucharist) consecrated at the Divine Liturgy the previous Sunday. It is an opportunity to receive the sustaining spiritual strength of Christ during the difficult journey of Lent. Although the church forbids the celebration of the Eucharist on weekdays of Lent (except the Annunciation), it recognizes the need for spiritual food. The consecrated Gifts may be offered on Wednesdays and Fridays of Lent. (Check your local church calendar.)

Friday

Check local schedule for Divine Liturgy of the Presanctified Gifts.

On the first five Friday evenings of Lent, the Small Compline service and "The Akathist Hymn" honor the Virgin Mary. The Compline is a worship service with prayers and psalms. "The Akathist Hymn," one of the most beautiful and beloved hymns of Orthodoxy, is an ecclesiastical poem about The Annunciation of the Mother of God (which occurs during Lent) and The Nativity of Jesus Christ. Parishioners stand during the hymn; the word *"akáthistos"* means "not seated." The hymn contains twenty-four stanzas in order of the Greek alphabet. Each stanza begins with a letter of the alphabet starting with Alpha and ending with Omega. A different stanza (referred to as "Salutations to the Virgin Mary") is sung on the first four Friday evenings of Lent. On the fifth Friday, "The Akathist Hymn" is sung in its entirety.

Preamble to The Akathist Hymn

Rejoice, through whom joy shall shine forth;
Rejoice, through whom the curse shall vanish.[10]

Each service concludes with the singing of "Ti Ipermacho" ("The Invincible Commander")[11] by the entire congregation, a triumphant song about the Virgin Mary, the protector of Constantinople. During the seventh century, she appeared in Constantinople during a siege by the Persians. The enemy fled after their fleet had sunk, and the grateful citizens stayed up all night in church composing the following hymn in her honor. The most popular hymn in Orthodoxy, it is also sung along with the national anthem at major ethnic holidays and during times of crisis.

Saturday— Third Saturday of Souls (The Feast of Two Theodores and The Miracle of the Kollyva)

This is the third and most prominent Saturday of Souls. It celebrates the Feast of Two Theodores and the Miracle of the Kollyva. Saints Theodore of Tyron and Theodore Stratilates are symbols of Christian obedience. During the fourth century, Emperor Julian the Apostate, in an attempt to break the Christian fast from meat, ordered the blood of animals to be sprayed on the food in the market. But the two Theodores appeared in a vision to the patriarch warning him of contamination and urging the Christians

Ti Ipermacho

Ti i - per - má - cho   stra - ti - gó - ta

ni - ki - tí - ri - a.   Os li - tro-

THí - sa   ton thi - nón ef - cha - ri - stí -

ri - a.   A - na - grá - fo si i

pó - lis   sou   THe - o - tó - ke.   All' os

é - chou - sa   to   krá - tos   a - pro - smá -

chi - ton,   ek pan - dí - on me kin-

thí - non   e - lef - THé - ro - son,   i - na   kra - zo

si;   ché - re   ním - fi a - ním - fef   te.

To you we attribute victory, the invincible commander in chief, and sing praises of thanksgiving, O Theotokos. Keep us all unassailable and deliver us from all dangers that beset us that we may sing: Hail, O bride unwedded.

Spring

to eat *kóllyva* to remain clean. Commemoration of this miraculous vision reminds the faithful to obey the fast of Lent.

It has been traditional for Orthodox Christians to fast during the first week of Lent and receive communion on this third Saturday of Souls. Relatives visit the graves of the deceased taking flowers and *kóllyva*. (See *Death and Mourning*)

The majority of individuals named "Theodore" celebrate their name day on this day, although some honor St. Theodore Stratilates on February 8 and St. Theodore Tyron on February 17.

Week #2

Sunday of Orthodoxy

The Sunday of Orthodoxy celebrates the restoration of the icons to the church and the affirmed dogma of Christ's humanity as shown in the icons of Christ, the man. In 726 A.D. icons were banned because many believed that Christ as God should not be depicted and that icons were being worshiped as idols. In 843 the Empress Theodora ordered them restored. This event is commemorated each year with a procession of icons through the church and the reading of the Synodikon Proclamation of the Seventh Ecumenical Council:

> As the prophets beheld, as the Apostles have taught, as the Church has received, as the Teachers have dogmatized, as the universe has agreed, as grace has shown forth, as truth has revealed, as falsehood has been dissolved, as wisdom has presented, as Christ awarded: thus we declare, thus we assert, thus we preach Christ our true God and honor his saints in words, in writings, in thoughts, in sacrifices, in churches, in holy icons; on the one hand worshiping and reverencing Christ as God and Lord, and on the other hand honoring them as true servants of the Lord of all and accordingly offering them veneration.

> This is the faith of the Apostles, this is the faith of the Fathers, this is the faith of the Orthodox, this is the faith which established the universe. To these all, teachers of piety and faith, we cry out in brotherly love, "Memory eternal." Amen.[12]

Wednesday

Check local schedule for Liturgy of the Presanctified Gifts.

Friday

Check local schedule for Liturgy of the Presanctified Gifts. The "Salutations to the Virgin Mary" (second stanza) is sung during the evening.

Week #3

Sunday — Feast of St. Gregory Palamas

St. Gregory Palamas is recognized on this day for his scholarly contributions to the church and for his example of asceticism (praying and fasting), major components of Lent.

Wednesday

Check local schedule for Liturgy of the Presanctified Gifts.

Friday

Check local schedule for Liturgy of the Presanctified Gifts. "Salutations to the Virgin Mary" (third stanza) is always sung during the evening.

Week #4

Sunday — Veneration of the Holy Cross

The cross on which Christ died is honored this day, the most important Sunday of Lent. This is the half-way point of the long journey of fasting, prayer, and philanthropy. The Veneration of the Holy Cross reminds the faithful how Jesus carried the cross, letting no obstacle prevent him from carrying it to the end. It is the same with the life of the Christian during Lent. Easter is reached only through the crucifixion of one's passions.

A cross is carried in procession to the middle of the church during the Divine Liturgy and left there all week for veneration as a symbol of strength. At the end of the Divine Liturgy, everyone receives a flower from the cross to be saved at the home *ikonostási*.

Wednesday

Check local schedule for Liturgy of the Presanctified Gifts.

Friday

Check local schedule for Liturgy of the Presanctified Gifts. The "Salutations to the Virgin Mary" (fourth stanza) is sung during the evening.

During Lent two significant events celebrated on March 25 break the solemn mood: The Annunciation of the Mother of God and Greek Independence Day. March 25 is a fixed date, but the dates of Lent change each year. March 25 is inserted here arbitrarily.

THE ANNUNCIATION OF THE MOTHER GOD AND GREEK INDEPENDENCE DAY
MARCH 25

March 25, one of the most important Greek holidays, celebrates The Annunciation of the Mother of God and Greek Independence Day. Although one event is religious and the other secular, the two are linked together by the common themes of birth and liberty. One event marks the good news that the Virgin Mary will give birth to the Son of God. The other commemorates the birth of the modern Greek state in 1821 and the proclamation that freedom would come to the enslaved Greek nation.

THE ANNUNCIATION OF THE MOTHER OF GOD

The Annunciation is the revelation by the Angel Gabriel to the Virgin Mary, that she would become the Mother of God. It confirmed that Christ, born of a human mother, would also be

Ο ΕΥΓΓΕΛΙΣΜΌΣ ΤΉΣ ΘΚΎ
Ο ΡΧ ΓΒΡΗΛ

The Annunciation of the Mother God

human and elevated Mary to sainthood and the highest position in the Orthodox church.

> And [Gabriel] said to her, "Do not be afraid, Mary, for you have found favor with God.
> And behold, you will conceive in your womb and bear a son, and you shall call his name Jesus.
> He will be great, and will be called the Son of the Most High; and the Lord God will give to him the throne of his father David,
> And he will reign over the house of Jacob forever; and of his kingdom there will be no end."
> And Mary said to the angel, "How shall this be, since I have no husband?"
> And the angel said to her, "The Holy Spirit will come upon you and the power of the Most High will overshadow you; therefore the child to be born will be called holy, the Son of God." Luke 1:-26-35

A Divine Liturgy always commemorates this major feast day. Annunciation falls during Lent, but fish may be eaten.

GREEK INDEPENDENCE DAY

HISTORY OF THE REVOLUTION

March 25 is the Greek "Fourth of July." Greece's modern revolution began on March 25, 1821, with a declaration of independence from the Ottoman Empire and subjugation since 1453. A popular theory claims that Greek Orthodox clergyman, Bishop Germanos of Patras, Greece, was the first to declare Greece free when he raised a flag over the monastery of Ayia Lavra (Holy Laura). Others say the declaration occurred in St. George's Square in Patras. His declaration, *"Elefthería i thánatos"* (pron. *THánatos*) ("Liberty or death"), became the rallying cry for the ensuing war.

Bishop Germanos

Although independence was granted in 1829, fighting continued until 1833. The devastating war resulted in bloodbaths throughout the Ottoman Empire, including Smyrna, Cyprus, and Chios. The Greek cause eventually captured the imagination of Philhellenes (lovers of Greece) throughout the world who contributed money and time and sacrificed their lives to secure freedom for the birthplace of democracy. British romantic poets like Byron and Shelley inspired sympathizers with their poetry in *Don Juan* and *Hellas*, respectively. For Greeks today all around the world, the liberation from the Ottoman Empire evokes great pride and passion for their oppressed and courageous ancestors. It also explains the continuing animosity between Greece and Turkey today.

INDEPENDENCE DAY AND THE CHURCH

The Archdiocese of North and South America mandates a short service (doxology) and program in recognition of the church's vital role in preserving the Greek religion, culture, and language during the four hundred years of occupation. The close relationship between church and state continues today. Orthodoxy is the state religion in Greece, and a cross graces the modern Greek flag.

Greek Flag

CELEBRATIONS IN AMERICA

In the United States, city, state, and national governments issue proclamations recognizing the day. Some communities with large Greek-American populations sponsor Independence Day parades. Three major parades take place each year: In New York City on

March 25 on Fifth Avenue; in Tarpon Springs, Florida, on the Sunday nearest March 25; and in Chicago during May (date varies). The Greek Embassy in Washington, D.C., holds an open house. Churches, Greek schools, and secular Hellenic organizations sponsor a variety of events. A typical program includes speeches by dignitaries about Greek history and current issues. Children in national costumes recite patriotic poems in Greek.

Many children wear the *foustanéla*, the traditional uniform adopted by the military men in central Greece and the Peloponnesus during the time of the occupation. The costume with its short, white pleated .skirt (*foustanéla*), includes a hat with tassel, blue jacket, and red shoes with pompoms (*tsaroúhia*). (See *illustration*) It has become a national symbol and is worn by a popular group of soldiers known as *évzones* who guard the Tomb of the Unknown Soldier in front of the parliament building in Athens. Although it was sanctioned as the official costume after liberation, there are other popular costume styles, including the *vráka*, baggy pants that stop short at the knees and are worn primarily in the islands. The girls' costumes are more diverse, reflecting the different regions of Greece. Most costumes are handed down through the generations or may be purchased in Greece. The largest selection may be found on Pandrossou Street in the Monastiraki area in Athens.

Foustanéla

Pictures of revolutionary heroes such as Kolokotronis, Bishop Germanos, and Bouboulina decorate the walls, and Greek music and folk dancing often complete the program. Inspired audiences shout *Zíto i Ellás* (Long live Greece!) and robustly sing the Greek national anthem, "Ethnikos Imnos" by Greek poet, Dionysios Solomos.[13] Greek people popularly call it, "Se Gnorizo Apo Tin Kopsi" from the opening line, but the correct title is "Imnos is tin Eleftherian" ("Hymn to Liberty").

Kolokotronis

Bouboulina

271

I know you by the cutting edge
of your dread sword;
I know you by your look
that fiercely scans the land.

Risen from the bones,
the sacred Greek bones,
and brave as of old,
Hail, O Liberty, Hail.

CELEBRATIONS IN GREECE

On March 25, white and blue bunting and flags decorate villages, towns, and cities throughout Greece. Greeks observe Independence Day with church services, parades, speeches, and parties. School children dress in their best clothes or in national costumes to participate in the marches. The festivities parallel America's Independence Day on the fourth of July.

The solemn atmosphere of Lent resumes as the devout continue preparing for Easter.

Week #5

Sunday — St. John of the Ladder

St. John Climacus is honored for the book he wrote for monks called *The Ladder to Paradise.* It detailed the self-discipline, sacrifice, and hard work necessary to reach moral perfection. His example and wisdom in the seventh century are inspirational during the Lenten season.

Wednesday

Check local schedule for Liturgy of the Presanctified Gifts.

Friday

Check local schedule for Liturgy of the Presanctified Gifts. The entire "Akathist Hymn" is sung on the fifth Friday evening of Lent. During the four previous Fridays, "Ti Ipermacho" concludes the service, but on the fifth evening, the dismissal hymn, "To Prostachthen Mistikos," takes a place of prominence:

> When the bodiless learned of the secret command, he came in haste to Joseph's house and said to her who knew not wedlock: He who bowed the heavens by coming down is contained wholly and unchanged in you. Seeing him take the form of a servant in your womb, I stand in awe and cry out to you: Rejoice, O Bride unwedded.[14]

Week #6 — Deaf Week (Kouphi Evdomada)

The week before Holy Week, known as "Kouphi (Deaf) Week," is silent and short. No services, other than Sunday, are held.

Sunday — St. Mary of Egypt

Known as the penitent saint of the church, St. Mary is one of the church's most positive examples of repentance. Before conversion she lived a licentious life of pleasure pursued by many men. A turning point came, however, when she visited the Church of the Holy Sepulchre in Jerusalem and found it impossible to enter because of an unseen power. She immediately repented and then lived as an ascetic in the wilderness of Egypt for the next forty years. Her example reminds the faithful of the importance of the virtue of repentance.

After a quiet week, the celebratory services for the Saturday of Lazarus and Palm Sunday provide a distinct break between Lent and the sorrow of Holy Week.

Saturday of Lazarus

Church Service

On Saturday morning a Divine Liturgy commemorates the resurrection of Lazarus from the dead by Christ. This important miracle, sometimes called the "first Easter," previews Christ's own Resurrection that occurs the following Saturday. Christ brings Lazarus back to life in Bethany and leaves from there to enter Jerusalem the following day.

Food and Social Customs

In some parts of Greece children go door to door singing an old folk song about Lazarus called *lazarákia* that describe his resurrection. In Cyprus, one child of the group, decked in yellow flowers and representing Lazarus, pretends to be dead during the song. He springs to his feet when his friends shout, "Lazarus, come out!" Special buns called *lázari* are made and decorated in different ways. Some are twisted like a man in sheet. In Mitilini, the roll is long and thin and crossed at the ends. A cross is made in the dough with currants. Children roll the buns down small hills, hoping to find a bird's nest where the buns stop.

Palm Sunday (The Entry of Jesus Christ into Jerusalem)

Word of the resurrection of Lazarus by Christ in Bethany spread quickly to Jerusalem, and Christ was triumphantly welcomed into the city by enthusiastic crowds the next day. The church commemorates this high point in Christ's public life at a Divine Liturgy in the church decorated with palms and/or laurel leaves. (Laurel is a symbol of triumph.) A procession through the church reenacts Christ's entry into Jerusalem, sometimes including children carrying lighted candles they have decorated. Small crosses made of palms are given to everyone at the end of the service and kept in the home *ikonostási.*

Palm Cross

Fasting is modified because of the triumphant nature of Palm Sunday, and fish is permitted. *Bakaliáros* (fried cod) with *skorthaliá* (garlic sauce) and fried vegetables is a traditional dish, but any fish may be served.

Holy Week

PURPOSE

Holy Week serves as the ultimate preparation to face and worship the risen Lord. The joy of Easter cannot be complete without reliving the events that lead to it. During Holy Week all the passions and pathos of the last week of Christ's life are retold and reenacted. From Palm Sunday evening to Good Friday, the services recount everything Jesus endured to fulfill the will of the Father. On Good Friday God's will is completed on the cross and then with the Resurrection. By reliving Christ's experience of Holy Week, the faithful can be resurrected and come closer to becoming like God (*théosis*).

DEMEANOR

The faithful reaffirm their faith during Holy Week by preparing physically and mentally for Easter. Social activities are curtailed and marital relations avoided. Spiritual reading and acts of sharing should be substituted for plays, movies, and television. The somber demeanor parallels mourning for a deceased loved one.

In Greece, businesses shut down on Holy Friday, and people return to their family villages for the rest of the week. Many *kafenia* (coffee houses) hang the Jack of Spades from a light fixture during Holy Week, and card playing is suspended until the Monday after Easter.

FASTING

Most Orthodox fast in some way during Holy Week. The very devout follow a strict fast of no fish, meat, animal products, olive oil, and alcohol for the entire week. Others adopt a modified version for all or part of the week. Meals parallel those of Lent, utilizing legumes such as beans and lentils. Lentils are said to represent the tears of the Mother of God.

<hr />

TYPICAL HOLY WEEK MEAL

Lentil soup and bread
Olives and boiled vegetables
Halvah and fruit

<hr />

PREPARATIONS FOR EASTER

Cleaning, shopping, and food preparation for Easter is traditional, making this a hectic week. New outfits, symbolic of new life after the Resurrection, are purchased for the Anastasi service held at midnight on Saturday. Some godparents buy new clothing for a young godchild, along with an Anastasi candle decorated with a ribbon and flower.

Food preparation begins well in advance of Easter day. Of special note are the red eggs, *tsouréki* (bread) and *mayerítsa* (soup). The red eggs, always dyed on Thursday, have great symbolic significance (see "Holy Saturday"). The traditional *tsouréki* and *mayerítsa* appear on every table, as essential as red eggs and lamb. (See recipes below.)

CHURCH SERVICES

Since the church day always begins the evening before the secular day, confusion arises when scheduling and publicizing services. For example, the matins (morning service) of Holy Friday are sung on Holy Thursday evening. Thus the readings from the twelve Gospels are presented on Holy Thursday evening according to the secular calendar, but in the church it is Friday morning. Events and themes below are listed under the secular day or evening they occur.

The services of Holy Week contain some of the most Orthodoxy's most beautiful Byzantine poetry. You may want to purchase English translations of the services as mentioned above in "Suggested Readings and Translations."

Sunday

Evening Service — The Matins of Christ the Bridegroom

On Sunday evening, six days of sorrow begin. The service celebrates the allegory of the church (the people) as a bride and Christ as a bridegroom. Like a bride who must be ready to meet her bridegroom, the people must be prepared for an eternal union with Christ.

Two parables are told. One concerns the Old Testament figure of Joseph who was betrayed by his brothers, just as Jesus will be betrayed later in the week. The other makes an example of a fig tree destroyed for not bearing fruit. The faithful are reminded that they too will not have life if they ignore God's word.

The icon of Christ is carried through the church and placed in the center until Holy Thursday. Parishioners should venerate the icon at the end of a service and when entering the church if a service is not in progress.

Holy Monday

Evening·Service — The Matins of Christ the Bridegroom

The theme of Christ as a bridegroom and the church (the people) as the bride is repeated again. Several parables are read, including that of the ten virgins. The virgins cannot meet Christ the bride-groom without lamps lit by oil, the oil of charity and love obtained only through the Holy Spirit. Likewise, the believer will not be ready for Christ at Easter without the genuine light of love.

Holy Tuesday

Evening Service — The Matins of Christ the Bridegroom

This service commemorates the anointing of Christ with myrrh by a sinful woman. While visiting the home of a Pharisee, Christ was approached by a woman who suddenly entered the house. While "…standing behind him at his feet, weeping, she began to wet his feet with her tears, and wiped them with the hair of her head, and kissed his feet, and anointed them with the ointment." (Luke 7:38) Despite the Pharisee's dismissal of her unworthiness to touch Christ, Jesus forgave her sins. She is presented to sinners as an example of how to repent and be saved. To honor this woman, one of the most beautiful and beloved hymns in the Byzantine repertoire, Kassiane's Hymn, is sung at the service. Written by one of only four Orthodox women hymn writers, Kassia the Melodos (ninth century), it relates the sinner's agony and repentance.

Holy Wednesday

Morning Service — The Liturgy of the Presanctified Gifts

Check local schedule.

Afternoon and/or Evening Service — The Sacrament of the Holy Unction

With compassion and mercy, the church offers the faithful the sacrament of holy unction on Holy Wednesday. Through this sacrament God provides both mental and physical healing with the administering of holy oil (*efchéleon*) for those in need:

> Is any one of you sad? Let him pray. Is any one in good spirits? Let him sing a hymn. Is any one among you sick? Let him bring in the presbyters of the Church and let them pray over him, anointing him with oil in the name of the Lord. And the prayer of faith will save the sick man, and the Lord will raise him up, and if he be in sin, they shall be forgiven him. James 5: 13-15

At the end of the service, parishioners go to the front of the church where the priest with a cotton swab dipped in oil makes the sign of the cross on the forehead, cheeks, chin, and front and back of the hands of each parishioner. Upon request you may take additional oil home and keep it at the *ikonostási* for later use. In Greece, it is customary to send the swabs to men away at sea. (See *Holy Unction*)

Holy Thursday

Morning Service — The Divine Liturgy of St. Basil the Great

This Divine Liturgy by St. Basil the Great commemorates the first Eucharist when Christ and his disciples shared the Last Supper. He appealed to them to remember him by consuming bread and wine changed into his Body and Blood. This is a meaningful and popular time to take communion.

Dyeing Eggs

Red Easter eggs are traditionally dyed on Holy Thursday, also known as Kokkinopempti (Red Thursday). Red symbolizes the blood of Christ shed on the cross. (See "Holy Saturday") Some consider the first egg in the dye, the "egg of the Virgin Mary," and save it in their home *ikonostási* to protect the household from the evil eye. Others save the egg from the church service at Anastasi. Eggs can be dyed on Holy Saturday or any other day except Good Friday, the most intense day of mourning. (See recipe below)

Cleaning the Home Ikonostási

Holy Thursday is the traditional day to dispose of the previous year's degradable items at the home *ikonostási*: Vasilopita, palm cross, flowers, and Easter egg. Burn the items in a small metal container outside the house, burying the ashes in a location where no one will walk over them.

Evening Service — The Crucifixion

Holy Thursday is the climax of Christ's suffering, the day of his Crucifixion. At the evening service, the altar is draped in black, and twelve readings from the Gospels are delivered describing all the events: Christ's farewell at the Passover meal, the betrayal, arrest, trial, Crucifixion, death, and sealing of the tomb. A candle is lit after the reading of each Gospel. (A few parishioners practice the custom of knotting a small ribbon after each reading and using it later as a *filaktó*.) After the fifth Gospel, the cross is taken out of the altar area, carried in procession, draped with flower wreaths, and placed in the center of the church. At the end of the service, parishioners come forward, make the sign of the cross, and kiss the body or feet of Christ as he hangs on the cross. People wear mourning clothes, and in some churches an all-night vigil is held.

*Holy
Thursday
Cross*

Holy Thursday is also known in English as "Maundy Thursday," the day Christ washed the feet of his disciples at the Last Supper. This act reveals Christ's great humility and teaches that the faithful should allow Christ to purify them from their sins. Some Orthodox churches commemorate this event with a reenactment. The priest imitates Christ and washes the feet of twelve boys or men seated in a semicircle. A play called *Niptir* (Washing) on the island of Patmos, Greece, has become one of the most famous reenactments. The washing takes place in the town square where a large wash basin is erected.

Holy Friday

Holy Friday, the most solemn day of the year, is a time of mourning and fasting. In Greece, it is a national holiday with no school or work, and flags are flown at half-mast. Church bells toll funeral knells, and the dead are honored at cemeteries. In Mitilini, Crete, and Thrace large bonfires are built, and Judas is burned in effigy. Many devout families in America take time off from work and school to emphasize the importance of the day and to attend church services.

Decorating the Kouvoúklion

Early Friday morning the women of each parish decorate the *kouvoúklion* (funeral bier) that will hold the *epitáphios* (an icon of Christ's burial embroidered on cloth). The women decorating the *kouvoúklion* represent the women who prepared Christ's body for the tomb. Hundreds of white, red, and purple flowers are used to cover the bier. Anyone can help with the decorating and/or contribute money for the flowers.

Attending Church

The devout reserve this day for church, attending three important services: The Reading of the Royal Hours, the Descent from the Cross, and the Matins of Lamentation. The dress for church is dark clothing. Upon entering the church (if a service is not in progress), venerate the cross in the center and the *epitáphios* with the sign of the cross and a kiss.

Morning Service — The Reading of the Royal Hours

Readings of prophecies from the Old Testament and church hymns relevant to the passion and death of Christ constitute this service.

Afternoon Service — The Descent from the Cross (Apokathilosis)

At this dramatic service, parishioners solemnly watch the priest take down the body of Christ from the cross, wrap him in a white sheet and place him on the black-draped altar. The priest reenacts the same steps taken by Joseph of Arimathea who took Christ's body to the tomb. The *epitáphios* is put in the decorated *kouvoúklion*. (People popularly refer to the *kouvoúklion* and *epitáphios* together as "the *epitáphios.*") Parishioners venerate the icon at the end of the service, and some children go under the *epitáphios* in the form of a cross to receive God's blessing.

The *epitáphios* remains at the front of the church for the entire afternoon and into the evening service. Parishioners come to church and pay their respects to the buried Christ, with the same regard accorded the viewing of a deceased family member or friend.

Evening Service — The Matins of Lamentation (Epitaphios)

A somber, sad atmosphere pervades this service, well attended by parishioners wearing dark clothing appropriate for mourning. Sorrowful funeral dirges, the "Encomia," are similar to those sung in ancient times. Young girls dressed in white stand at the *epitáphios*, like the women who guarded Christ's tomb. During the evening, the congregation joins the choir in singing one of the most famous Orthodox hymns, "Lamentations," presented in three stanzas: "E Zoi En Tafo" ("Thou, O Christ, the Life"); "Axion Esti Megalinin Se Ton Zoothotin" ("It is Meet to Magnify Thee, the Giver of Life"); and "E Genee Pase Imnon Ti Tafi Sou" ("All Generations Offer Adoration").

Kouvouklion and Epitaphios

The procession with the *epitáphios* through the church is the high point, a solemn but extraordinary spectacle. Some churches hold the procession outside as the congregation follows with lit candles. The *kouvoúklion* is brought to the entrance of the church and raised high above everyone's head as the parishioners file underneath to receive God's blessing. To symbolize the death of Christ, the candles are extinguished and rosewater, representing tears, is sprinkled on the congregation.

At the end of the service, each person venerates the *epitáphios* and receives a holy flower. People customarily wish each other, "*Kalí Anástasi*" (Happy Resurrection) outside the church. After arriving at home, the holy flowers are placed at the *ikonostási*.

The procession with the *epitáphios* in Greece is held outside. From Athens to the smallest village, the procession winds through the streets. In large cities, bands play funeral marches, and in Athens the head of state and other dignitaries take part in the ceremony. In some places the bier is taken to the cemetery and carried over the graves. Effigies of Judas are hung in some towns or burned in bonfires.

Holy Saturday

Morning Service — The Descent into Hades and Anticipation of the Resurrection — The Divine Liturgy of St. Basil

The first service of Holy Saturday takes place in the morning and breaks the somber spell. Jesus' descent to Hades where he preached his message to the dead is observed. Those who believed in him received eternal life and salvation. The heavy sorrow of Good Friday begins to lift when the priest, wearing a bright robe, chants, "Arise, O God, to the world," while sprinkling bay leaves or flower petals throughout the church to celebrate the triumph over death.

EASTER

EVENING — THE MATINS OF EASTER SUNDAY AND THE RESURRECTION (ANASTASI)

The Anastasi service is the climax of the Orthodox year. Before midnight throngs of people dressed in new, bright clothing, especially red, arrive at church. Even those who do not attend religious services during the calendar year make an appearance. This is a universal event for believers and nonbelievers alike, those who observe Lent, and those who do not. They are brought together in a rare emotional harmony for Anastasi.

Participants buy white candles upon entering church or bring decorated ones of their own. Hymns of anticipation for the great event are sung at the matins before midnight as the church gets more and more crowded. A few minutes before twelve, the church is darkened to resemble a tomb. The only light in the church is that of an oil candle on the holy altar. At midnight the royal gates open, the chief celebrant (patriarch, bishop, or priest) appears holding a lighted candle and joyfully proclaims: "Come receive the light from the unwaning light, and glorify Christ who rose from the dead."

The light is given to the congregation, and parishioners pass it along to each other. In moments the church is aglow with the light of Christ. In the bright and colorful atmosphere the good news of the Resurrection is read from the Gospel, followed by the most joyful and triumphant hymn of Orthodox Christianity, "Christos Anesti" ("Christ is Risen"). [15] The entire congregation sings while making the sign of the cross with their candles.

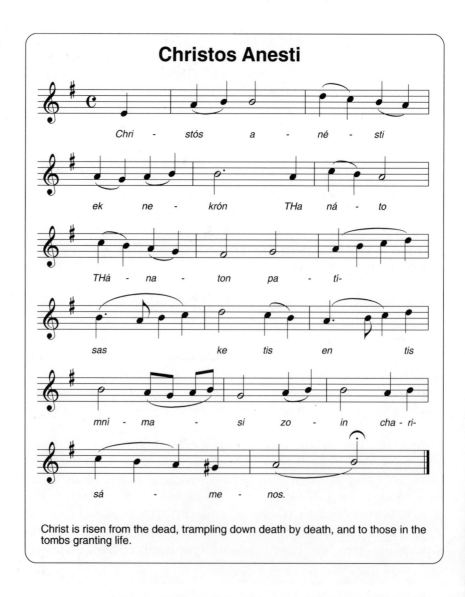

Christ is risen from the dead, trampling down death by death, and to those in the tombs granting life.

Many parishioners exit after lighting their candles, but they miss the true celebration of Anastasi that follows at the Divine Liturgy and a brief sermon written by St. John Chrysostom. The sermon explains that God welcomes, rewards, and comforts all of those who come to him, whether they have come early or come late. Christ has risen. Death and evil are conquered.

At the end of the service each parishioner receives a red egg wrapped in netting, a symbolic Orthodox tradition. The red color represents the blood shed by Christ for mankind, and the egg symbolizes the new life of the Resurrection. The enclosed shell is Christ's tomb; and when the egg is cracked, it represents Christ's emergence.

As everyone leaves the church, they greet each other with, *"Christós anésti"* (Christ has risen) and respond with, *"Alithós anésti"* (Truly he has risen) or *"Alithós o Kírios"* ("Truly the Lord") and exchange the kiss of the Resurrection. This is a time of forgiveness, peace, and joy.

Parishioners hurry home with their lit candles, trying to keep them from extinguishing. The light of Christ is used for three customs: To make a cross of smoke over the entryway of the home, to light the *kandíli* at the home *ikonostási,* and to light the candles on the dinner table. The holy light is believed to have miraculous powers of protection and to bring blessings for the entire year. If you wish to do so, save the candle and bring it back forty days later, on the day of Ascension or the Sunday following it. Light it and leave at church.

The traditions for Anastasi in Greece are similar, but include a grand public display at midnight. When the light is passed at church, fireworks explode, crowds cheer, bells ring, and ships and cars toot their horns. In Corfu an electric sign lights up the hillside, and in Athens, Lycabettus Hill glows with candle light as people wind down the slope from St. George's church.

ANASTASI MEAL

A delicious supper of traditional foods follows the service even though the hour is late. Instead of a prayer before the meal, "Christos Anesti" is sung three times in honor of the Trinity, and everyone chooses a red egg to crack with someone else. Eggs are cracked large end to large end and small end to small end with the competitors saying, *"Christós anésti"* and *"Alithós anésti,"* symbolizing Christ's emergence from the tomb. Through the process of elimination a "champion" unbroken egg is left. The holder is declared the winner and expected to have good luck all year. If complete fasting has been observed, the egg is the first food consumed, since it was the last thing eaten on Cheese Fare Sunday. ("With an egg I close my mouth, and with an egg I open it.")

The *tsouréki*, the Easter bread with a red egg peeking out from its three braids for the Trinity, is cut. The traditional Easter soup, *mayerítsa*, is shared. The delicate soup with its chopped lamb parts is considered a gentle way to introduce meat back into the diet. Some families share a modified menu similar to a light breakfast, serving Easter eggs, *tsouréki*, cheese, and hot chocolate. (Recipes for *tsouréki* and *mayerítsa* below.)

Tsouréki

ANASTASI MEAL

Red Easter eggs, *tsouréki*,
and *mayerítsa*
Salad, cheese, olives, and wine
Fruit and *koulourákia*

EASTER SUNDAY (PASCHA OR LAMBRI)

The joyous day of Easter — a day of happiness, love, and delicious smells and tastes — finally arrives after the arduous journey through the Triodion.

Church Service — Great Vespers of Agape

The Great Vespers of Agape (God's love) takes place on Easter Sunday, encouraging love, forgiveness, and reconciliation: "…let us embrace one another. Let us, brothers and sisters, forgive all things to those who hate us…" [16]

The Gospel is read in as many different languages as readers can be found, showing the universality of God's message. After the service, the Kiss of Agape is exchanged.

The Greeks use the terms "Pascha" and "Lambri" interchangeably with "Easter." "Pascha" is from the Hebrew word for "Passover," referring to the Jewish holiday celebrating the deliverance of the Jews from slavery in Egypt. Christ was crucified during this holiday season. For Christians the passover is deliverance from death to life. "Lambri" ("Bright") describes the brilliant light of the resurrected Christ.

Easter Dinner

The Greek Orthodox literally feast on Easter Sunday. Even the church calls Pascha the most important feast day of the year, the Feast of Feasts, the Festival of Festivals. Spring lamb is the traditional meat along with a rich array of *pítes* and tasty *mezédes*. Some Greek Americans prepare the lamb outdoors on a spit as it is done in Greece, but more often it is roasted in the oven.

EASTER DINNER

Oúzo and wine
Taramosaláta, dolmathákia, kokkorétsi
Red Easter eggs and *tsouréki* • *Mayerítsa*, cheese, and olives
Roast lamb and roast potatoes • Salad with green onions and dill
Spinach and cheese *pítes*
Fruit and *Galaktoboúriko*

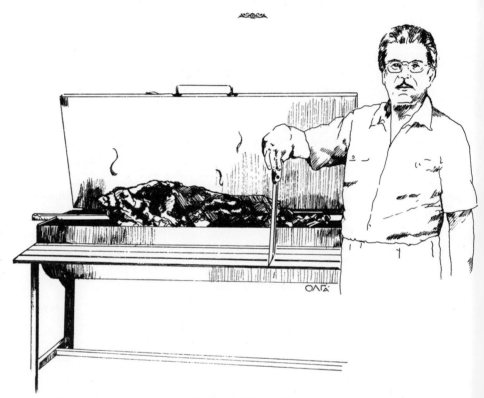

Roasting Easter Lamb

Easter Baskets and Easter Egg Hunts

Some Greek Americans give their children Easter baskets and conduct Easter egg hunts in keeping with American traditions. While these activities add to the festivities, they are secular, non-Orthodox customs.

AFTER EASTER

BRIGHT WEEK

The joy of Easter radiates into the following week, called "Bright Week," referring to the bright light cast by the Resurrection. For Greek Americans life returns to normal after Easter Sunday, except for the traditions mentioned below in "Forty-day Observances." There is no fasting during Bright Week as it is considered a time of complete joy. The doors of the church *ikonostásion* remain open for the week, symbolizing the open tomb of Christ.

In Greece the Easter celebration continues in the countryside for a week. In Megara on White Tuesday, for example, young and newly wed girls dance the famous "Dance of Trata," where they imitate fishermen pulling nets out of the ocean. At Karystos on Evia Island on New Thursday, a dance is done to appease the north wind. A common superstition is not to wash hair because it might turn white!

FORTY-DAY OBSERVANCES

The following customs should be observed for forty days after Easter, the time Christ was on earth before his Ascension.

Greetings   Say *"Christós anésti"* and *"Alithós anésti"* instead of "Hello" to fellow Orthodox.

Dinner   Light candles on the dinner table with the light from the *ikonostási kandíli* and sing "Christos Anesti" three times.

Liturgy   Do not kneel during the consecration of the Gifts during the Divine Liturgy. Christ's Resurrection provides the opportunity to rise, not fall. (Some theologians dispute this practice and recommend kneeling.)

Prayer   Sing "Christos Anesti" three times as a prayer.

RECIPES

RED EASTER EGGS

3 dozen white eggs (room temperature)
1 package imported red egg dye from specialty store
½ cup white vinegar

Wash eggs with soapy water and rinse. (If you wish, make crosses on the eggs with white wax.) Dissolve the egg dye in a glass of warm water. Add dye mixture and vinegar to enough water to cover eggs. Bring the solution to a boil without eggs and simmer for about five minutes. Skim if frothy. Cool mixture by removing from heat and adding a few ice cubes. Add eggs to pot and return to heat, boiling gently for 20 minutes or until desired color. Remove eggs. When cool, wipe each egg with a lightly oiled soft cloth. Dye may be reused by adding a little more vinegar. To dye eggs for Easter bread, let uncooked eggs sit in cool dye until desired shade. (Boiled eggs baked in bread may crack open.)

Always use dye approved by the U.S. Food and Drug Administration. The practice of using textile dye is not recommended and could cause ill effects if consumed.

Easter Bread

(*Tsouréki* or *Lambrópsomo*)

2 envelopes dry yeast	1½ cups whole milk
1 tablespoon sugar	2 teaspoons *machlépi*
⅓ cup warm water	½ scant teaspoon crushed *masticha*
1 cup unsalted butter	5 eggs
1½ cups sugar	9-10 cups flour

Decoration: 3 red eggs, uncooked
1 egg, plus 1 tablespoon of water for wash
⅓ cup of sesame seeds or ⅓ cup sliced blanched almonds

Mix yeast and 1 tablespoon of sugar in slightly warm water in a large cup. Cover, put in a warm place for 10-15 minutes until yeast activates (becomes bubbly). Warm the butter, sugar, milk, *machlépi*, and *masticha* in a pan until the butter melts and sugar dissolves. Cool. Beat 4 eggs until foamy. Put 2 cups of flour in a large bowl. Add cooled butter mixture, yeast, and eggs and stir thoroughly. Add most of the remaining flour. While dough is still sticky, add 1 unbeaten egg. Continue to add flour until dough is very soft but no longer sticky. Knead dough about 10 minutes. Put in a lightly greased bowl, cover with a damp cloth, and let rise in a warm place for about 2 hours. When doubled, punch down the dough and divide into four balls. For each ball: form three ropes the length of a cookie sheet. Braid the three ropes on a greased cookie sheet. Squeeze the ends together so they do not separate. (For a round loaf, braid the bread and coil in a 9" round cake pan.) To decorate: Tuck at least one red egg in between the braids, and brush the dough with a wash of 1 whole egg beaten with 1 tablespoon of water. Sprinkle generously with sesame seeds or sliced blanched almonds. Cover with a damp cloth and let rise about a half hour. Bake at 350°F for 40-45 minutes or until bread browns. Reduce heat to 250°F and bake until bread sounds hollow when tapped. Makes three medium loaves.

Note: The spices, *machlépi* and *masticha*, found in specialty stores or gourmet shops, give the bread its unique flavor. *Machlépi* is a ground seed from Syria. *Masticha* comes from the sap of the *mastichódendro* bush grown primarily on the Greek island of Chios and used in the production of gum. The translucent, light yellow chunks of *mastícha* must be crushed to powder before use. Greeks generally use the word *"tsouréki"* for Easter bread. The word *"Lambrópsomo"* refers to the bright (*lambró*) light of the Resurrection, and *"psomí"* means "bread."

━━━━━►►◦◄◄━━━━━

EASTER SOUP

(*MAYERÍTSA*)

16 cups broth (10 of lamb and 6 of chicken or 16 of chicken – l split lamb head for broth)
12 cups finely chopped boiled parts of two spring baby lambs (may include liver, heart, and lungs)

2 cups finely chopped green onions	8 cups water
½ pound butter	7 eggs, separated
2 cups fresh chopped dill	1½ cups fresh lemon juice
1 heaping cup of converted rice	Salt to taste

Optional lamb broth: Wash split lamb head and place in a large pot with water salted to taste. Add 12 cups water, salt to taste, and simmer covered for about 1½ hours. If necessary, add enough water to make 10 cups. Remove meat, chop fine, and contribute toward the 12 cups of meat. Skim the broth and strain. (Chicken broth may be substituted for lamb broth.)

Wash desired lamb parts and place in a large pot of boiling water for 15-30 minutes. Drain and rinse with cold water. Chop into small pieces. Lightly saute onions in butter in a large pot. Add chopped meat and saute for several minutes. Add fresh dill, 8 cups water, and 16 cups broth. Cover and bring to a boil. Reduce heat and simmer covered for 1 hour. Add rice. Cover and simmer for 20 minutes. Meanwhile, in the bowl of an electric mixer or large blender, beat 7 egg whites until thick and foamy. Add egg yolks, 1½ cups fresh lemon juice and ⅓ cup ice water. Continue beating until well blended. Slowly add 2 cups hot soup from pot. Gradually add egg mixture back to main pot and warm. DO NOT BOIL. Makes about 35 cups.

THE ASCENSION OF JESUS CHRIST
Forty Days after Easter

Christ ascended to heaven forty days after his Resurrection. During those forty days he appeared at various times to his disciples, exhorting them to spread the gospel. The Ascension is described in Luke 24:51: "While he blessed them, he parted from them, and was carried into heaven." The church commemorates the Ascension with a Divine Liturgy.

The Orthodox believe that the soul of a deceased person, like Christ, remains on earth for forty days. A memorial service is always held on or before forty days after a death. (See *Death and Mourning*)

PENTECOST
Fifty Days after Easter

Pentecost celebrates the founding of the Christian church fifty days after the Resurrection of Christ. According to scripture, the Holy Spirit descended upon Christ's disciples to enable them to spread his message throughout the world.

> When the day of Pentecost had come, they were all together in one place. And suddenly a sound came from heaven like the rush of a mighty wind, and it filled all the house where they were sitting. And there appeared to them tongues as of fire, distributed and resting on each one of them. And they were all filled with the Holy Spirit and began to speak in other tongues, as the Spirit gave them utterance. Acts 2:1-4

This significant event is recognized with the service of kneeling. The congregation kneels three times with the priest as he prays for the repose of the dead and for the descent of the Holy to give spiritual strength to all.

❦ *Summer*

HOLY APOSTLES LENT
Eighth Sunday after Easter to June 28

This fast commemorates all the apostles of the Orthodox church. It begins on the eighth Sunday after Easter (All Saints Sunday) and ends the evening of June 28. Some parishioners take communion on June 29, the Feast Day of Saints Peter and Paul, but the majority receive it on June 30, the Feast Day of the Holy Apostles. For those who observe this Lenten period, the fast is generally light, and fish, for example, is often eaten.

FEAST DAY OF SAINTS PETER AND PAUL
June 29

Saints Peter and Paul, the great missionary pillars of the church in its early years, are honored together for their tremendous contributions to Christianity. St. Peter, the leader of Christ's apostles, conducted an extensive ministry for Jesus, founding the church in Rome and Antioch. St. Paul was the greatest missionary of the church. A fervent Jew, he was converted to Christianity during a blinding light on the road to Damascus, and proceeded to convert thousands to Christ. His extensive writings (almost half of the New Testament) have greatly influenced Christian thought. Parishioners attend church and take communion. In Greece an evening church service is held on the hill of the Areopagus in Athens from which St. Paul made a speech to the Athenians.

FEAST DAY OF THE HOLY APOSTLES
June 30

Although each of the apostles has his own feast day, the church honors all of them together on June 30. It reminds people of the great contributions they made and the positive role models they provide for generations of Christians. Most parishioners extend their fast to this day and take communion.

DORMITION OF THE MOTHER OF GOD LENT
August 1 — August 14

Preparation for one of the greatest feast days in the church, the Dormition of the Virgin Mary on August 15, begins on August 1. The faithful fast through the eve of August 14. Eating fish is permitted on August 6, The Transfiguration.

THE TRANSFIGURATION OF JESUS CHRIST
August 6

The Transfiguration celebrates the revelation of Christ's divine nature to three of his disciples shortly before his betrayal and crucifixion. To convince the apostles of his divinity before his death, Christ took Peter, James, and John to Mount Tabor where he was transformed in front of them. His face became bright as the sun, his clothing became white as light, and the voice of God said, "This is my beloved Son in whom I am well pleased, hear him." Moses and the Prophet Elias appeared beside Christ. For the first time the veil of his humanity was lifted. The event reminds all Christians of the brilliance of Christ and that his light brings hope and change to mankind. Transfiguration occurs during the Dormition Lent, but fish may be eaten on this feast day.

In Greece the harvest season traditionally began on the Transfiguration. Grapes, in particular, were not eaten before August 6. In some parishes, the first grapes would be brought to church for a blessing and distributed to parishioners.

THE DORMITION OF THE MOTHER OF GOD
August 15

The Orthodox revere the Mother of God (Theotokos) above any other saint in the church. She always stands on Christ's right-hand side in each church *iconostásion,* and an enormous icon of her with the Christ child dominates the space above the altar. Through her, the Virgin Mary, Christ proves his humanity. Four of the church's twelve great feast days are devoted to her, of which The Dormition is the most significant. Two weeks of fasting and special prayer services precede August 15 when the faithful crowd the church to honor her and remember her feast day. People commonly refer to the day as "Tis Panayias" ("Panayia's [feast day]").

The Dormition of the Mother of God

APOCRYPHA

Unlike most of the events related to Christ's death and Resurrection, The Dormition (Falling Asleep) of the Mother of God was not recorded by eye witnesses in the four Gospels. Writings and legends exist about her death, but they have not been historically verified. They are known as "apocrypha." Therefore the Orthodox church has not promulgated dogma concerning this important event. Yet some of these legends have become an inseparable part of the Orthodox belief. There is the popular view that when the Virgin Mary was about to give up her spirit, all the apostles, except for Thomas, miraculously appeared in Jerusalem from all parts of the world to pay their respects and receive her blessing. As they were preparing for her funeral and burial, angels came in the presence of the apostles and took her body to heaven. When the Apostle Thomas, who had not come earlier, went to her grave, he found it empty.

In the hymnology of the Orthodox church and especially in the beautiful poetry of St. John of Damascus, reference is made to this belief of the assumption of the body to heaven. St. Andrew of Crete also makes reference to it in his sermon on The Dormition of the Mother of God.

The Orthodox and the Roman Catholics differ on this belief. The Catholics have made the Assumption a part of dogma. As yet, Orthodox have not done so. In addition, the Orthodox believe that the Virgin Mary died in Jerusalem, whereas the Roman Catholics believe she died and was buried in Ephesus. The Orthodox visit the site of her tomb in Jerusalem at the Mt. of Olives.

PREPARATION

The Dormition of the Mother of God Lent (August 1 — August 14)

The devout prepare for this great feast day by fasting for two weeks, from August 1 to the evening of August 14. Fish is permitted on August 6, The Feast of the Transfiguration of the Lord. No weddings may be performed during these two weeks.

Great and Small Paraklisis (August 1 — 13)

A *paráklisis* is a service of supplication and prayer. The Orthodox church traditionally holds one every evening during the first two weeks of August, except Saturdays, the feast day of the Transfiguration (August 6), and on the eve of the Dormition when a vesper service is held instead. The Small Paraklisis, shorter than the Great Paraklisis, expresses the troubles of the soul surrounded by sin and asks for help in being restored both physically and spiritually to original health and beauty. The Great Paraklisis prays for society in general, including the captured city of Constantinople, calling on the Mother of God, the protector of the city, to free her from the enemy. Some parishioners give the priest a list of names of individuals for whom they want prayers to be said. The Small and Great Paraklisis alternate evenings. Check your church schedule, however, some churches do not hold a service each night. Your church may have copies of *The Service of the Small Paraklesis to the Most Holy Theotokos*,[17] or a copy may be purchased from Holy Cross Orthodox Book Store in Brookline, Massachusetts.

OBSERVANCES

Significance and Church Service

The feast day celebrates the death of the Virgin Mary, but the focus goes beyond her passing from the earth. Mary is the mother of all humanity and, through her, mankind also reaches heaven. Her special death in which her body did not become corrupted in a tomb but was carried to heaven glorifies her unique nature. This glorification of her soul and body is the true celebration of August 15.

The four services of the feast day (vespers, matins, litany, and Divine Liturgy) are outpourings of praise and supplication for the Theotokos in some of the church's most beautiful poetry.

> When the Translation of thy most pure tabernacle was being prepared, the apostles surrounded thy deathbed and looked upon thee with dread, and as they gazed at thy body, they were filled with awe. In tears Peter cried aloud to thee: 'O undefiled Virgin, I see thee who are the life of

all mankind lying here outstretched, and I am struck with wonder: for He who is the delight of the future life made His dwelling in thee. Pray, then fervently to thy Son and God to save thy flock from harm.'

— Matins for the Dormition of Our Most Holy Lady from *The Festal Menaion* [18]

Families honoring the Virgin Mary come primarily to the Divine Liturgy and often take communion. Some bake *prósforo* and/or bring a single flower or small bouquet to decorate her icon. After the service everyone greets each other with, *"Ke tou chrónou"* (And to next year) and to those celebrating their name day, *"Chrónia pollá."*

Name Day

August 15 may be the most popular name day of the year. Many names for both men and women come from the Virgin Mary or Panayia such as Mary, Maria, Despina, Panayiota, Mario, and Panayiotis.

Celebrations in Greece

In Greece August 15 is a national holiday with dances, fireworks, and *paniyíria* (festivals). Some churches and monasteries hold all-night vigils from the late evening of August 14 to the early morning of August 15.

You may want to make a pilgrimage during this time as a special tribute to the Theotokos or to fulfill a *táma*. The most famous pilgrimage site in Greece relating to the Virgin Mary is on the island of Tinos. Thousands of pilgrims jam the docks and city streets to visit the Church of the Evangelistria that safeguards a miraculous healing icon of Mary. Revealed in a vision, it was found buried in a field in 1823, and the church was built to house it. Pilgrims bring items of precious metals and other gifts to leave at the church. On August 15 and March 25 (The Annunciation) the icon is carried through town in a grand procession.

1. "I Yennisis Sou" adapted from Nick and Connie Maragos, eds., *Sharing in Song,* 9.

2. Mother Mary and Kallistos Ware, trans. *The Festal Menaion,* 277.

3. George A. Megas, *Greek Calendar Customs,* (Athens: Press and Information Department, Prime Minister's Office, 1958), 50.

4. St. Basil, "Exhortation to Youths as to How they shall best Profit by the Writings of Pagan Authors," In *Patrology,* vol. 3, by Johannes Quasten (1960; reprint, Westminster, Md.: The Newman Press, 1963), 214.

5. Mother Mary and Kallistos Ware, trans. *The Lenten Triodion.*

6. A. C. Calivas, *Great Week and Pascha in the Greek Orthodox Church* (Brookline, Mass.: Holy Cross Orthodox Press, 1992). Alexander Schmemann, *Great Lent* (Crestwood, N.Y.: St. Vladimir's Seminary Press, 1969).

7. Mother Mary and Kallistos Ware, trans., *The Lenten Triodion.* Nomikos Michael Vaporis, *The Services for Holy Week and Easter* (Brookline, Mass.: Holy Cross Orthodox Press, 1993). Holy Transfiguration Monastery, trans., *Pentecostarion.*

8. Holy Cross Orthodox Bookstore, 50 Goddard Avenue, Brookline, MA 02146; and Light and Life Publishing Company, 4836 Park Glen Road, Minneapolis, MN 55416.

9. Alexander Schmemann, *Great Lent,* 46.

10. N. Michael Vaporis and Evie Zachariades-Holmberg, trans., *The Akathist Hymn and Small Compline* (Brookline, Mass.: Holy Cross Orthodox Press, 1992), 16.

11. "Ti Ipermacho" adapted from Nick and Connie Maragos, eds., *Sharing in Song,* 16.

12. From "Sunday of Orthodoxy Vespers" Service conducted by the Orthodox Christian Clergy Council of Metropolitan Washington, D.C.

13. "Ethnikos Imnos" adapted from Nick and Connie Maragos, eds., *Sharing in Song,* 39. English translation by Thanasis Maskaleris, "Hymn to Liberty" in *Hellenic Journal,* 11 March 1976.

14. N. Michael Vaporis and Evie Zachariades-Holmberg, trans. *The Akathist Hymn and Small Compline,* 7.

15. "Christos Anesti" adapted from Nick and Connie Maragos, *Sharing in Song,* 20.

16. Nomikos Michael Vaporis, *The Services for Holy Week and Easter,* 304.

17. Demetri Kangelaris and Nicholas Kasemeotes, *The Service of the Small Paraklesis to the Most Holy Theotokos* (Brookline, Mass.: Holy Cross Orthodox Press, 1984).

18. Mother Mary and Kallistos Ware, trans. *The Lenten Triodion,* 514.

❧ BIBLIOGRAPHY

Athenagoras. "Encyclical on the Greek Language Schools." August 7, 1937. In *The Odyssey of Hellenism in America* by George Papaioannou. Thessaloniki, Greece: Patriarchal Institute for Patristic Studies, 1985.

————. "An Encyclical on Marriages and Family." September 27, 1948. In *The Odyssey of Hellenism in America* by George Papaioannou.

Calivas, A. C. *Great Week and Pascha in the Greek Orthodox Church.* Brookline, Mass.: Holy Cross Orthodox Press, 1992.

Callinicos, Constance. *American Aphrodite: Becoming Female in Greek America.* New York: Pella Publishing Company, 1990.

Chiochios, Mary (producer) and George Chiochios (director and editor). *My Sweet Village.* Watertown, Mass.: Hellenic Images, 1990.

Coniaris, Anthony M. *Making God Real in the Orthodox Christian Home,* Minneapolis: Light and Life Publishing Company, 1977.

————. *These are the Sacraments, the Life-Giving Mysteries of the Orthodox Church.* Minneapolis: Light and Life Publishing Company, 1981.

Cummings, D. *The Rudder.* Chicago: The Orthodox Christian Educational Society, 1957.

D'Aulaire, Ingri and Edgar Parin d'Aulaire. *Book of Greek Myths.* Garden City, N.Y.: Doubleday and Company, 1962.

Economou, Steven G. *Greek Proverbs.* N.p., 1976.

Fitzgerald, Thomas. "The Treasures of Orthodoxy" Pamphlets 1-10. Brookline, Mass.: Greek Orthodox Archdiocese of North and South America, n.d.

"Future Theological Agenda of the Archdiocese — Conclusion." *Orthodox Observer.* March 1991.

Gage, Nicholas. *Eleni.* New York: Random House, 1983.

———. *Hellas: A Portrait of Greece*. American Heritage Press, 1971. 2d. ed. New York: Villard Books, 1986. 3d ed. Greece: Efstathiadis Group, 1987.

———. *A Place for Us*. Boston: Houghton Mifflin Company, 1989.

Georgakas, Dan and Charles Moskos. *New Directions in Greek-American Studies*. New York: Pella Publishing Company, 1991.

Gillquist, Peter E. Project Director. *The Orthodox Study Bible*. Nashville, Tenn.: Thomas Nelson Publishers, 1993.

GOTELCOM (Greek Orthodox Telecommunications). Videos entitled: *Akathist Hymn; Divine Liturgy; Great and Holy Week; Holy Image, Holy Space: Icons and Frescoes from Greece; March 25: Independence Day; Twelve Days of Christmas*. Brooklyn, N.Y.: GOTELCOM.

Greek Orthodox Archdiocese of North and South America. *The Priest's Handbook and Ceremonial Guide*. New York: Greek Orthodox Archdiocese of North and South America, 1987.

———. *Yearbook 1999*. New York: Greek Orthodox Archdiocese Press, 1999.

Gvosdev, Matushka Ellen. *The Female Diaconate: An Historical Perspective*. Minneapolis: Light and Life Publishing Company, 1991.

Harakas, Stanley S. *Contemporary Moral Issues Facing the Orthodox Church*. Minneapolis: Light and Life Publishing Company, 1982.

Holst, Gail. *Road to Rembetika: Music from a Greek Sub-culture*. Athens: Anglo-Hellenic Publishing, 1975.

Holy Transfiguration Monastery, trans. *Parakletike*. Brookline, Mass.: Holy Transfiguration Monastery, 1990.

———, trans. *Pentecostarion*. Brookline, Mass.: Holy Transfiguration Monastery, 1990.

Kangelaris, Demetri and Nicholas Kasemeotes, *The Service of the Small Paraklesis to the Most Holy Theotokos*. Brookline, Mass.: Holy Cross Orthodox Press, 1984.

Kazantzakis, Nikos. *Report to Greco*. Translated by P. A. Bien. New York: Simon and Schuster, 1965. Reprint. New York: Bantam Books, 1966.

Kochilas, Diane. *The Food and Wine of Greece*. New York: St. Martin's Press, 1990.

Kourvetaris, George. "The Greek American Family." In *Ethnic Families in America: Patterns and Variations*. Edited by Charles H. Mindel, Robert W. Habenstein, and Roosevelt Wright, Jr. 3d ed. New York: Elsevier Science Publishing Company, 1988.

Laografia. Dalia Miller, ed. Irvine, Ca.

Litsas, Fotios K. *Our Roots: Holidays & Customs*. New York: Greek Orthodox Archdiocese of North and South America, n.d. (In Greek only).

————, ed. *A Companion to the Greek Orthodox Church*. New York: Department of Communication, Greek Orthodox Archdiocese of North and South America, 1984.

Maragos, Nick and Connie Maragos, eds. *Sharing in Song: A Songbook for Greek Orthodox Gatherings*. Sherman Oakes, Calif.: The National Forum of Greek Orthodox Church Musicians, 1988.

Maskaleris, Thanasis. "Hymn to Liberty" in *Hellenic Journal*, 11 March 1976.

Mastrantonis, George. "Holy Communion, The Bread of Life." St. Louis, Mo.: Ologos, n.d.

Megas, George A. *Greek Calendar Customs*. Athens: Prime Minister's Office, Press and Information Department, 1958.

Members of the Faculty of Hellenic College/Holy Cross Greek Orthodox School of Theology, trans. *The Divine Liturgy of Saint John Chrysostom*. Brookline, Mass.: Holy Cross Orthodox Press, 1985.

Moskos, Charles C. *Greek Americans: Struggle and Success*. Englewood Cliffs, N.J.: Prentice-Hall, 1980. 2d. ed. New Brunswick, N.J.: Transaction Publishers, 1989.

Mother Mary and Kallistos Ware, trans. *The Festal Menaion*. London: Faber and Faber, 1969. Reprint. South Cannan, Pa.: St. Tikhon's Seminary Press, 1990.

————, trans. *The Lenten Triodion*. London: Faber and Faber, 1978.

Orthodox Christian Clergy Council of Metropolitan Washington, D.C.
    "The Synodikon of Holy Orthodoxy." N.p., n.d.

Ouspensky, Leonid. *Theology of the Icon*. Translated by E. Meyendorff.
    Crestwood, N.Y.: St. Vladimir's Seminary Press, 1978.

Ouspensky, Leonid and Vladimir Lossky. *The Meaning of Icons*. Rev. ed.
    Crestwood, N.Y.: St. Vladimir's Seminary Press, 1982.

Papaioannou, George. *The Odyssey of Hellenism in America*.
    Thessaloniki, Greece: Patriarchal Institute for Patristic Studies, 1985.

————. "Tell Me Father." *Orthodox Observer*. 11 February 1987.

Paroulakis, Peter H. *The Greeks: Their Struggle for Independence*.
    Darwin, Australia: Hellenic International Press, 1984.

Patrinacos, Nicon D. *A Dictionary of Greek Orthodoxy*. New York:
    Greek Orthodox Archdiocese of North and South America,
    Department of Education, 1984.

————. *All That a Greek Orthodox Should Know*. New York: Greek
    Orthodox Archdiocese of North and South America, Department of
    Education, 1986.

Petrakis, Harry Mark. *A Dream of Kings*. New York: David McKay
    Company, 1966.

————. *Stelmark: A Family Recollection*. New York: David McKay
    Company, 1970.

Poulos, George. *Orthodox Saints: Spiritual Profiles for Modern Man*. 4
    vols. Brookline, Mass.: Holy Cross Orthodox Press, 1976-1982.

————. *Lives of the Saints and Major Feast Days*. 1981. Reprint.
    Brookline, Mass.: Department of Religious Education, Greek
    Orthodox Archdiocese of North and South America, 1989.

Recipe Club of St. Paul's Greek Orthodox Cathedral. *The Complete Book
    of Greek Cooking*. New York: Harper and Row, 1990.

Sadie, Stanley, ed. *The New Grove Dictionary of Music and Musicians*.
    Vol. 7. London: Macmillian Publishers.

St. Basil. "Exhortation to Youths as to How they shall Best Profit by the
    Writings of Pagan Authors." In *Patrology* by Johannes Quasten. Vol.
    3. 1960. Reprint. Westminster, Md.: The Newman Press, 1963.

St. Demetrios Cookbook Committee. *Greek Cooking in an American Kitchen.* Seattle, Wash., 1982.

Saloutos, Theodore. *The Greeks in the United States.* Cambridge: Harvard University Press, 1964.

———. "Growing Up in the Greek Community of Milwaukee," *Historical Messenger of the Milwaukee County Historical Society* 29, no. 2. Summer 1973. In *The Greek Americans* by Alice Scourby. Boston: Twayne Publishers, 1984.

Schmemann, Alexander. *Great Lent.* Crestwood, N.Y.: St. Vladimir's Seminary Press, 1969.

Scourby, Alice. *The Greek Americans.* Boston: Twayne Publishers, 1984.

———. "Ethnicity at the Crossroads." *The Greek American.* 3 October 1992.

Sendler, Egon. *The Icon: Image of the Invisible.* Translated by Steven Bigham. Redondo Beach, Calif.: Oakwood Publications, 1988.

Stavropoulos, Christoforos. *Partakers of Divine Nature.* Translated by Stanley Harakas. Minneapolis: Light and Life Publishing Company, 1976.

Topping, Eva Catafygiotu. "Sacred Songs in Byzantium: Orthodox Hymnography." In *A Companion to the Greek Orthodox Church,* edited by Fotios K. Litsas. New York: Department of Communication, Greek Orthodox Archdiocese of North and South America, 1984.

———. *Holy Mothers of Orthodoxy: Women and the Church.* Minneapolis: Light and Life Publishing Company, 1987.

———. *Saints and Sisterhood: The Lives of Forty-eight Holy Women.* Minneapolis: Light and Life Publishing Company, 1990.

U.S. Bureau of the Census. *1990 Census of Population and Housing, Population Ancestry.* Summary Tape File 3A (CD-ROM).

———. *1990 Detailed Ancestry Groups for States.* CP-S-1-2.

———. *1990 Foreign-born Population in the United States.* CPH-L-98.

Vaporis, N[omikos] M[ichael], ed. *An Orthodox Prayer Book.* Brookline, Mass.: Holy Cross Orthodox Press, 1977.

————, trans. *The Services for Holy Week and Easter.* Brookline, Mass.: Holy Cross Orthodox Press, 1993.

Vaporis, N. M. and Evie Zachariades-Holmberg, trans. *The Akathist Hymn and Small Compline.* Brookline, Mass.: Holy Cross Orthodox Press, 1992.

Vardoulakis, Mary. *Gold in the Streets.* New York: Dodd, Mead, 1945.

Ware, Timothy. *The Orthodox Church.* 1963. Reprint. London: Penguin Books, 1987.

————, Kallistos [Timothy]. *The Orthodox Way.* Oxford: A.R. Mowbray and Company, 1979. Reprint. Crestwood, N.Y.: St. Vladimir's Seminary Press, 1986.

Wellesz, Egon. *A History of Byzantine Music and Hymnography.* 1949. Reprint. London: Oxford at the Clarendon, 1971.

Welts, Eve Primpas. "Greek Families." In *Ethnicity and Family Therapy,* edited by Monica McGoldrick, John K. Pearce and Joseph Giordano. New York: The Guilford Press, 1982.

Winterer-Papatassos, Mary. *Experiencing the Feast Days of Festal Menaion in Greece.* Minneapolis: Light and Life Publishing Company, 1987.

World Council of Churches. "Report on the Consultation of Orthodox Women, 11-17 September 1976, Agapia, Roumania." Geneva, Switzerland: World Council of Churches, 1977.

————. "The Place of Women in the Orthodox Church and the Question of the Ordination of Women, Rhodes, Greece," 30 October-7 November 1988. Istanbul: The Ecumenical Patriarchate, 1988. (Available through World Council of Churches)

————. "Church and Culture: Second International Orthodox Women's Consultation, 16-24 January 1990, Orthodox Academy of Crete." Geneva, Switzerland: World Council of Churches.

Yiannias, John. "Orthodox Art and Architecture." In *A Companion to the Greek Orthodox Church.* Edited by Fotios K. Litsas. New York: Department of Communication, Greek Orthodox Archdiocese of North and South America, 1984.

INDEX

Abgar, King of Edessa, 107
Abortion, 168
Address, forms of, 37, 77, 78, 180-181
    see also Etiquette
Adoption, of children, 168
Aegina, 226
Afterlife, Orthodox beliefs about, 133, 137, 143
Age, calculation of, 168
Agrypnía (prayer vigil), 119
AHEPA. *See* American Hellenic Educational
    Progressive Association
Aiparthenos. *See* Mary, Mother of God
The Akathist Hymn (hymn), 264, 273
Alexander, Saint, 86, 101
Alexandra, Saint, 98
All Saints Day, 95, 98, 101
Altars, 17, 84
    see also Sanctuary
American Hellenic Alliance, 212
American Hellenic Educational Progressive
    Association (AHEPA), 211, 212
American Hellenic Institute
    Business Network, 211
    Public Affairs Committee, 212
American Hellenic Lawyers Society of Wash-
    ington, D.C., 211
Anastasi (Resurrection), 283
    candles, 283-284, 285
    Christos Anesti (hymn), 284
    church service, 283-285
    greetings for, 285
    meal, 286
    traditions in Greece, 286
    see also Easter
Anastasios, name day, 86
Andrew of Crete, Saint, 297
Andrew, Saint (*Protóklitos*), 86, 100
Anna, Saint, 83, 86, 100, 123, 232, 235
Annunciation (Evangelismos), 90, 101, 231,
    235, 262, 268-269
    celebration on Tinos, 299
    icons of, 103, 269
    name day, 90, 101
    see also Mary, Mother of God
Annunciation Cathedral (Baltimore), 211
Annunciation Greek Orthodox Church
    (Milwaukee), 14
Anthony the Great, Saint, 79, 87, 101
Antídoron, how to receive, 29
Antiques, export from Greece, 110, 228
Apocrypha, 297
Apokriá (Carnival), 257, 258
Apostles. *See* Holy apostles

Archbishop of the Greek Orthodox Archdio-
    cese of North and South America, 77, 238,
    251
Archdiocese of North and South America. *See*
    Greek Orthodox Archdiocese of North and
    South America
Architecture
    Byzantine, 14, 224-225
    of Orthodox churches, 13-14, 105
Artoklasia service, 125-126
    bread for, 99, 125-126, 127, 148
Artophórion, 17
Ascension of Jesus Christ, 231, 289, 293
Asimósi to pethí (to silver a child), 166
Assumption of the Virgin Mary, 297
Astoria, New York, 214
Athanasios the Great, Saint, 12-13, 87, 100, 101
Athena, 184
Athenaeum University Club, 211
Athenagoras, Ecumenical Patriarch, 20, 175
The Athenian Society, 210
Athens, 184, 198, 224, 263, 271
    Byzantine art & architecture in, 224
    Holy Friday procession, 283
    museums, 224
    Oxi Day celebrations in, 234
    pre-Lenten carnival in, 258
    shopping in, 110, 227-228
Axios, 211
Ayia Lavra monastery (Patras), 225, 270
Ayios O Theos (hymn), 26, 27

Babies
    circumcision, 165
    eighth-day prayer, 165
    expressions for birth, 164, 177
    filaktó for, 166
    first-day prayer, 165
    gifts for, 108, 166
    gold coins for, 166, 201
    silver gifts for, 166
    superstitions about, 167
    sweets for visitors, 165-166
    see also Baptism; Children
Baby showers, 164
Baptism of Jesus Christ, 231
Baptism, Sacrament of, 33-34
    of adults, 42-43
    age for, 35
    by air, 43
    candles, 35, 39, 42
    ceremony, 15, 33-35
    ceremony explanation for guests, 38
    dance of joy, 35, 38

Baptism *(cont.)*
    days not permitted for, 35
    in emergencies, 43
    expressions for, 41, 177
    godparent's role, 33, 35, 204
    grandmothers' role, 38
    gratuities, 41
    invitations to, 37
    items needed for, 39-43
    martiriká (lapel crosses), 40
    new white clothing for, 35, 40
    of non-Orthodox Christians, 43
    oiling of baby, 34, 40, 201
    parents' preparations for, 37-38
    post-ceremony celebrations, 37-38
    proof of Orthodoxy needed for, 39
    theósis and, 33
    white sheet for, 34, 42, 139
    see also Chrismation
Barbara, Saint, 83, 87, 100
Bartholomew I, Ecumenical Patriarch, 88
Bartholomew, Saint, 88, 101
Basil the Great, Saint, 79, 82, 83, 91, 244, 246,
   254
    Divine Liturgy of, 21, 279, 283
    feast day, 230, 231, 245, 247-248
    gifts to children from, 92, 243, 246
    name day, 92, 96, 101, 114, 230, 248
    see also Three Hierarchs; Vasilopita
Basil (plant), 185, 232-233, 252
Bean soup *(fasolátha)*, 183, 262
Benaki Museum (Athens), 224
Beverages, 186-187
Birth control, 58
Birthdays, 168, 177
Bishops, 76
Blessings, 118
    of grapes, 295
    of homes, 118-119, 252
    of icons, 110, 119
    of vehicles, 119
Bonboniéres
    at baptisms, 38, 40-41
    how to make, 40
    at weddings, 50, 54, 58
Book of Greek Myths (d'Aulaire), 223
Bouboulina, Lascarina, 271
Bouzoúki, 189, 191, 198, 223
Brandy, 132, 134, 142, 187
Breads
    lázari buns, 274
    for *artoklasia* service, 99, 125-126, 127,
      148
    Christmas (Christopsomo), 240, 242
    for Clean Monday *(lagána),* 262, 263
    Communion bread *(prósforo),* 70, 73, 99,
      123-125, 147, 148

Breads *(cont.)*
    Easter *(tsouréki),* 183, 276, 286, 291, 292
    at engagement party, 49
    paximáthia, 142, 143, 151
    Vasilopita, 183, 244-246
    see also Food; Recipes
Bright Week, 289
Burial service *(endaphiasmós),* 141-142
Byron, Lord (George Gordon), 225, 270
Byzantine Empire, 89
Byzantine Museum (Athens), 110, 224

Calendar
    days not permitted for baptism, 35
    days not permitted for marriage, 51, 61
    fast days, 130
    fast-free days, 130
    Julian, 257
    of observances, 231
Calivas, A. C., 261
Candles, 25
    Anastasi candles, 276, 283-284, 285
    baptismal candles, 35, 39, 42
    as form of prayer, 25
    kandíli, 114-115, 285
    in marriage service, 46
    preserving wicks, 58
    symbolism of, 25
    to remember the deceased, 25, 147
    as wedding decorations, 53, 56
Canon law, 11-12
Carnival *(apokriá),* 257, 258
Caskets, 138-139, 141
Censers *(thimiatá)*
    in the *ikonostási,* 114
    use of, 116-117
Chanters *(psáltes),* 18, 19
Cheese Fare Sunday, 260
Cheese Fare Wednesday, hymn for, 261
Cheese Week (Tirini), 259
Cheeses, 185, 286, 259
    féta cheese, 185, 188
Chicago, 214, 215
Children, 163
    adoption of, 168
    gender preferences, 50, 164
    terms of endearment for, 163
    see also Babies
Chochios, George, 221
Chochios, Mary, 221
Chrismation, Sacrament of, 33
    for adults, 43
    tonsuring at, 34
    see also Baptism
Christmas, 231, 237-238
    Archbishop's message, 238
    bread (Christopsomo), 242
    carols, 176, 238-239, 240, 241

Christmas *(cont.)*
    church services, 238
    dinner, 242
    gifts, 243
    greetings, 177, 242
    kálanda, 176, 240, 241
    as name day, 100, 243
    Santa Claus, 237, 243, 247
    see also Nativity of Jesus Christ
Christmas Lent, 68, 231, 235, 237
Christos Anesti (hymn), 284
Church of the home *(kat' íkon ekklisía),*
    113-117
Church services, 20-21
    etiquette for, 24-29
    in Holy Week, 277-283
    language of, 19-20
    on name days, 98, 99
    seating for, 28, 141, 144
    see also Divine Liturgy; *names of specific*
      services
Churchill, Winston, 234
Circumcision, 165
Circumcision of Jesus Christ, 231, 247
Clean Monday (Kathari Deftera), 262-263
Clean Week (Kathara Evdomada), 262-266
Clergy-Laity Congress, 209
Clothes. *See* Dress
Coffee, 134, 187
Communion bread *(prósforo),* 123-125
    division by priest, 123
    from holy unction flour, 73
    names to be honored by, 124, 148
    religious seal for, 123-124
    when to bring to church, 70, 73, 99, 123,
      299
Communion, Sacrament of, 67
    before marriage, 56
    during menses, 69
    eligibility for, 67
    fasting before, 69, 129
    frequency of receiving, 68
    how to receive, 29, 67
    last communion, 133
    of newly baptized children, 17, 35, 42
    at non-Orthodox churches, 70
    preparation for, 68-69
    reservation of, 17
    wine for, 67, 70
    see also Divine Liturgy
A Companion to the Greek Orthodox Church
    (Litsas), 106
Confession, Sacrament of, 63
    before holy unction, 72
    frequency of, 64
    Orthodoxy required for, 64
    penance after, 65
    preparation for, 64

Confession *(cont.)*
    priest for, 64
    private confession, 65
Constantine the Great, Saint, 89, 94, 101, 108,
    232
Constantinople, 42, 89, 106, 245, 264
Corfu, 82, 100, 226
Cosmas, Saint, 82, 105
Costumes, Greek, 271
    foustanéla, 271
    sources of, 198, 227, 271
    as wedding gowns, 53
Cremation, 137
Crete, 166, 280, 283
Cross *(stavrós)*
    Exaltation of the Holy Cross, 100, 231,
      232-233
    name day for, 94, 100
    sign of the, 25-27, 127
    Veneration of the Holy Cross, 267-268
Crosses
    at chrismation, 35
    church crucifixes, 17
    in homes, 18
    martiriká, 40
    styles of, 18
    wearing of, 18, 35
Crowns *(stéphana),* 52, 57
    case for, 50, 57, 116
    in casket, 139
    in marriage service, 46
    provided by *koumbáros(a),* 52
    style of, 52
    symbolism, 46, 57
Cummings, D., 11
Cyprus Children's Fund, 212

Dalaras, Giorgos, 193
Damian, Saint, 82, 105
Dance of Isaiah, 47
Dancing, 195
Dancing, folk, 194, 196
    at Easter, 289
    geographic diversity, 195
    participating in, 195-196
    popular dances, 196-197
    ways to learn, 196, 198
Daphni, Monastery of (near Athens), 224
D'Aulaire, Edgar Parin, 223
D'Aulaire, Ingri, 223
Deaconesses, 78
Deacons, 78
Deaf Week (Kouphi Evdomada), 274
Death
    anniversaries of, 145-147
    autopsies, 148
    cremation, 137
    embalming, 137

Death *(cont.)*
exhuming of bones, 137, 138, 146-147
expressions about, 134
grave markers, 137
notice of, 136
organ donations, 148
Orthodox beliefs about, 133, 137, 143
praying for the deceased, 259
preparation of body for burial, 137
remembering the deceased, 147-148, 259
théosis and, 133
transferring remains to Greece, 138
Triasagion service, 134, 140, 141
see also Funerals; Mourning
Demetrios the Great, Saint, 83, 89, 100, 172, 227
Desby, Frank, 19
Descent from the Cross (Apokathilosis), 281
Despina. *See* Mary, Mother of God
Dimotiká (music), 189-190
Divine Liturgy, 13, 21-22
antídoron, 29
etiquette for, 28
Lord's Prayer in, 23-24
music in, 19
Nicene Creed in, 10-11
participating in, 22
priest's role in, 21, 23, 78
of St. Basil the Great, 21, 279, 283
of St. James, 21
of St. John Chrysostom, 21, 22-24
see also Church services; Communion
Divorce, 58-59
Doctrine, 9-10
Dodecameron, 237, 243
Don Juan (Byron), 225, 270
Dormition of the Mother of God, 119, 231, 296, 298-299
celebration on Tinos, 299
celebrations, in Greece, 299
church services, 298-299
see also Mary, Mother of God
Dormition of the Mother of God Lent, 68, 231, 295, 297-298
fish days in, 295, 297
paráklisis services in, 84, 119, 298
Dowry *(príka),* 48, 50, 164
A Dream of Kings (Petrakis), 213
Dress
for adult baptism, 42-43
for babies at baptism, 35, 40
bridal headpieces, 53
chefs' hats, 184
for church services, 24, 280, 281
clothing for deceased person, 138
during Great Lent, 261, 280, 281
for funerals, 139

Dress *(cont.)*
Greek costumes, 53, 271
for mourning, 135
of priests, 75, 75-76
wedding gowns, 53
see also Etiquette
Drosinis, George, 219

Easter (Lambri; Pascha), 231, 287
baskets, 288
bread *(tsouréki),* 183, 276, 286, 291, 292
church service, 287
dinner, 287-288
food for, 183, 276
forty-day observances, 289
greetings, 178, 285, 289
as name day, 101
new clothes for, 276
soup *(mayerísta),* 183, 286, 292
see also Anastasi (Resurrection)
Easter eggs, 260
dyeing, 276, 279, 290
hunts for, 288
in the *ikonostási,* 114, 115
symbolism of, 183, 279, 285, 286
see also Eggs
Ecumenical Patriarchate of Constantinople, 12, 81, 135, 230
Education, 158-159
Greek schools, 174-176, 211
hidden schools, 157, 159, 173-174
organizations for, 211
patron saints of, 159
universities, 212-213
upward mobility via, 159
Eggs, 259
on Cheese Fare Sunday, 260
see also Easter eggs
Eighth-day prayer, for infants, 165
Elafrolaiká (music), 190, 191
Elafrolaiká, modern (music), 190, 191
Eleftherios, Saint, 82, 163
Eleni (Gage), 213
Elias, Prophet, 83, 90, 101, 295
Emmanuel (Christ)
name day for, 88, 100
see also Jesus Christ
Encomia (hymns), 281
Encyclopedia of Associations, 210
Endaphiasmós (burial service), 141-142
Engagements, 47
expressions for, 178
hope chests, 50
parties, 48-49
premarital counseling, 49
rings, 48
superstitions about, 49

Engagements *(cont.)*
    wedding showers, 49-50
    see also Marriage
English language
    in church services, 4, 19-20
    conversion of Greek names, 172
Entry of Jesus Christ into Jerusalem, 231, 275
Eonia i Mnimi (hymn), 143-144
Epiphany (Theophania), 231, 249-250
    church services, 250, 251
    exorcising *kalikántzari,* 251
    fasting for, 249
    Feast of Lights, 251
    Greater Blessing of the Water, 249, 250
    holy water, 249, 250, 252-253
    Lesser Blessing of the Water, 249, 250
    name day, 101
    in Tarpon Springs, Fla., 251-252
Epitáphios (icon of Christ's body), 148, 281, 282-283
Ethnikos Imnos (national anthem), 271-272
Etiquette
    between priests and laity, 77
    for church services, 24-25, 28
    for Divine Liturgy, 28-29
    godparent selection, 36-37
    for memorial services, 28
    see also Address, forms of; Dress
Eucharist. *See* Communion; Divine Liturgy
Evangelismos. *See* Annunciation
Evangelistria, Church of the (Tinos), 37, 92, 120, 227, 299
Evangelists, 16, 17
Evil eye *(vaskanía),* 120, 203
    máti (talisman), 166, 205
    dispelling of the, 120
    Easter eggs and, 114
    expressions against, 178, 204
    identifying, 203
    prayer against *(ksemátiasma),* 120, 205
    preventing, 53, 204-205
Evil spirits, exorcising of, 120, 251
Evropaiká (music), 192, 193
Exaltation of the Holy Cross, 231, 232-233
Excommunication, 49, 65, 131

Family, in Greece, visits to, 220-221
Family values, 55, 154-156, 163
Fasolátha (bean soup), 183, 262
Fasting, 124
    before Communion, 69, 129
    canonical flexibility, 131
    Cheese Fare Sunday, 260
    days for, 129-130
    demeanor during, 128-129
    dietary restrictions, 129
    in Dormition of Mother of God Lent, 297

Fasting *(cont.)*
    dry eating *(xeropháyi),* 129
    expression for, 130
    in Great Lent, 260, 261-262, 266, 275
    for holy unction, 72
    in Holy Week, 276
    levels of, 129
    Meat Fare Sunday, 259
    see also Food
Feast days, 231
    see also names of specific feast days, saints
The Female Diaconate (Gvosdev), 78
The Festal Menaion, 19, 30n, 238, 299
Festivals *(paniyíri)*
    at churches, 99, 209-210
    in Greek villages, 99-100, 221, 299
Filaktó (talisman), 166, 280
Films, about Greek Americans, 213
First-day prayer, for newborns, 165
Fish, 142
    in Dormition of Mother of God Lent, 295, 297
    in Great Lent, 130, 262, 269, 275
Flowers
    decoration of *kouvoúklion* with, 280
    holy, 282
Food
    for Easter, 183
    for Great Lent, 183, 261-262
    Greek cuisine, 183-188
    for *makaría,* 142
    for New Year, 183, 248
    for Palm Sunday, 275
    in Pre-Lent, 259, 260
    social life and, 183
    see also Breads; Fasting; Meals; Recipes; Soups; Sweets; *names of specific foods*
Forty-day blessing *(sarantismós),* 17, 167-168
Forty-day memorial observance, 143-146
Forty-day observances (after Easter), 289
Funerals *(kithíes)*
    breaking pottery after, 141
    burial service, 141-142
    burial site, 136
    caskets, 138
        items in, 139, 141
        open-casket, 138
    church seating for, 28, 141
    church service, 140-141
    clothing for deceased person, 138
    dress for, 139
    eligibility for Orthodox, 135
    expressions of sympathy, 144, 177, 179
    funeral home selection, 135-136
    icon cards, 139
    makaría (meal), 142

Funerals *(cont.)*
    pallbearers, 140
    scheduling of, 136
    shrouds, 42, 138
    superstitions about, 140
    ushers, 140
    viewing of the deceased, 140
    see also Death; Memorial services

Gabriel, Archangel, 16, 92, 100, 235, 268, 269
Gage, Nicholas, 213, 223
Gallos, Anna, 19
Garlic, 185, 201, 204, 275
George the Great, Saint, 83, 90, 100, 101, 108
Georgia, Saint, 98
Germanos, Bishop of Patras, 225, 270, 271
Gifts
    at Christmas, 243
    for family in Greece, 220
    from St. Basil, 92, 243, 246
    for godparent at baptism, 38
    icons as, 108
    for new babies, 166, 201
    for priests, 77
    superstitions about, 207
    sweets for hosts, 188
    to fulfill a *táma,* 120
Godparents, 36
    for adult baptism, 43
    baby's name announcement, 38-39, 163, 171
    baptismal ceremony role, 33, 35, 204
    Easter preparations by, 276
    for firstborn child, 36
    forms of address for, 37, 180
    gift for, 38
    koumbári as, 36, 51
    name day observance, 99
    name selection by, 38-39, 163, 169, 171
    qualifications, 36
    responsibilities of, 41, 42
    selection of, 36-37, 51
    sex of child and, 37
    see also Baptism
Gold in the Streets (Vardoulakis), 213
Good Friday. *See* Holy Friday
Good luck, 178, 201
GOTelecom (Greek Orthodox Telecommunications), 216
Grandmothers, baptismal ceremony role, 38
Grandparents, naming children after, 169-170, 172
Grapes, 295
Great Lent, 68, 130, 231, 260
    books about, 261
    Clean Monday, 262-263
    Clean Week, 262-266

Great Lent *(cont.)*
    Deaf Week, 274
    Eucharist during, 263
    fasting in, 260, 261-262, 266, 275
    fish days during, 130, 261, 275
    Fridays in, 264
    greeting for, 178
    observance of, 261
    Saturday of Lazarus, 145, 274-275
    weekly schedules, 262-268, 273-275
    see also Holy week
Great Lent (Schmemann), 261
Great Paraklisis, 84, 119, 298
Great Vespers of Agape, 287
Great Week and Pascha in the Greek Orthodox Church (Calivas), 261
Greece
    carnival celebrations in, 258
    classical period, 1, 223-224
    daily routine in, 222
    Embassy of (Washington, D.C.), 271
    Greek-American contributions to, 158, 220
    Independence Day, 176, 268, 270-271, 273
    leisure activities in, 222
    national anthem, 272
    nightclubs in, 223
    Ottoman occupation, 1, 157, 173, 184, 190, 270
    Oxi Day, 176, 231, 233-234
    pilgrimages to, 99, 226-227
    restaurants in, 222
    roadside shrines in, 85
    sightseeing in, 223-225
    transferring human remains to, 138
    travel accommodations, 220-221
    village reunions, 221
    war of independence, 225, 270
    see also names of specific places
The Greek American (newspaper), 216
Greek Americans: Struggle and Success (Moskos), 161, 213
Greek Americans, 1
    ancestry, 4, 158
    church festivals, 99, 209-210
    contributions in Greece, 158
    ethnic pride, 157-158
    family values, 154-156, 163
    "Greek towns," 5, 214-215
    honor, personal, 159
    hospitality, 160, 183
    literature about, 213
    population, 158
    scholarly works about, 213
    studies of, 213
    upward mobility through education, 159

Greek Americans *(cont.)*
    work ethic, 160-161
    see also Immigrants, Greek
The Greek Americans (Scourby), 3, 213
Greek heritage. *See* Hellenism
Greek Independence Day, 268, 270
    celebrations, 176, 270-271, 273
Greek language, 157, 176
    in church services, 19-20
    church-sponsored classes in, 4
    converting names to English, 172
    expression for tragic events, 167
    expressions for special occasions,
        177-180
    folk sayings, 199-200
    forms of address, 37, 77-78, 180-181
    Greek schools in U.S., 174-177, 211
    as means of preserving Hellenism, 4, 174
    newspapers, 216
    pronunciation, xiv
    terms of endearment, 163
    toasts, 179
    transliteration, xiv
Greek Letters Day, 159, 254
Greek National Tourist Organization, 221, 222,
    223, 227
Greek Orthodox Archdiocese of North and
    South America, 4, 130, 157, 208, 209
    Clergy-Laity Congress, 209
    headquarters, 208
    marriage guidelines, 59-62
    programs, 208-209
    schools, 175-176, 211, 254
    theological schools, 76
Greek Orthodox Church
    architecture, 13-17
    canon law, 11-12
    excommunication from, 49, 65, 131
    festivals, 99, 209-210
    Greek culture and, 157
    preservation of Hellenism by, 3, 4,
        156-157
    women's role in, 78-79
    see also Orthodoxy
Greek Orthodox Ladies' Philoptochos Society,
    142, 184, 209
Greek revolution, 270
    sites connected with, 225
Greek schools, in U.S., 174-176
Greek Star (newspaper), 216
Greek Towns, in U.S. cities, 5, 214-215
Greek Video Records & Tapes, 193
Greek Women's Institution, 227
Greek-American Women's Network, 211
The Greeks in the United States (Saloutos), 213
Gregory Palamas, Saint, 267

Gregory the Theologian, Saint, 83, 91, 101
    see also Three Hierarchs
Gvosdev, Matushka Ellen, 78

HANAC. *See* Hellenic American Neighborhood
    Action Committee
Handicrafts, sources of, 198, 210, 227
Hasápiko (dance), 197
Hasaposérviko (dance), 197
Hatzidakis, Manos, 191
Helen, Saint, 89, 94, 101, 108, 232
Hellas: A Portrait of Greece (Gage), 223
Hellas (Shelley), 270
Hellenic American Academy, 211
Hellenic American Neighborhood Action
    Committee (HANAC), 212
Hellenic Artisan Trades Cooperative in, 227
Hellenic Cardiac Fund for Children, 212
Hellenic Chronicle (newspaper), 216
Hellenic College/Holy Cross Greek Orthodox
    School of Theology, 76, 209, 212
Hellenic Cultural Museum (Salt Lake City), 214
Hellenic Foundation, 212
Hellenic Journal (newspaper), 216
Hellenic Museum & Cultural Center (Chicago),
    214
Hellenic University Club, 211
Hellenism
    Greek-American media and, 215-216
    organizations for, 211
    preservation of, 3, 4, 173, 174
    scholarly journals on, 213
    university study programs, 212-213
Hidden schools *(krifá scholiá),* 157, 159,
    173-174
Holy Apostles, feast day, 231, 294
Holy Apostles, Church of the (Thessaloniki),
    225
Holy Apostles Lent, 68, 231, 294
    see also Lent
Holy Communion. *See* Communion
Holy Cross, Exaltation of the, 100, 231,
    232-233
Holy Cross Greek Orthodox School of
    Theology, 76, 209
Holy Cross Orthodox Bookstore, 109, 261, 298
Holy Cross, Veneration of the, 267-268
Holy Friday, 275, 276, 279, 280
    church services, 281-283
    decorating the *kouvoúklion* (funeral
        bier), 280
    epitáphios, 148, 281, 282-283
    greetings, 282
    observance of, 276
    see also Holy Week
Holy Mothers of Orthodoxy (Topping), 78
Holy orders, Sacrament of, 75

Holy Thursday
    Communion on, 279
    Crucifixion service, 279-280
    disposal of *ikonostási* items on, 115, 279
    dyeing Easter eggs on, 276, 279
    foot washing reenactment, 280
    see also Holy Week
Holy Tradition, 9
Holy Transfiguration Monastery (Brookline, Mass.), 109
Holy Trinity Cathedral, Hellenic Cultural Museum (Salt Lake City), 214
Holy Trinity Cathedral (New York), 214
Holy Trinity Church (New Orleans), 2
Holy Trinity, Convent of the (Aegina), 82, 226
Holy unction, Sacrament of, 71-72
    Communion bread and, 73
    on Holy Wednesday, 72, 278-279
    oil for, 71
    private service for, 72-73
Holy water *(ayiasmós)*
    annual blessing of the home with, 252
    at blessing of a new home, 118-119
    at Epiphany, 249, 250
    personal use of, 253
Holy Week, 231, 275
    abstinence from sex during, 58
    church services, 277-283
    demeanor during, 275-276
    fasting in, 276
    Holy Monday, 277
    Holy Saturday, 283
    Holy Tuesday, 278
    Holy Wednesday, 278
        holy unction on, 72, 278-279
    see also Great Lent; Holy Friday; Holy Thursday
Home
    church of the *(kat' íkon ekklisía)*, 113-117
    spiritual atmosphere of the, 117
Home and Overseas Mission, 209
Honor *(philótimo)*, 50, 159
Hospitality, *(philoxenía)*, 160, 183, 220
Hymns, 19
    see also Music (of songs); *names of specific hymns*

Iakovos, Archbishop, 20, 154, 175
Iconographers, 104, 110
Icons, 81, 103, 116
    artistic styles, 105, 106
    banning of, 104, 266
    blessing of, 110, 119
    in caskets, 139, 141
    of Christ, 15, 16, 103-104, 106, 107, 144, 277
    in church nave, 15-16

Icons *(cont.)*
    color symbolism, 105
    commissioning of, 110
    export from Greece, 110, 228
    as gifts, 108
    healing powers of, 107-108
    historical controversies over, 103-104, 266
    in the home, 114, 116
    in the *ikonostási*, 114
    inheritance of, 108
    inscriptions, 106
    media for, 104-105
    metal coverings, 105, 120
    miracles attributed to, 107
    name day decoration, 99
    for personal worship, 116
    purchasing, 109-110, 227
    restoration of antique, 106
    selling of, 111
    Sunday of Orthodoxy, 104, 107, 266
    in vehicles, 119
    veneration, 25, 28, 84, 107, 277
    Western art contrasted, 103
    see also names of specific saints, events
Ikonostási, 113
    arrangement of, 115
    contents, 113-115, 124, 275, 282
    disposal of seasonal items, 115, 279
    location, 115
    marriage crowns and, 116
    use of the, 115, 118
Ikonostásion, 16, 17
    icons on, 15-16, 28, 107
    veneration of, 28, 107
Illuminations (television program), 216
Immigrants, Greek, 2-3
    population, 2
    values, 154-161, 163
    visits to Greece by, 219-220
    see also Greek Americans
Imnos is tin Eleftherian (national anthem), 271-272
Incense, 114, 116-117
Infants. *See* Babies
Ionian Village (Bartholomio, Greece), 209, 226
Irene, Saint, 83

James, Saint, 295
    Divine Liturgy of, 21
Jesus Christ, 88, 103-104
    emulation of, 13, 33, 129-130, 143, 167
    icons of, 15, 16, 103-104, 106, 107, 144, 277
    as model for *théosis*, 12-13
    see also Emmanuel
Jinxing, 202
Joachim, Saint, 83, 86, 123, 232, 235

Joanna, Saint, 171
John the Baptist, Saint, 83, 91, 250
    feast day, 231, 249, 253
    icons of, 16
    name day, 97, 101, 171, 253
John Chrysostom, Saint, 91, 131, 134
    Anastasi sermon by, 285
    Divine Liturgy of, 21, 22-24
    see also Three Hierarchs
John Climacus, Saint, 273
John of Damascus, Saint, 297
John, Saint (Apostle), 226, 295
Joseph of Arimathea, 281
Judas, burned in effigy, 280, 283

Kalamata, 196
Kalamatianós (dance), 196
Kalanda, 176, 238, 240, 250
Kalanda Christouyennon (song), 241
Kalanda Protochronias (song), 245
Kalikántzari (evil spirits), 243, 251
Kandíli (*ikonostási* candle), 114-115, 285
Karas, Simon, 198
Kassia the Melodos, 278
Kassiane's Hymn, 278
Kastelorizo, Greece, 165
Kathara Evdomada (Clean Week), 262
Katherine, Saint, 83, 91, 100
Kazantzakis, Nikos, 160
Kithía (funeral), 140-141
Knives, superstitions about, 50, 206, 207
Knocking on wood *(ktípa ksílo),* 179, 202
Kóllyva, 144-145, 183, 259, 266
    Miracle of the, 264-266
    recipe, 149-150
    for Saturday of Souls, 147, 150, 259
    symbolism of, 144, 150
Kolokotronis, Theodore, 271
Kontakion (hymn), 238
Kontoglou, Photios, 106
Kouféta (candied almonds), 40, 41, 48-49, 52, 58
Koumbári
    as godparents, 36, 51
    godparents as, 36
    marriage service role, 45, 46, 51-52
    selection of, 36, 51
Kouvoúklion (funeral bier), 280, 281, 282
Kreatini (Meat Week), 259
Krifá scholiá (hidden schools), 157, 159, 173-174
Ksemátiasma (prayer against evil eye), 205
Ktípa ksílo (knock on wood), 179, 202

The Ladder to Paradise (John Climacus), 273
Lagána (Bread for Clean Monday), 262, 263
Laiká (music), 190-191, 193

Lamb, 183, 188
    for Easter, 276, 286, 287, 288, 292
Lambri. See Easter
Lambropsomo (Easter bread), recipe, 291-292
Lamentations (hymn), 281
Language. *See* English language; Greek
    language
Lazarus, 143, 274, 275
Lazarus, Saturday of, 145, 274-275
Lemons, 185
Lent. *See* Christmas Lent; Holy Apostles Lent;
    Dormition of the Mother of God Lent;
    Great Lent; Pre-Lent
The Lenten Triodion, 19, 30n, 130, 258, 261
Light and Life Publishing Company, 109, 261
Literature, Greek-American, 213
Liturgy of the Presanctified Gifts, 15, 21, 263, 278
Lord's Prayer (*Pater Imon*), 23-24
Lossky, Vladimir, 106
Luke, Saint, icon of, 108
Lyceum Club of Greek Women, 198, 227

Macedonia, 210
Machlépi (spice), 291
Makaría (funeral meal), 142
Makarios, Patriarch, 232
Mani, 2
Marina, Saint, 82, 100
Marriage, Sacrament of, 45
    betrothal, 45
    birth control, 58
    bonboniéres at, 50, 54, 58
    bridal headpieces, 53
    church decorations, 55-56
    church guidelines for, 49, 59-62
    Communion before, 56
    crowns *(stéphana),* 46, 52, 57, 116, 138-139
    days prohibited for, 51, 61
    dowry, 50
    expressions for, 178-179
    gratuities, 53
    interfaith, 4, 49, 60, 61-62, 156
    koumbari, 45
    matchmakers, 48
    parental permission for, 48
    planning the wedding, 50-51
    prohibited relationships for, 12, 62
    second and third marriages, 59, 60
    service, 45-47, 55, 163
        Dance of Isaiah, 47
        music for, 55
        text of, 55
        wedding program, 55
    superstitions about, 58, 206
    wedding bed, 56

Marriage *(cont.)*
    wedding gowns, 53, 206
    wedding reception, 56
    wedding rings, 48
    wedding tray, 52
    see also Engagements
Martiriká (baptismal lapel crosses), 40
Mary Magdalene, Saint, 78, 105
Mary, Mother of God (Theotokos), 92, 123, 296
    Assumption of, 297
    burial place, 92, 297
    as Constantinople's protectress, 246
    feast days, 296
    icons of, 16, 17, 92, 102, 105, 296, 299
    name days, 98, 101, 299
    names for, 92
    nativity, 231, 232
    paráklisis services, 84, 119, 298
    pilgrimage sites, 92, 227, 299
    prayers to, 119, 143
    Presentation in the Temple, 231, 235
    see also Annunication; Dormition of the
      Mother of God
Mastícha (spice), 291, 292
Mastrantonis, George, 69
Matchmakers, 48
Matins. *See* Orthros service
Matins of Christ the Bridegroom, 277-278
Matins of Lamentation, 281-282
Maundy Thursday. *See* Holy Thursday
Mayerísta (Easter soup), 183, 286, 292
Meals
    Anastasi meal, 286
    Christmas dinner, 242
    Easter dinner, 287-288
    Holy Week menu, 276
    Lenten menu, 262
    makaría, 142
    New Year, 248
    typical Greek, 187-188
    see also Food
The Meaning of Icons (Ouspensky & Lossky), 106
Meat Fare Sunday, 259
Meat Week (Kreatini), 259
Megara, 289
Meletios, Saint, 171
Memorial services *(mnimósino)*, 143-145, 146, 147
    Eonia i Mnimi, 143-144
    expressions for, 179
    forty-day memorial, 143, 146
    kóllyva for, 144-145, 183
    see also Funerals
Messolongi, Greece, 225
Metánia, 26
Metaxas, Ioannes, 233

Meteora, monasteries at, 79, 87, 224
Michael, Archangel, 92, 100
    icons of, 15, 114, 227
    pilgrimage site, 92, 227
Miracle of the Kollyva, 264-266
Miscarriage, 168
Mistra, Greece, 224
Mitilini, 42, 138, 166, 186, 280
Mitropolis Cathedral (Athens), 110, 227
Monasteries, 224-225, 226-227, 270
    at Meteora, 79, 224
    on Mt. Athos, 79, 225, 226
    pilgrimage arrangements, 226
Monastic orders, 79
Mosaics, 105, 224, 225
Moskos, Charles, 2, 161, 213
Mother Mary (author), 130, 258, 261
Mothers, expectant, 163, 164, 179
Mt. Athos, 79, 86, 88, 225, 226
Mourning
    demeanor during, 135
    dress for, 135
    food for guests during, 134
    memorial dates, 145-147
    period of, 143, 146
    see also Death
Museums
    in Greece, 224, 228
    of Greek-American culture, 214
Music (church)
    Byzantine, 18-19, 189-190
    in Divine Liturgy, 19
    at funerals, 141
    hymns, 19
    organs, 19
    at weddings, 55
    see also names of specific hymns
Music (Greek), 189
    bouzoúki, 189, 191, 198, 223
    composers, 193
    dimotiká, 189-190, 192, 193
    elafrolaiká, 190, 191
    elafrolaiká, modern, 190, 191
    Evropaiká, 192, 193
    Greek-American, 192
    laiká, 190-191, 193
    patriotic songs, 190
    performers, 193
    rebétika, 190, 191, 192, 197, 198
    recordings, 192, 193
    regional differences, 190
    at wedding receptions, 56
    Western influences on, 190, 191
    see also names of specific songs
Music (of songs)
    I Yennisis Sou, 239
    Ayios O Theos, 27
    Christos Anesti, 284

Music *(cont.)*
    Eonia i Mnimi, 144
    Ethnikos Imnos, 272
    Kálanda Christouyennon, 241
    Kálanda Protochronias, 241
    Ti Ipermacho, 265
Mussolini, Benito, 233
"My Bright Shiny Moon" (poem), 173-174
My Sweet Village (film), 221
Mystírion. See Sacraments

Name days, 96, 168, 171-172
    celebration activities, 96, 98-99
    choosing a, 97-98
    of the deceased, 148
    expressions for, 96, 98, 179, 299
    religious significance of, 97
Names
    after saints, 85, 171-172
    announcement of baby's name, 38-39,
        171
    baptismal name, 33, 163, 171
    church preferences, 171
    converting from Greek to English, 172
    family traditions for, 169-170
    legal name, 171
    middle name, 169, 170
    nonreligious names, 172
    patronymic, 170
    selection
        by godparent, 38, 163, 171
        name day considerations, 171-172
        as a *táma,* 164
Narthex, 15
    preparing for worship in, 25, 28
The National Archeological Museum (Athens),
    224
National Dance of Greece Ensemble, 198
National Family Week, 154
National Herald (Ethnikos Kiryx) (newspaper),
    214, 216
National Welfare Organization (Greece), 227
Nativity of Jesus Christ, 103, 231, 236
    see also Christmas
Nativity of the Mother of God, 231, 232
Nave, 15-16
Nektarios, Saint, 81-82, 100, 226
New Smyrna, Florida, 2
New Thursday, 289
New Year's Day, 231, 243, 247-249
    church services, 247-248
    food, 183, 248
    greetings, 179, 246, 248
    name day celebrations, 248
    superstitions, 248-249
    Vasilopita cutting on, 244-246
New Year's Eve, 244-246
New York City, 214

Newspapers, Greek-American, 216
Nicene Creed, 10, 11, 33, 89
Nicholas, Saint, 83, 92, 100
Nightclubs, in Greece, 223
Niptir (play), 280

Obituaries, 136
The Odyssey of Hellenism in America
    (Papaioannou), 160, 213
Oikonomía, 12
Oil
    at baptism, 34, 40, 201
    for chrismation, 34
    for holy unction *(efchéleon),* 71, 278, 279
Olive oil, as food, 183-184, 262
Ordination. *See* Holy Orders
Organizations
    business & professional, 4, 211
    church-sponsored, 208-209
    educational, 211
    Greek-American community, 4, 212
    for Hellenism, 211
    political, 212
    regional societies, 4, 210
Organs, 19
"Orthodox Art and Architecture" (Yiannias),
    106
The Orthodox Church (Ware), 9
Orthodox Observer (newspaper), 148, 216
The Orthodox Way (Ware), 10
Orthodoxy
    doctrine (dogma), 9-11
    eligibility for Communion and, 67-68
    funeral eligibility and, 135
    marriage and, 49, 60
    required for sacraments, 31, 39
    Sunday of, 104, 107, 266
    see also Greek Orthodox Church; *Théosis*
Orthros service, 17, 20
Ouspensky, Leonid, 106
Ouzo (beverage), 186-187
Oxi Day, 176, 231, 233-234

Palm Sunday, 231, 262, 275
Panayia. *See* Mary, Mother of God
Pancyprian Association of America, 212
Panormites, Monastery of (Simi), 92, 227
Panteleimon Saint, 82
Paniyíri (festivals), 99-100, 209-210, 299
Papaioannou, George, 148, 160, 213
Papapostolou, Harilaos, 19
Parakletike, 19, 30n
Paráklisis services, 84, 119, 298
Paraskevi, Saint, 82, 84, 101
Parios, Giannis, 192
Parnassos Society, 211
Pascha. *See* Easter
Pater Imon (Lord's Prayer), 23-24

Patmos, 86, 226, 280
Patras, 86, 225, 258
Paul, Saint, 93, 101, 113, 294
    on family roles, 155
Paximáthia (bread), 134, 142, 151
Peloponnesus, 194, 221, 224
Penance, 65, 68
Pentecost, 231, 293
Pentecostarion, 19, 30n, 261
Pericles, 208
Peter, Saint, 93, 101, 294, 295
Petrakis, Harry Mark, 50, 107, 213
Phanourios, Saint, 83, 121
Phanouropita (cake), 121-122
Phîllo (pastry dough), 186
Philoptochos Society, 142, 184, 209
Philótimo (personal honor), 50, 159
Philoxenía, (hospitality), 160, 183, 220
Pilgrimages, 99, 226-227
    see also names of specific sites
Piraeus, 191, 222
A Place for Us (Gage), 213
Plato, 158
Platytera ton Ouranon, 17
Poulos, George, 85
Prayers
    against the evil eye, 120, 205
    for the deceased, 259
    paráklisi, 119
    to saints, 81, 84
    vigils, 119
Pre-Lent, 257
    carnival celebrations, 257, 258
    Cheese Fare Sunday, 260
    Cheese Week, 259
    Meat Fare Sunday, 259
    Meat Week, 259
    Sunday Gospel readings, 258, 259, 260
Pregnancy, 163, 179
    abortion, 168
    miscarriage, 168
Presanctified Gifts, Liturgy of the, 15, 21, 263, 278
Presentation of Jesus Christ in the Temple, 167, 231, 255
Presentation of the Mother of God in the Temple, 231, 235
Priests, 75
    for confession, 64
    education of, 76
    forms of address, 77, 181
    ordination, 75
    parishoner relationship with, 77
    qualifications, 76, 78
    responsibilities of, 76
    role in Divine Liturgy, 21, 23, 78
    women as, 78
Príka (dowry), 48, 50, 164

Procopius, Saint, 83
Proini (newspaper), 214, 216
Pronunciation guide, to Greek, xiv
Prósforo (Communion bread), 70, 73, 99, 123-125, 147, 148
Proskomithî, 17, 123
Proverbs, Greek, 183, 199-200
Psáltes (chanters), 18, 19
Psychosavato (Saturday of Souls), 147, 150, 259, 264-266
Purification, after childbirth, 167-168

Radio programs, 216
Reading of the Royal Hours, 281
Rebêtika (music), 191, 197, 198
Recipes
    Artoklasia service bread, 127
    Christmas bread (Christopsomo), 242
    Clean Monday bread *(lágana),* 263
    Communion bread *(prósforo),* 125
    Easter bread *(tsouréki),* 291
    Easter eggs, 290
    Easter soup *(mayerísta),* 292
    kóllyva, 149, 150
    paximáthia, 151
    Phanouropita (cake), 122
    Vasilopita (bread), 246
    Vasilopita (cake), 247
    see also Breads; Food; Sweets
Relics, 17, 84
    see also names of particular saints
Report to Greco (Kazantzakis), 160
Resurrection. *See* Anastasi
Retreats, centers for, 209, 226
Retsína (wine), 186
Rings, 45, 48
Rublev, Andrei, 106
The Rudder (Cummings), 11

Sacraments *(mystírion),* 31
    administration of the, 31
    as aid to *théosis,* 13, 31
    essential, 31, 64
    Orthodoxy required for, 31
    see also Baptism; Chrismation;
        Communion; Confession; Holy orders;
        Holy unction; Marriage
St. Augustine, Florida, 2, 209, 214
St. Basil Academy (New York), 82, 175, 209
St. Demetrios, Church of (Thessaloniki), 225, 227
St. Demetrios Greek Orthodox Church (Chicago), 215
St. Michael's Home for the Aged (Yonkers, N.Y.), 209
St. Photios National Shrine (St. Augustine, Fla.), 2, 209, 214

St. Sophia Cathedral (Constantinople), 13, 19, 104, 105
St. Sophia Cathedral (Washington, D.C.), 14, 19
St. Spyridon Cathedral (Corfu), 82, 94, 226
Saints, 15, 81, 85
    canonization of, 81-82
    feast days, 84, 100-101
    icons of, 84
    as models, 81, 159, 171
    naming children after, 85, 171-172
    patron saints, 82-83, 85, 159, 163, 171
    praying to, 81, 84, 119
    as protectors, 81
    relics, 17, 84
    roadside shrines, 85
    táma to, 83, 120-121
    see also names of specific saints
Saints Peter and Paul, feast day of, 231, 294
Saints and Sisterhood (Topping), 85
Saloutos, Theodore, 174, 213
Sanctuary, 16-17, 167-168
    see also Altar
Santa Claus, 237, 243, 246
Saturday of Lazarus, 145, 274-275
Saturday of Souls *(Psychosavato)*, 147, 259, 264-266
    kóllyva for, 150, 266
Schmemann, Alexander, 261
Schools. *See* Education
Scourby, Alice, 3, 213
Seal for Communion bread *(Sfrayítha)*, 114, 123-124
Second Coming of Christ, 136, 143
The Service of the Small Paraklesis to the Most Holy Theotokos, 298
Services. *See* Church services
The Services for Holy Week and Easter (Vaporis), 261
Seventh Ecumenical Council (783 A.D.), 12, 266
Sfrayítha (seal for Communion bread), 114, 123-124
Shelley, Percy Bysshe, 270
Shopping, in Greece, 222, 227-228
Shrines, roadside, 85
Sifnos, 42, 165
Sightseeing, in Greece, 223-225
Sign of the Cross, 25, 27
    how to make the sign, 26
    when to make the sign, 26-27, 127
Silver
    coin for announcement of baby's name, 39, 41
    gifts for newborn babies, 166
    on icons, 105, 120
    táma offerings, 120

Simeon, Saint, 255
Simi, 92, 114, 227
Sirtáki (dance), 197
Sirtós (dance), 197
Small Paraklisis, 84, 119, 298
Societies. *See* Organizations
Society for the Dissemination of National Music, 198
"The Soil of Greece" (poem), 219
Solomos, Dionysios, 271
Songs, music for. *See* Music (of songs)
Sophia, Saint, 93, 100, 107
Soups
    bean soup *(fasolátha),* 183, 262
    Easter soup *(mayerísta),* 183, 286, 292
Sparta Fraternity, 210
Speros Basil Vryonis Center for the Study of Hellenism, 211
Spices, 185-186, 291-292
Spyridon the Miracle Worker, Saint, 82, 94, 100, 226
Stavrós (cross), 17, 18, 35, 40 94, 100
Stelianos, Saint, 83
Stelmark: A Family Recollection (Petrakis), 50, 107, 213
Stéphana (marriage crowns), 46, 52, 57, 116, 138, 139
Stephen the Protomartyr, Saint, 94, 100
Stratou, Dora, 198
Sunday of Orthodoxy, 104, 107, 266
Sunday of St. Thomas, 145
Superstitions, 201, 205-207
    about dreams, 202-203
    about engagements, 49
    evil eye, 53, 114, 166, 203-205
    about funerals, 140
    for good luck, 201
    kalikántzari, 243, 251
    about knives, 50, 206, 207
    about marriage, 49, 58, 206
    neráithes, 203
    New Year's Day, 248-249
    about newborn babies, 167
    predictions, 187, 202-203
    spirits, 203
    to prevent misfortune, 202
Sweets, 142, 188
    for baby's visitors, 165-166
    bonboniéres, 38, 40-41, 50, 54, 58
    for Christmas, 240
    as hostess gift, 188
    kouféta (candied almonds), 40, 41, 48-49, 52, 58
    loukoumáthes (pastry), 166, 244
    Phanouropita (cake), 121-122
    Vasilopita (cake), 246, 247
    see also Food; Recipes

Symbolism
    in baptismal ceremony, 33, 34
    of breaking pottery after funeral, 141
    of candles, 25
    in chrismation ceremony, 34-35
    of crosses, 18
    in Divine Liturgy, 21, 22, 23, 78
    in icons, 105
    of *kóllyva,* 144, 150
    in marriage service, 46, 47, 57
    of the nave, 15
    of red Easter eggs, 183, 279, 285, 286
    of sign of the cross, 26
Symeon, Saint, 82
Sympathy, expressions of, 134, 144, 177, 179

Táma (vow), 83, 120-121
    for conception and delivery, 164
    godparent selection and, 37
Tarpon Springs, Florida, 214, 215
    Epiphany celebrations in, 215, 251-252
Television programs, 216
Theodora, Empress, 104, 266
Theodorakis, Mikis, 191
Theodore Stratilates, Saint, 83, 95, 101, 264, 266
Theodore Tyron, Saint, 83, 95, 101, 264, 266
Theology. *See* Doctrine
Theology of the Icon (Lossky), 106
Theophanes the Greek, 106
Théosis, 12, 260
    achieving, 12-13, 31
    baptism and, 33
    Communion and, 67
    death and, 133
    Holy Week and, 275
    of saints, 81
    see also Orthodoxy
Theotokos. *See* Mary, Mother of God
Thessaloniki, 89, 100, 225, 227, 234
Thimiatá (censers), 114, 116-117
Thomas, Saint, 145, 297
Thrace, 280, 100
Three Hierarchs, 83, 159, 247-248
    feast day, 159, 231, 254
    patron saints of education, 83, 88, 159, 254
    see also Basil the Great; Gregory the Theologian; John Chrysostom
Ti Ipermacho, (hymn), 264-265, 273
Tinos, 37, 87, 92, 120, 227, 299
To Pistevo (Nicene Creed), 10-11, 33, 89
To Prostachthen Mistikos (hymn), 273
Toasts, 179
Ton Photon (Feast of Lights), 251-252
Topping, Eva Catafygiotu, 78, 85
Transfiguration of Jesus Christ, 231, 295, 297

Travel Agent's Manual, 223, 227
Triasagion service, 134, 140, 141
Triodion, 231, 257
Tsámiko (dance), 197
Tsiftetéli (dance), 197
Tsouréki (Easter bread), 183, 276, 286, 291, 292
Turkokratia (Ottoman rule of Greece), 1, 157, 173, 184, 190, 270
Two Theodores, feast of the, 95, 101, 264-266

Unction. *See* Holy unction
United Hellenic American Congress (UHAC), 212
Universities, 212-213

Vaporis, Nomikos Michael, 261
Vardoulakis, Mary, 213
Vasilikós (basil plant), 185, 232-233, 252
Vasilopita (bread for St. Basil), 183, 244
    cake, 246, 247
    cutting the, 244-246
    in the *ikonostási,* 114, 115, 246
    legend of, 244
    public observances, 246
    see also Basil the Great, Saint
Vaskanía (evil eye), 114, 120, 178, 203-206
Veneration of the Holy Cross, 267-268
Virgin Mary. *See* Mary, Mother of God

Ware, Kallistos [Timothy], 9, 10, 130, 258, 261
Weber, Max, 160
Weddings. *See* Marriage
Widows, 135
Wines
    in *Artoklásia* service, 125, 126
    common cup in marriage service, 47
    for Communion, 67, 70
    from Greece, 186
Women
    family role, 55, 155
    Greek Orthodox Church and, 78-79
    purification after childbirth, 167, 168
    receiving Communion during menses, 69
    sanctuary closed to, 17, 167-168
Work ethic, 160-161
Worry beads, 222, 227
Wright, Frank Lloyd, 14

Yearbook (Greek Orthodox Archdiocese of North and South America), 59, 130, 210, 216
Yennitoúria, 165-166
Yiannias, John, 106

Zeibékiko (dance), 197-198

320

NOTES